The Utopian PMO:
Reengineering the Project Management Office

www.theutopianpmo.com

A J A Y   K U M A R   D

M.Tech, PMP, PMI-RMP, CISSP, CISA, CISM, ITIL

Limit of Liability/Disclaimer of Warranty: While best efforts were taken in the preparation of this book, the author makes no representations or warranties with respect to the accuracy or completeness of the contents of this book and specifically disclaim any implied warranties of merchantability or fitness for a particular purpose. The advice and strategies contained herein may not be suitable for all situations. The author is not engaged in rendering professional services, and you should consult a professional where appropriate. The author shall not be liable for any loss of profit or any other commercial damages, including but not limited to special, incidental, consequential, or other damages.

For reprint requests and other enquiries, please contact the author at *info@theutopianpmo.com*

PMBOK®, PMP®, PMI-RMP®, PMI-SP®, PgMP® PfMP® are registered trademarks of the Project Management Institute, Inc. which is registered in the United States and other nations.

PRINCE2® is a registered trade mark of AXELOS Limited.

For further information on the Utopian PMO, process maps in full-color, training, assessment and testing options on the UPMO framework, visit www.theutopianpmo.com

To Mom,
You exist in all the words

TABLE OF CONTENTS

6.2

7

THE UTOPIAN PMO PROCESSES QUICK REFERENCE

Thank you SR

Chapter 1
The Utopian PMO

Historically, there always existed a need for a PMO. From time immemorial, strategic projects such as the Pyramids at Giza or the Colossus of Rhodes have always been executed using some form of strategic management that could loosely be defined as the modern day equivalent of project management. The Romans, stepped up project management by executing massive programs across their empire that included cities and infrastructure (roads, aqueducts and sewers). The Roman's ability to plan and execute projects successfully stemmed from their military prowess and resulting ability to execute strategic war plans. Reporting to the senate and later to the triumvirate, Roman project managers were required to keeps project durations and costs to a minimum and changes to both were often met with criticism. This led to projects that created the Colosseum in the year 70 A.D and the Pantheon in the year 126 A.D.. Surprisingly, these projects were delivered in relatively short timeframes, Colosseum in 9 years, and the Pantheon in 7 years. Like the projects of today, the focus was primarily to keep the project sponsors happy.

In the west, the first signs of project management did not show up until the 11th or 12th century, with the end of the dark ages, as towns and cities expanded and grew. European cities vied with one another to build the most splendid of cathedrals to woo pilgrims. The renaissance period that followed, germinated artists such as Masolino da Panicale and

Donatello, who developed the art of perspective drawing aiding in better visualization and architectural planning. The industrial revolution and the invention of the steam engine brought about complexities, which the project management methodologies prevalent then, could not keep up with. Projects executed during that time were often so fraught with cost-overruns that they often bankrupted their sponsors. Notable examples are the Suez Canal and the Brooklyn Bridge both of which exceeded their original estimates, several-fold.

The First World War brought about the real need for projects to be delivered with no leverage for failure or overruns as the consequences were far reaching. Project management was finally recognized as a management function and the first frameworks for project delivery were formulated. As projects increased in criticality, there arose a need for a specific organizational entity to manage the delivery of these critical projects. The first use of a PMO is often credited to the US Air Corps who developed a 'Project Office' function to monitor aircraft development in the 1930s.

In 1942, the height of the Second World War, US Air Force's project offices, coordinated the development of the B-29 bomber and then in 1951, the Joint Project Office (JPO) coordinated the development of the B-47, with its engines carried in pods under the swept wing, the B-47 was a major innovation in post-World War II combat jet design, and helped lead to more complex aircraft such as the Convair B-58 Hustler. The B-58 was a major engineering challenge and the JPO adopted a monitoring and controlling role, integrating design, manufacturing, bombing and navigational expertise to deliver the first operational supersonic jet bomber capable of Mach 2 flight. The evolution of complex technologies such as the ICBM saw the JPO evolve to become the Weapon System Project Office (WSPO), where the practice of formal project management principles became the norm. These project offices saw the first use and development of both CPM (Critical Path Method) and PERT (Program Evaluation and Review Technique) techniques and charts giving project managers greater control. Projects began to be developed in a phased approach and improvements in budgets and predictions were seen.

The advent of the information technology age ushered in an era where companies began to deliver a multitude of projects, both for internal and external customers. These projects often spanned across various verticals in a company, often requiring the expertise of many, if not all departments of an organization and practitioners began to look for a common framework to deliver projects with PMOs as a general overseer.

During the dot-com boom of the 1990's, the PMO that we now know of today, was established. Project management became main-stream and organizations began undertaking more and more radical, cutting-edge, cross-functional projects whilst PMOs evolved to become complex entities and the strategic PMO with cross-functional expertise was born.

PMOs play a variety of roles, from merely existing due to the whimsical desires of a wishful senior management, to being a purveyor of project management practices and effort in an organization.

PMOs can be classified based on a variety of factors. Crawford JK and Cabanis-Brewin, classify PMOs based on its hierarchy in an organizational map.

PMO Type	Organizational Position
Type 1: Project Office	Operational Level
Type 2: Departmental Level PMO	Tactical Level
Type 3: Enterprise/ Strategic PMO	Strategic Level

PMOs that operate at the operational and tactical levels fail to see the big picture and are often seen fire-fighting as they constantly vacillate between shifting organizational priorities. These PMOs do not have the 'mile-high' view that is intrinsically important to plan and manage future demand. There is often redundant work being done across various departments. In some cases, projects with the same scope may be under execution within the same department. PMOs operating at this level are often over-loaded due to this redundancy and hence they are unable to put in place or administer standardized project management practices. Management loses trust in this kind of a PMO, is looked upon as a loss-center and scrapped to oblivion when any reformation exercises take place.

The Enterprise PMO (EPMO) or the strategic PMO, on the other hand, operates at a much higher level than the other PMOs. Typically reporting to one of the CxO positions, the EPMO consolidates the project management effort across various entities in the organization. Since the

Project Office's view of the strategic objectives

Departmental Level PMO's view of the strategic objectives

Strategic PMO's view of the strategic objectives

EPMO reports at a senior level, it has visibility towards the primary strategy (ies) of the organization and can hence manage a strategically-aligned portfolio. Every project delivered by the EPMO, contributes to the strategy in some form or the other, while adhering to organizationally mandated project management principles and processes. The EPMO is able to foresee and predict future demand due to its strategic position in the organizational hierarchy and is able to make proactive decisions in ramping up (or down) its capability to support and deliver. The EPMO can also prioritize projects, based on the project's strategic importance versus the PMO's capacity to deliver. The EPMO, by virtue of not being a customer of the project, is better suited to independently recording the ROI and intended benefits of implementing projects. A PMO such as the EPMO is often viewed by the management as a strategic asset.

Gerald I. Kendall and Steven C. Rollins further classify PMOs based on their value proposition based on two philosophical approaches. PMOs that focus purely to contain costs, called the "Cost-containment Model" and PMOs that focus on achieving organizational goals, called "Throughput Model". The authors in their publication "Project Portfolio Management and the PMO" (JRoss & IIL Pub., 2003) state that cost is not ignored in the throughput model but rather spending is validated on activities that create better throughput or efficiency thereby creating an intrinsic system of cost containment.

Peter Taylor from the APMG group classifies PMOs based on their operating approach. In his paper titled "Leading successful PMOs", he says PMOs can adopt four styles of engagement.

- Supportive

- Controlling

- Directive

- Blended

A supportive PMO as the name suggests, lends its support by way of expertise, processes and know-how to the project management effort underway in the organization, in more of what is known typically as "a pull" approach where help is solicited from the PMO by those requiring it.

A controlling PMO has a stronger hold on the project management effort in the organization, by forcing the adoption of a project management approach and model. The Directive PMO takes this, a step further and actually delivers projects for the organization. In this model of engagement, project managers actually belong to the Directive PMO, are assigned to projects and return to the PMO once the project is delivered. The fourth is a blended approach, which takes the best elements of the other three or any of the other two approaches to suit the needs of the organization or a particular project.

The core framework of the Utopian PMO

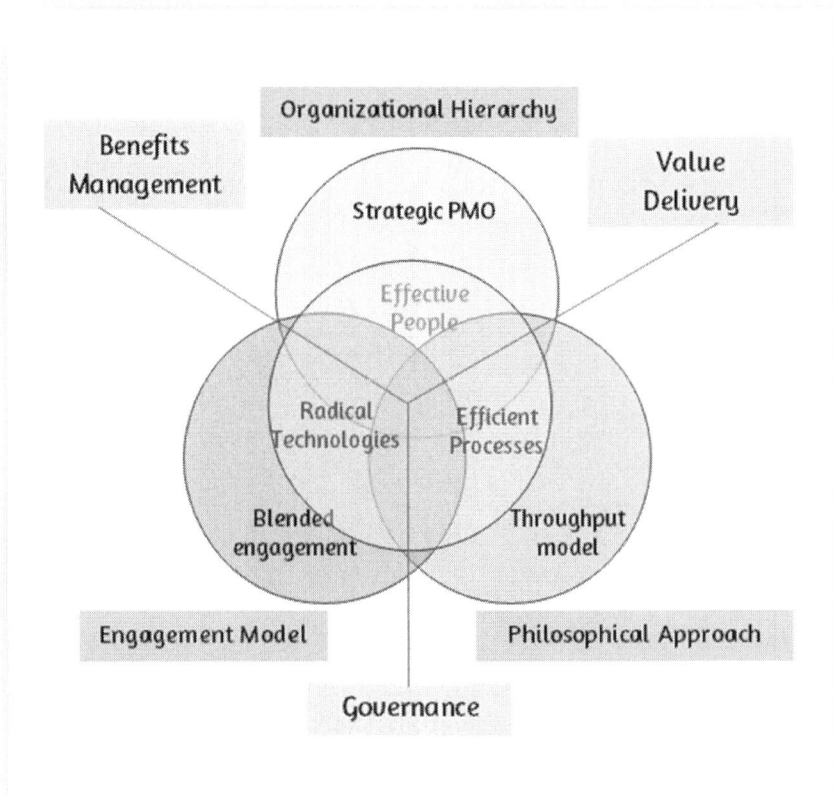

Organizational Hierarchy

Benefits Management

Value Delivery

Strategic PMO

Effective People

Radical Technologies

Efficient Processes

Blended engagement

Throughput model

Engagement Model

Philosophical Approach

Governance

The Utopian PMO

The Utopian PMO is defined as a strategic engine, consuming organizational resources on one end and efficiently and effectively delivering strategic projects on the other with minimal operational losses.

In other words, a Utopian PMO is the ultimate PMO, a pinnacle of its kind and like the very definition of Utopia, is an entity possessing highly desirable or near perfect qualities. Reengineering an existing PMO to a Utopian PMO will create a strategic engine that will ensure that:

- The organization's portfolio is a right mix of strategic, tactical and operational projects.

- Organizational strategy is an intrinsic part of all project work that the organization undertakes.

- Value and ROI of projects are delivered and benefits realized even if the benefit realization cycle is long.

- The organization is steeped in a culture of learning, coaching and mentoring with inter-departmental teams working in total synergistic balance. The PMO will also possess capabilities to take over failing projects under its wing to nurture and nourish them back on track, provisioning a blended engagement approach.

- Organizational resources are managed at an enterprise-level with periods of high capacity being forecast accurately and the PMO being able to support the same when the need arises.

- A standardized set of project management methodologies, practices and tools are used throughout the organization aligned to a standard and improved on a regular basis.

- A master road-map, reporting on delivered projects, current progress and future plans of all project management effort in the organization exists.

- Supporting structures, key to the functioning of a Utopian PMO such as resources, skills, templates and information systems are in place.

- A maturity measurement and improvement system is implemented to keep the Utopian PMO evolving to the next level.

- A skills development and assessment system is in place to ensure that the Utopian PMO staff is kept at the forefront of knowledge, aiding delivery success.

- It exists in a strategic position within the hierarchy such that it can raise an alarm if any of the above ceases to function or perform inefficiently.

Chapter 2
The Case for Reengineering

Now that the "what" question has been answered, we can proceed to the "why" part of it. This chapter discusses the business need for a re-engineering effort. A Utopian PMO is prescribed as the *reengineered* solution for any organization, that already has a PMO in place *but* the existing entity is one:

- that has no defined processes, for both its own operation and for that of the projects and programs within it purview. Each project manager in this kind of PMO is held hostage in case any project fails and there exists a general environment of chaos and poor reliability. These PMOs are often viewed as liability-centers and slated for shutdown at the first opportunity.

- that has no presence in project status meetings and is a sub-divisional entity within a division in an organization. This PMO produces no substantiated reports and has low staffing and high turnover of staff. This PMO also has no visibility on the status of any project management work currently underway in the entire organization. If questioned, the concerned project manager is sought hurriedly and a quick, often wrong status obtained.

- that has no involvement in hiring project management staff and therefore has no say in their promotions or career progressions, which usually in an environment of this type, are politically motivated. Favored project managers are always under allocated and the unpopular ones overburdened.

- that has no KPIs defined for all of its processes. There is no internal or external check for compliance and maturity assessment is, but a pipe dream.

- that has no benefits measurement team in place.

- that has no periodic reporting in place but sporadic, ad-hoc information on projects exist. Senior management has no idea where the current portfolio stands and may, in some cases, contact the project manager directly for updates, bypassing the PMO entirely.

- that has no supplier management function and each project manager handles their own vendors independently. Project managers are often left to their own discretion regarding whether a vendor should be monitored for compliance to processes and policies.

- that has no business relationship function and operates independently from the rest of the organization.

The US General Accounting Office (GAO) defines BPR as an activity that involves fundamentally rethinking of how organizations do their work in order to dramatically improve customer service, cut operational costs, and become world-class competitors.

Any process reengineering activity must be preceded by a business case that clearly establishes the need for this activity. Such a document must also define the purported benefits that are intended as a result of undertaking process reengineering.

Davenport (1990), defines a business process as a set of logically related tasks that enable a business related outcome to be achieved. BPR undertakes a fundamental rethink of these business processes, as opposed

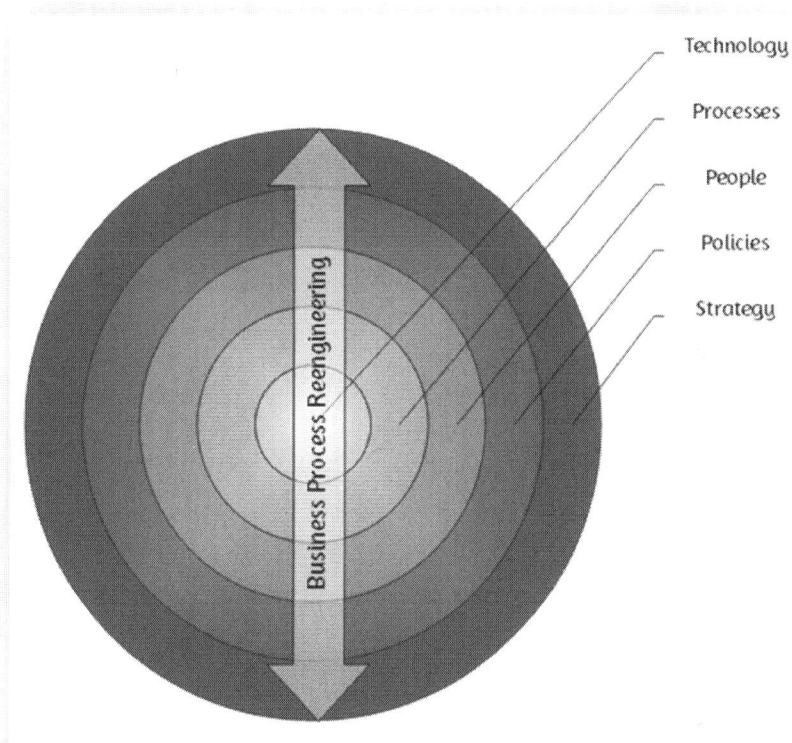

to ventures that result in incremental improvements. BPR is not a light-weight solution but rather a massive re-vamp at the organizational level. When an organization is not ready for dramatic changes or when business processes are already fundamentally sound, options other than BPR, especially those that emphasize marginal improvements must be considered.

The diagram above helps us infer two things. Firstly, BPR is an all-encompassing effort designed to strike at the operational, tactical and strategic levels in an organization. Secondly, that BPR can only be undertaken by organizations that already have a fundamental operating framework consisting of strategy, processes and people already in place.

We can also extrapolate this to mean than those organizations that have recently been incorporated, or those that have no strategy would find business process re-engineering to be an exercise in futility and to attempt BPR would result in no meaningful consequences.

Kevin B. Lowe (1995), sums it up best when he says BPR can show a company "how to do things right," but it is limited in its ability to show "the right things to do."

We have so far established two fundamental pre-requisites for an organization to consider and benefit from re-engineering. Let us now look at some of the other considerations that warrant merit, before an organization chooses to reengineer itself.

The US GAO provides guidance on the pre-requisites, through its seven-item checklist. This checklist, though created primarily for government agencies equally applies to organizations in the private sector as well. The GAO has also sufficiently caveated this checklist with the clause that, though the seven items are important to consider, they are by no means rigid or exhaustive. An organization or the person considering BPR has to be able to study the need for reengineering on a situational or case-by-case basis, considering the unique aspects that make up each organization.

The following assessment questions help an organization determine if reengineering the PMO is an appropriate direction to take.

Assessment Question 1: Has the Mission and/or Strategic Goal changed

An organization may choose to reassess its mission and strategic goals if it has been determined that:

- The original goals and mission of the organization no longer stand valid either due to lines of business being added / removed / modified due to changing market conditions or also because the original goals have already been fulfilled or even nullified.

- The organization is currently, facing external and internally mandated compliances, laws and regulations.

Reassessment of the mission and goals will inevitably involve:

- Identifying obstacles and the very feasibility of achieving the newly formed mission and goals.

- Reevaluation of the restructured mission and goals, with an aim of keeping the organization market-competitive.

- Validating if the organizational goals are in alignment with customer / client needs.

- Identifying core processes that are business differentiators. The BPR effort must always, focus on reengineering core processes such that, the primary improvements in efficiency are witnessed immediately, post-BPR.

- Considering out-sourcing non-core processes to improve operational efficiency, by focusing on the core business and reduction in risk (E.g. A financial institution may be able to gain a competitive advantage by outsourcing its IT support, those activities being non-core in nature). Reengineering non-core supporting processes will bring about changes in operational efficiency, but only if the primary processes are reengineered first.

Conclusion: Assessment question 1, allows us to consider going ahead with reengineering the PMO if:

- An enterprise- PMO already exists with basic processes, procedures and a methodology.

- This soon-to-be reengineered PMO is expected to execute strategic projects as part of its core business activities.

- There is a change in organizational direction, mission and overall strategy.

Assessment Question 2: Does the cut-over to the new strategic direction, warrant reengineering?

After answering the first assessment question, an organization may find that the PMO is indeed a core business activity that warrants reengineering, to meet the new strategic goals of the organization. It may also, on the other hand, find that the changes required to meet the new direction, to be marginal and not requiring a full-fledged BPR program. If BPR is the strategic direction, then the entity considering BPR must now begin to move into phase 2 of the assessment:

- Identify senior management's commitment to the idea of reengineering. Though BPR is a grass-roots level change, it definitely needs to be driven by a top-down approach. Senior management buy-in is obligatory for any organizational level improvement.

- Getting the aforementioned buy-in will involve the creation of a business case depicting the predicted benefits of reengineering the PMO and the benefits to expect post-BPR. A study confirming that all other possible alternatives were considered, before proposing BPR as the potential answer, is mandatory. This business case will also explore, albeit at a high level, the potential costs, and internal capabilities to perform BPR. If the BPR exercise is being outsourced, an assessment must be made, to confirm the organization's ability to manage the BPR vendor.

- In almost every case, reengineering the PMO must never be undertaken in isolation and must be a part of an overall organizational-level, cross-functional improvement effort.

Conclusion: Assessment question 2, allows us to consider going ahead with reengineering the PMO, if a clear business case for the BPR program was created and approved by the executive management of the organization and this business case has explicitly considered and concluded that:

- No improvement programs other than a BPR will suffice.

- The organization is ready for BPR and that capabilities exist, to either execute or manage an outsourced vendor performing this BPR.

- The PMO reengineering program is not being undertaken in isolation but is a part of larger transformation effort underway throughout the organization or planned in the near future.

Assessment Question 3: Do organizational capabilities for managing the BPR exist?

Assessment question 2 helped us determine, if a fundamental revamp of the PMO's processes was *the* solution that the organization required and a high-level business case was created to prove this need. This business case also establishes, at a high-level that capabilities exist within the organization to either execute or manage the BPR exercise.

Assessment question 3 determines very specific requirements that an organization must possess before undertaking a reengineering of the PMO. These controls must at a minimum include:

- Establishing the BPR as a strategic project with its own executive steering committee with the CEO, preferably as its head.

- Identification of resources to manage the project and an experienced team to perform the desired reengineering exercise. This presents a quandary. On one hand a team that has understood or has worked with the processes are best qualified to reengineer them, but on the other hand, they would possess the least process reengineering experience, especially when compared to professional consultants who specialize in BPR. Most often, organizations choose to employ BPR experts to reengineer processes as opposed to internal resources due to the following reasons:

  - External resources are free from organizational politics and are able to make decisions independent of them. For example, in a BPR exercise for a large government entity, executed using internal teams, requests were received, using covert channels, for designing processes such that new project requests are required to be reviewed by all six PMO staff so that they could choose which project they wished to be assigned to. The PMO staff, preferred, most often than not, to be assigned to small, non-critical projects, due to their reduced work load.

- BPR experts have far reaching insight into leading practices and are not inflicted by resistance to change that often plagues internal resources who are used to doing things a certain way.

- BPR experts are not practitioners of the processes they reengineer and this ensures that they are not creating processes that circumvent requisite controls with the intent of making them easy to execute.

- If a decision has been made to outsource the BPR effort, then a suitable vendor is selected, via a competitive outsourcing process (unless only a sole or single vendor exists).

- Dooley & Johnson, 2001 recommend a combination of resources including those familiar with the processes and some resources that have no familiarity of the processes (consultants). Covert (1997) recommends a team size of no more than ten members.

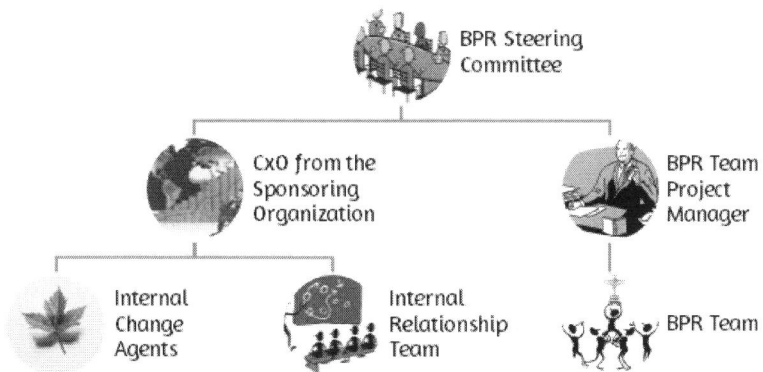

Conclusion: Assessment question 3, checks off the requirement to have:

- An independent authority, free from ulterior agenda to reengineer the PMO processes.

- A steering committee, properly represented by executive management, with sufficient vested powers to manage the exercise.

- Internal teams within the organization to support change and manage relationships.

Assessment Question 4: Does the reengineering team have a defined methodology and plan in place?

Assessment question 3 completes determining if the organization is ready to undertake a BPR. Assessment question 4 helps establish if the team performing the reengineering has:

- A clear plan and methodology for executing the BPR, such as the one outlined, in this book that has been agreed with the steering committee.

- Standards and leading practices have been referred to and an appropriate methodology for alignment has been agreed. Typically one of the industry leading frameworks such as the PMBoK®, PRINCE2® or any other leading frameworks for project management is selected. If there is a need, a combination comprising of the best of these methodologies are used. When consultants are reengineering PMOs that handle both projects and programs, any leading framework such as this or the P3O can be sought for guidance.

- Implementation plans, change management plans and training initiatives have been planned to the level possible and organizational-level awareness has been created about the upcoming exercise.

- Processes and teams for pilot implementation, change agents and other such implementation supports are planned.

- Benefits management and other such evaluations are considered and prior planning has taken place to ensure this.

- Sufficient allowances have been made, by the organization undergoing the BPR to accommodate a study period where the current state of processes is studied by the reengineering team.

- Quick wins for every phase identified and the approvals of the steering committee for implementation obtained.

A quick win is an improvement that is visible, has immediate benefit, and can be delivered quickly after the project begins. Quick wins, help garner immediate support and acceptance for an initiative.

- Appraised the steering committee about the use of supporting information technology options available and also ensured that it has the involvement of experts in these technologies.

- Prepared and received approvals for a funding plan to fund the project till completion (or handover as the case may be) and,

- Included all potential stakeholders in determining expectations from the BPR project, especially the organization's employees, who often mistake BPR to be an attempt to lay-off or down-size.

Conclusion: Assessment question 4, checks off the final requirements to consider a BPR exercise, including:

- A clear plan and methodology for the BPR exercise.

- Creation of awareness within the organization to support the BPR execution team.

- Identification of training and change management needs.

Assessment Question 5: Is a Utopian PMO the reengineered solution?

Assessment question 5 helps determine if a Utopian PMO is a solution that will fit the current organizational structure.

- A Utopian PMO can only function in an organization that is significantly large, has been in existence for several years, has several thousand employees, is matrix in nature and depends extensively on the delivery of strategic, internal and external projects for its survival and for the contentment of its customers. A government institution, or a multi-national corporation best defines the kind of organization where the Utopian PMO is the need of the hour and, if implemented, operates at its best.

Conclusion

The 5 assessment questions in this chapter, helps one think of BPR on a deeper level and determine organizational readiness from different perspectives. Each perspective probes at a level more profound than the previous. Starting with the viability of BPR as an improvement program to tangible checks such as those for management support and executional ability of the organization. The 4th assessment question ensures that the performing team has a definite plan for executing the BPR such as the one that the next few chapters detail. This plan can easily be ported to any strategic-level PMO, wishing to be reengineered. The 5th assessment checks if a Utopian PMO is an apt solution for the given situation.

The answers for each of the assessment questions will form the parts of a compelling business case, that can not only help win support for the reengineering exercise, but also ensure that the far reaching benefits of BPR are understood and the organization is in a position to embrace the benefits of a Utopian PMO.

Chapter 3
The Business Process Reengineering Framework

O nce a solid case for reengineering the PMO has been built, via the assessment questions and has the management's buy-in, the next step for the reengineering team, is to put together a framework for this exercise. The framework for reengineering the PMO is no different than other commonly used reengineering approaches that have the following main phases, often with differing terminologies:

- The Definition Phase
- The Study Phase
- The Develop Phase
- The Deploy Phase
- The Post-Deployment Phase

Though these phases are performed consecutively, there may be several iterations of feedback, between the develop and study phases. Each phase is comprised of a set of activities which have deliverables as an outcome, which feed into the subsequent phases as inputs.

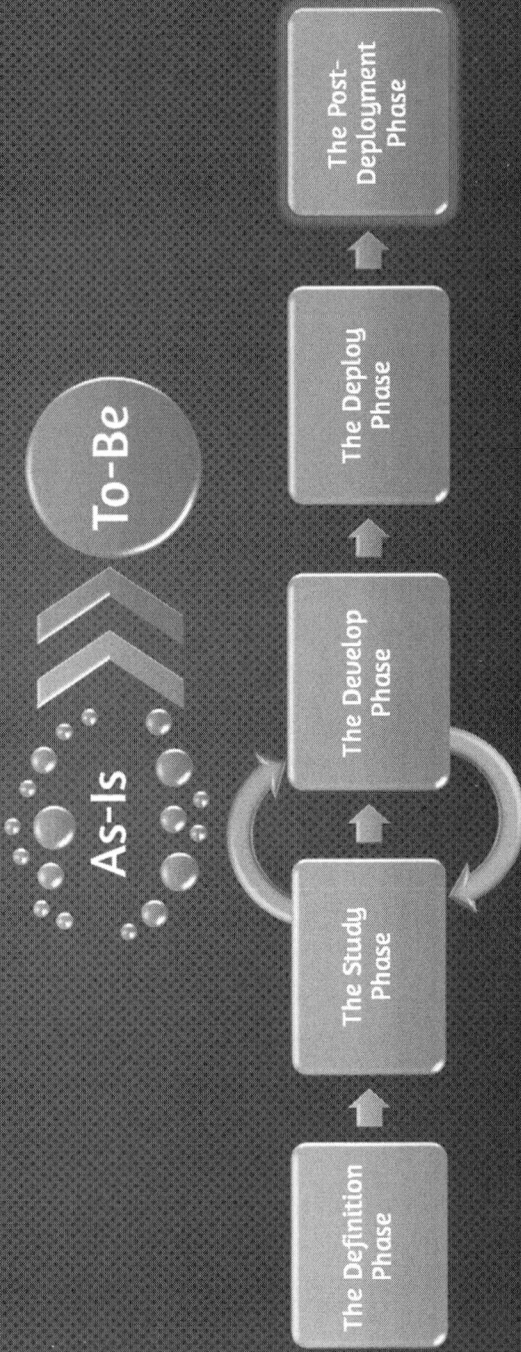

The Utopian Project Management Office – Reengineering Framework

As-Is

To-Be

The Definition Phase

The Study Phase

The Develop Phase

The Deploy Phase

The Post-Deployment Phase

Chapter 4

The Definition Phase

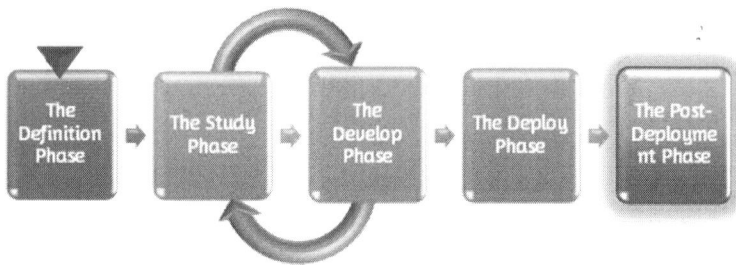

The BPR project for the PMO begins with the definition phase. The backbone for the BPR exercise is defined and a detailed framework for delivering the BPR is established. Some of the key steps in this phase include:

- **Preparation of the team**: The BPR team is assembled and an induction exercise is run, to acquaint the team with the high-level pre-requisites and expectations. This induction process must also include representatives from the internal change management and relationship building teams. The team is provided with the necessary tools and infrastructure. Laptops, e-mails and other information technologies necessities are set-up. A Project Management Information System (PMIS), for purposes of team collaboration and information storage purposes is highly recommended. A cloud based system will greatly enhance the efficiency of the team allowing quick review and approval cycles. The BPR team, could also consider open-source or free resources on the internet for sourcing collaboration software.

Key Outcomes:

- Team acquainted with each other.

- Communication infrastructure Set-up.

- Collaboration portal set-up.

- **BPR Team organization:** Team hierarchies are set-up and reporting relationships are established. A detailed team organization chart with contact details is created and stored on the collaboration portal. The reengineering team must be sponsored, preferably by a CxO position, with the necessary authority and intrinsic interest to bring about the proposed change to the present operating model. It is a necessity to have an exclusive project manager to manage the overall effort. It is preferable that this project manager not be a Subject Matter Expert (SME) in the same project to prevent possible conflicts of interest. This also ensures that the project manager is able to, dedicate his time towards managing the project. Also recommended, is a project support or a coordinator position to coordinate the various activities and maintain cohesiveness of the team, especially if some of the SMEs are virtually located and to help manage and bring some sense to the vast amounts of data, that a project such as this usually accumulates.

Key Outcomes:

- Team hierarchies established.

- Project hierarchical organization chart.

- Sponsor validated.

- Project Manager appointed.

- Project support / coordinator appointed.

- **BPR Project Setup:** The PMO BPR initiative is foremost, a project in its own right and any change the project hopes to have on the organization, is possible only if the BPR project is in itself managed properly. In that regard, the BPR project's charter, duly signed by the sponsor, the project plan, the risk and issues register are created and maintained on the PMIS. Weekly team meetings and meeting schedules with the sponsor are agreed. Also included in the project schedule are placeholders for weekly risk meetings. The methodology for delivering the BPR project is recommended to be aligned to any commonly accepted project management frameworks such as the PMBOK® or PRINCE2®. This includes creating all project-related documents that the framework recommends. Any project delivery approach consists of the following lifecycle phases, in one variation or the other.

  - Initiation or pre-project
  - Planning or directing
  - Execution or delivering
  - Monitoring and control
  - Closing the project

It would also be prudent at this juncture to determine the acceptance criteria for the delivered processes, as well any other specific outcome-related requirements that the sponsoring organization might have, including quality requirements.

Key Outcomes:

- BPR Project Charter

- BPR Project Plan (including subsidiary plans)

- BPR Project Risk Register

- BPR Project Issue Log

- BPR Project Schedule

- BPR Project Deliverables' Acceptance Criteria

- **BPR Project Stakeholders:** The BPR team, under the guidance of the project sponsor, as well as by a thorough analysis, ascertains the stakeholders of the BPR project. An enterprise PMO is usually an all-encompassing entity and the stakeholders for such a centralized division is usually spread out throughout the organization. Various functional managers who have until now run projects in their own disparate fashion will now either support or oppose the initiative depending on their mindset. Early identification of all stakeholders and appropriate tact in the way the reengineering team approaches them is key to garnering lasting support for the project. It does not suffice to just identify stakeholders, but rather elaborate information-gathering techniques are used, which can help stakeholders reveal their pain-points, that the performing team can attempt to resolve when designing new processes.

Key Outcomes:

- BPR Project Stakeholder Register

- Stakeholders ranked by Power and Influence

- **BPR Project Alignment:** A strategic enterprise PMO plays a huge part in interacting with several organizational departments. The BPR team must ensure that interaction points between the PMO processes and their internal processes are considered when designing the reengineered processes. The focus is usually on the following organizational entities, including but not limited to:

    - The Strategy Department / CEO's Office

    - Finance and Accounting Department

    - Contracts and Procurement Department

Key Outcomes:

- Inter-department alignment points

- **Leading Practices alignment:** One of the primary purposes of having a process reengineering exercise done is to ensure alignment of the PMOs processes to a global standard. Some organizations may express their preference upfront, by virtue of having staff with expertise in a particular global standard, or because they have tangible reason to believe that a particular standard is a best fit for their organization. In PMO reengineering projects, the sponsoring organization will often choose from leading frameworks for program and portfolio management guidance such as the PMBoK® or PRINCE2®. The BPR team can determine such preferences, if they exist. If no such preference exists then the BPR team can alternatively propose the Utopian PMO model, after a careful study of the organization in the study phase. Another factor that may play a role in considering the direction to take may be influenced by a strategic or organizational mandate. For example: A mandate requiring all federal government PMOs be aligned to a particular framework.

Key Outcomes:

- Preferred standard for alignment identified

- **BPR Project Awareness:** A crucial part of the BPRs success is lodged in the cooperation of the employees of the sponsoring organization. Getting this cooperation is dependent on the employees of the sponsoring organization having a clear understanding, that the reengineering effort is a step in the right direction for the organization, in terms of optimizing its operations and not an attempt to downsize or lay-off employees. The BPR team must also note that any attempt to estimate the present workload of the existing organization's staff, will usually yield in skewed results, as the employees take on more responsibilities than usual to demonstrate their extended contribution to the organization, in the hope that the BPR team exclude them from layoffs that the employees, wrongly perceive as imminent.

Key Outcomes:

- Awareness campaigns

- Launch of change management initiatives

- **Process Prioritization:** The BPR team must determine if any particular processes in the PMO need to be reengineered first, to overcome any current organizational pain points. Conversely, the sponsoring organization, by self-assessment may have already determined that a particular sub-set of their processes are sufficiently robust for their need. In this case, the BPR team is able to determine a priority list of those processes, where efforts need to be focused first.

Key Outcomes:

- Priority list of processes

- **Quick Wins:** The identification of those action items that can provide quick and lasting relief to existing problems in the organization must be the first order of priority. It is imperative that these action items have a short implementation time-span, so that the BPR team can demonstrate to the organization that change, can indeed be beneficial. Since no formal study of the existing "as-is" processes have been done, any quick wins that are identifiable at this point, will most likely be due to observation or perceived during conversations with key stakeholders. Any identified quick wins must be subject to detailed scrutiny and only after extensive internal vetting, must they be presented to the client for approval. It is imperative for the BPR team to get outcomes from identified quick wins right, the first time, in order to build trust and reliability.

Conclusion

The first phase of the BPR project aims to establish the BPR project's internal structure and operating framework. Also done at this stage are building of key relationships:

- Among the BPR team members
- Between the internal teams and the BPR team
- With key stakeholders

This phase also establishes points of alignment between key PMO processes and other departmental processes, such as those in strategy, finance and procurement. A standard for aligning the new operating model is established and awareness for the upcoming project activities is created in the sponsoring organization. This phase also includes a study of the quick wins and organization pain points to help establish a sense of what efforts to focus on, first. This phase in essence lays the foundation for the remainder of the reengineering effort, that is to follow in the subsequent phases.

Chapter 5
The Study Phase

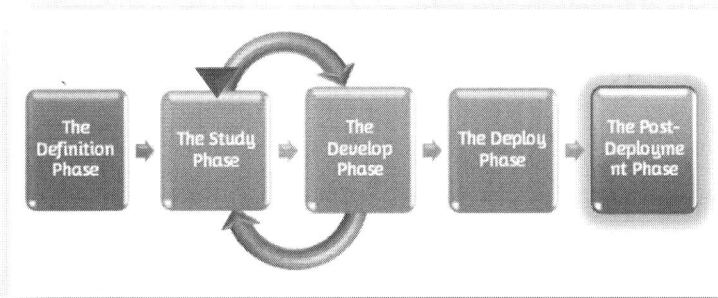

A fter the establishment of BPR as a project, in the sponsoring organization, the next course of business for the BPR team is to conduct a study or an "as-is" review of the existing processes.

A snap shot of the current state of processes is known as the "As-Is". This is used to form a baseline for future work and for purposes of comparison, once improvement activities have concluded.

To be able to conduct a meaningful study of the current state of processes, the BPR team must review any documentation of the processes that exist. It may not be unusual to find these legacy processes function entirely without any written documentation. This is a usual scenario in public sector reengineering projects where projects are run in some manner simply because they have been done the same way for the past years. Information, templates and processes are usually passed on as a word of mouth and a lot of it is lost when employees leave or retire. The key to understanding legacy processes lies in conducting detailed interviews.

The ability to conduct detailed interviews is again dependent on a competent stakeholder identification process. The initial list of stakeholders identified in the definition phase is further reinforced with key additional information such as their current levels of influence and support towards the reengineering effort. The key success of the BPR project or any project for that matter rests on getting the reengineered processes accepted by key stakeholders for transition into operations. Several tools that can be used to facilitate this.

A stakeholder matrix, like the one shown below will help document project stakeholders and assign a subjective rating for their levels of influence and support. This rating is usually subjective based on the perception of the interviewer and later ratified with the rest of the team if necessary. A range of scales can be chosen, for example: 1-10. Personal experience has shown that adopting an unequal interval scale of the kind: 1, 4,7,10 greatly reduces subjective errors and facilitates quicker consensus among the team members on the chosen scores.

Name	Role	Current Influence	Desired Influence	Current Support	Desired Support
Stakeholder1	PMO Head	7	10	7	10
Stakeholder2	Strategy Dir	4	10	7	10
Stakeholder3	Procur. Dir.	4	7	1	7

A pictorial depiction such as the one shown below will further help the BPR team in understanding the stakeholder effort involved. Other grids such as one proposed by Eden and Ackermann (1998) plot stakeholders by their power and interest in a 4x4 grid. Stakeholders are assigned their positions on the grid helping, identify true "players" from those that are irrelevant in the context of the project referred to as "crowds". Eden and Ackermann, also provide strategies for liaising with the stakeholders in various categories.

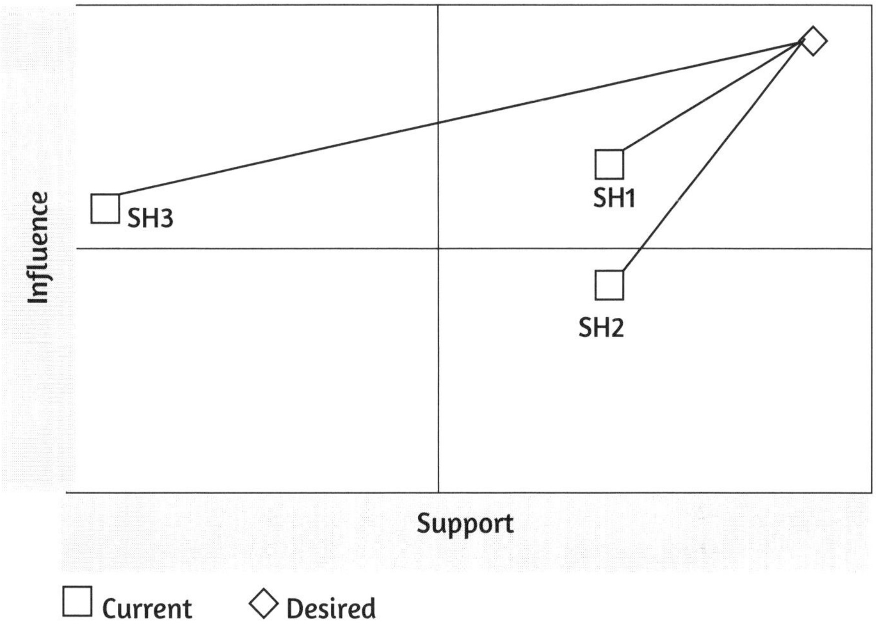
SH3
SH1
SH2
Influence
Support
Current
Desired

Andersen (1995);Kotler et al. (2002) suggest identifying stakeholders with competing requirements, also referred to as having supra-interests as opposed to common interests. The technique suggested by Bryant (2003), suggests the use of diagrams such as the one below to assess potential areas of cooperation among stakeholders with competing requirements to come up with those common requirements that contribute to the greater good of the organization as a whole.

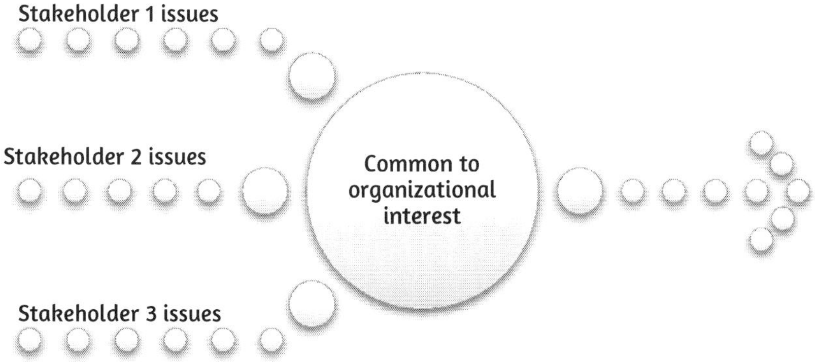
Stakeholder 1 issues
Stakeholder 2 issues
Common to organizational interest
Stakeholder 3 issues

Anderson et al (1999), suggest forming coalitions of larger groups of stakeholders to push for adoption of practices that could help the organization. The key items to remember are:

- Effective stakeholder identification is key to BPR success.

- The BPR team must act upon each of the stakeholders to achieve a cohesive, unified support structure to push for operational transformation.

"The Flight of Stairs" Maturity Assessment

Documenting the current state of PMO maturity is important to help establish an overall baseline. This baseline can help the BPR team two-fold. Firstly, it can help the team identify existing strengths and weaknesses in the present PMO and as a consequence identify the areas of effort. Secondly and most importantly, it can help the BPR team prove at the end of the BPR project, that improvements have indeed taken place, provided the benefits realization phase of this initiative effectively captures the post-BPR maturity of the PMO.

The maturity of the PMO as a whole is, the sum of the maturity levels of each individual lines of practice, within the Utopian PMO, which are delineated into the following:

- **Governance and Strategic Alignment**

- **Process Maturity Management**

- **Delivery Management**

- **Resource Management**

- **Quality Management , Compliance & Maturity**

- Benefits Management

- Reporting

- Supplier Management

- Business Relationship Management

The "flight of stairs" maturity model is an assessment model, which validates an organization's maturity on a scale of 1-3 points on the above assessment verticals. The present score vs. the desired score represents the vertical aspect of each stair. Greater the gap, higher the organization must "climb" to reach the desired level. Once the organization "climbs" all the steps that cover the above assessment verticals, the organization reaches its "to-be" maturity state. The order of depiction of the various assessment levels is non-consequential and each assessment level carries an equivalent level in importance. A scoring system of 1-3 was adopted to ease the scoring process, by attempting to draw analogies with the black-grey-white approach equated to the following incremental stages:

- Non-compliant
- Understanding the need for compliance
- Compliant

Taking an organization to the highest level of maturity in each of the assessment verticals involves, implementing the key PMO processes as well as other framework processes, described later in this book. The processes are recommended only if the desired maturity levels have not yet been attained. If an organization evaluates itself at the top maturity score of 3 for a particular vertical, it can ignore improvements in that vertical and focus on improving those verticals in which the organization was assessed at less than perfect scores. A detailed system for scoring maturity at each of the verticals is given below.

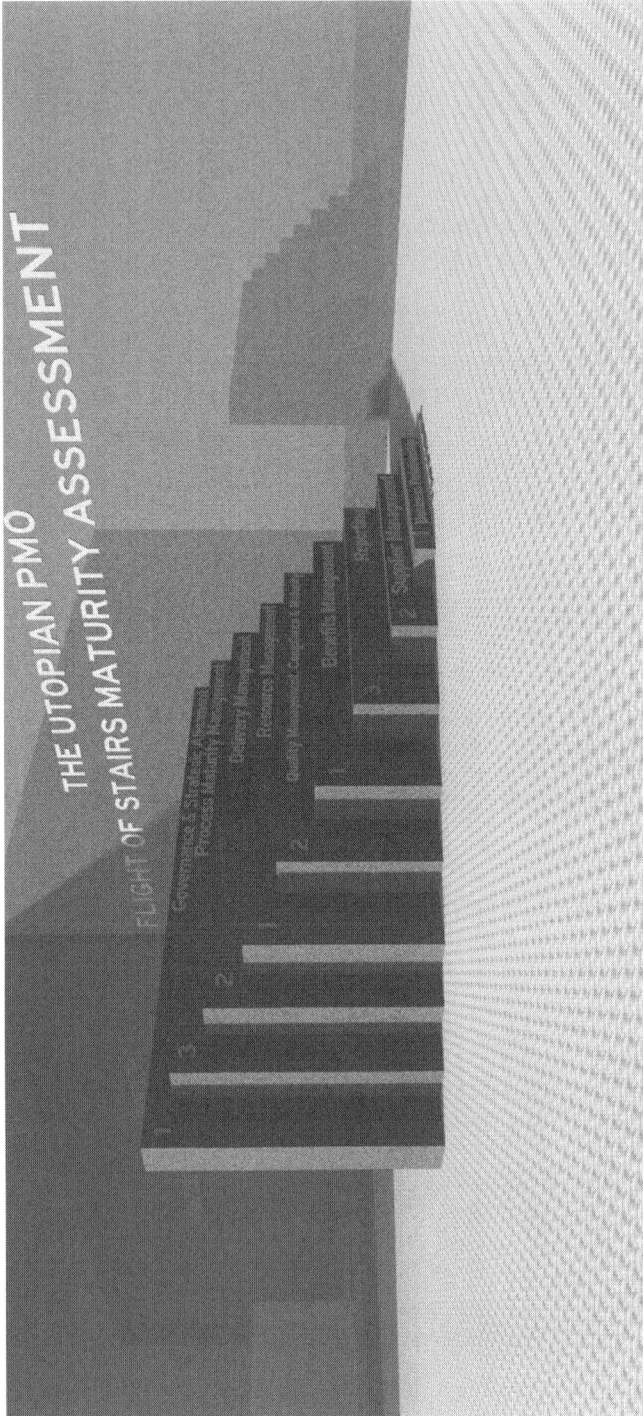

The Utopian PMO's 9- Step Maturity assessment model

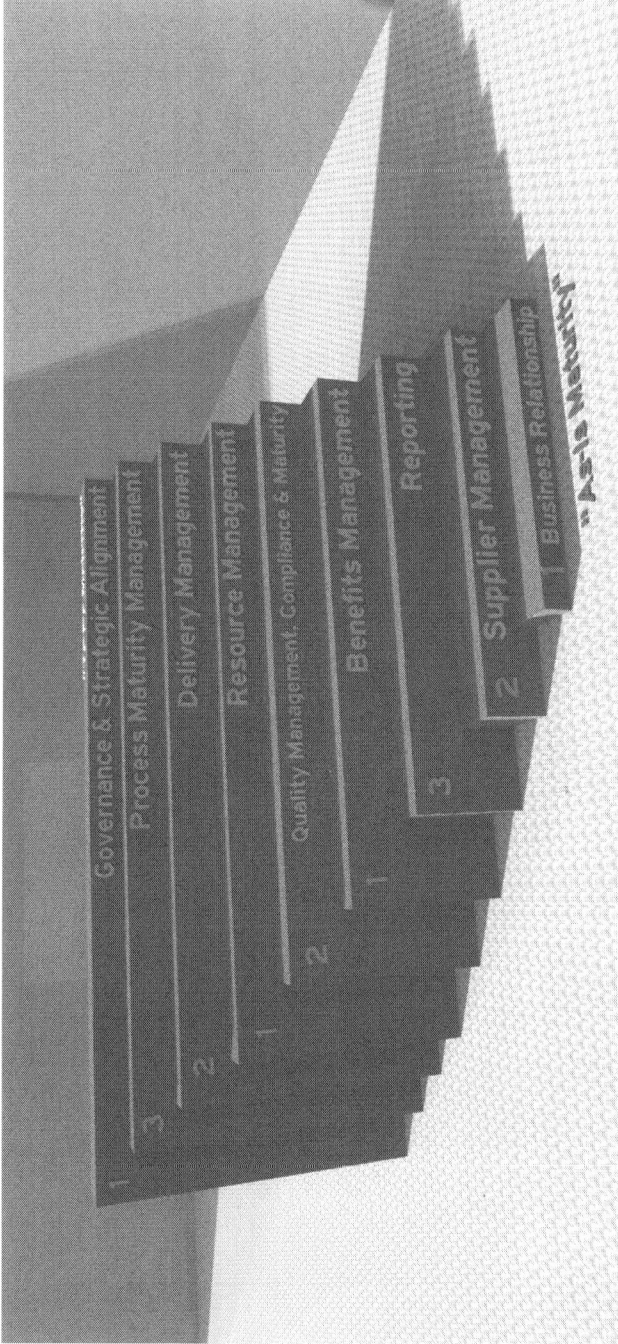

The 9 verticals of Assessment, depicted with the scores of a mock assessment

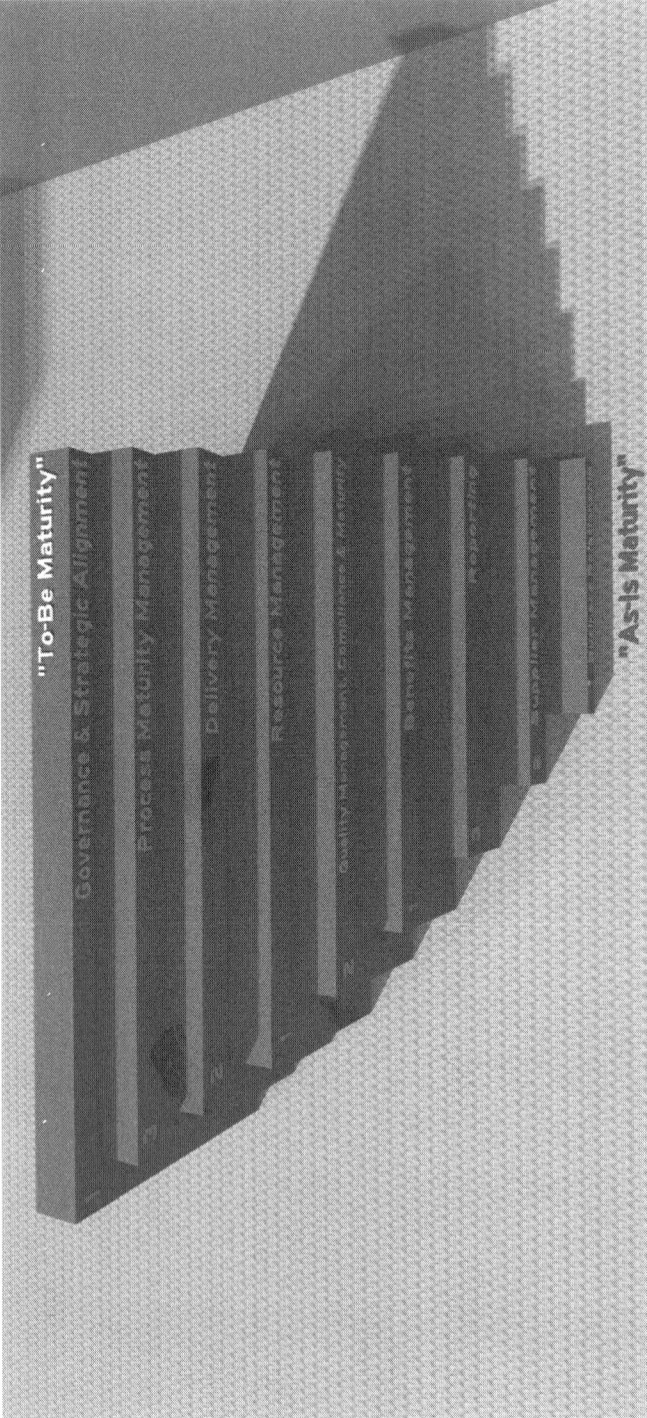

The 'flight of stairs' from "as-is" and "to-be"

Governance and Strategic Alignment

Governance and Strategic Alignment, quite possibly, the most important function of a PMO, serves to maintain strategic alignment of an organization's portfolio with its strategy. A Utopian PMO especially, has an established process for assessing this fit before the commencement of any project-related work, and therefore can be awarded a maximum score of 3 on a 3-point scale on this vertical. Any and all strategic work adopted for execution by the PMO must first be vetted by an executive team for the following:

- Is the proposed piece of work in alignment with the mission, vision and value statements of the organization?

- Is the proposed piece of work delivering a strategic, tactical or operational goal or parts thereof?

- Has a business case comprising the strategic, economic, commercial, financial and management cases been created and a value-proposition for each been articulated and agreed?

- Have the organizational-level risks arising from delivering this project been understood and agreed?

- Is the proposed work in violation of any regulations in effect or known to be imposed in the near future?

- Have other alternatives been considered and a rational check made to ensure that the solution selected has merits other than financial alone?

- Do any potential conflicts of interest exist?

- Can the scope of the proposed work be fit into any of the existing initiatives and can the present portfolio accommodate this initiative at its present capacity or can it be deferred for later delivery?

A PMO can be graded at less than the maximum points for maturity on the governance and strategic alignment vertical, in case of the following scenarios:

1 Point: for a PMO in an organization where projects and strategy have never historically met. Projects are undertaken due to the aspirations of stakeholders and departmental heads. Projects are never assessed for ROI and/or benefits and any such returns are purely coincidental. PMO is often blamed for execution failures and not included in any organization level decision making.

2 Points: for a PMO that is represented in strategy meetings and where a basic awareness exists that projects must be validated against the strategy of the organization. Some project managers in this kind of a PMO take a personal initiative to create business cases that are sporadically reviewed. However a PMO that does not review benefits or assess risks at a strategic level can only be awarded 2 points at this assessment vertical.

Process Maturity

Process maturity, is one single factor, in which most maturity assessments place their emphasis on. Though the maturity of project and program management processes in an organization, are primary determinants in assessing the maturity of the PMO, they can hardly be looked at in isolation but rather as a sub-set of other functions of an enterprise PMO.

A PMO can be awarded the maximum score of 3 on a 3-point scale if this PMO, unconditionally:

- Adopts a leading practice framework for its own operations as well as for the projects and programs under its purview and subsequently customizes the same to meet its internal needs and requirements.

- Has this customized framework extensively documented with each process having:

    - Process Maps
    - Standard Operating Procedures
    - Triggers
    - Owners
    - Alignment / hand-over points/ kill points
    - Review dates / cycles

- Has this framework published, on an enterprise-level collaboration portal.

- Has a feedback mechanism to enable process practitioners to provide operational-level feedback on the processes.

- Validates future updates to the public-framework against its own customized framework to identify improvement opportunities.

- Conducts systematic phase-gate exits and inspections on *all projects* in the organizational portfolio and not on a sample of projects.

- Has a dedicated function within the PMO to identify maturity improvements to the framework, processes and procedures. This function also has mandates to look for potential alignment points with other organizational functions.

- Has a training team to induct new project management staff into the customized framework.

- Holds periodic refresher sessions for all members of the project management community in the organization.

A PMO can be graded at less than the maximum points for maturity at the process maturity vertical in case of the following scenarios:

1 Point: for a PMO that has no defined processes for both its own operation and for that of the projects and programs within it purview. Each project manager in this kind of PMO is held hostage in case any project fails and there is a general environment of chaos and poor reliability. These PMOs are often viewed as liability-centers and slated for shutdown at the first opportunity.

2 Points: can be awarded for a PMO that has no defined PMO processes but project and program management processes, however exist. Most, if not all projects are in compliance. A rudimentary system of checking compliance exists and most processes in the framework are available in some form for reference. The project management community in the organization takes the initiative to study and follow defined processes.

Delivery Management

Delivery management takes accountability for the delivery of projects and ensures that project managers have no obstacles in keeping up their commitment of the delivery dates. The Utopian PMO has a proven track record of deliveries and thus has the management's confidence. A PMO of this type gets a score of 3 out of a maximum of 3, if all of the following happen consistently:

- The PMO has recorded sufficient historical information, to help the project managers provide accurate delivery dates.

- The PMO is present on project status and risk meetings to help provide solutions that may not be immediately apparent to the project manager and provides escalation paths for issues beyond its remit.

- The PMO has sufficient seniority in the organization structure to raise an alarm if a project is losing its grip on delivery or costs.

- The PMO has experts and the bandwidth to temporarily take over or assist project managers burdened with failing or slipping projects.

- The PMO uses discrete frameworks for delivery of initiatives depending on its classification as a project or as a program as opposed to a one size fits all approach.

A PMO can be graded at less than the maximum points for maturity at the delivery management vertical in case of the following scenarios:

1 Point: for a PMO that has no presence in project status meetings and is a sub-divisional entity within a division in an organization. This PMO has no visibility on the status of any project management work currently underway in the entire organization. If questioned, the concerned project manager is sought hurriedly and a quick, often wrong status obtained.

2 Points: can be awarded for a PMO that has limited presence in project status and risk meetings. This PMO supports some projects in the entity on an ad-hoc basis or on demand. However, this PMO cannot be awarded full points if it does not possess the capability to nurture and support sick projects.

Resource Management

The Resource management function is tasked with developing and retaining top-notch project management talent. The Utopian PMO aggressively pursues and retains top project management talent for the organization. This PMO also manages the career paths of the project managers within its purview. Also, the definition of resources in this context is not limited to human capital but also those resources that provide project management capability such as Enterprise Project Management (EPM) Software. This kind of a PMO:

- Pursues and retains project management talent on behalf of the organization.

- Maintains a detailed skills list and career paths for each of the project management staff in its purview that is free from organizational politics and based purely on merit.

- Maintains a current and up to date resource utilization level and ensures that spare bandwidth is always available to accommodate new strategic initiatives. Project management staff is constantly encouraged to keep themselves at the forefront of knowledge regarding frameworks and project management in general.

- Ensure that the project management community is not over-burdened and likewise not under-allocated.

- Monitors the utilization of other technology services that help deliver project management such as EPM and other collaboration services.

A PMO can be graded at less than the maximum points for maturity at the resource management vertical in case of the following scenarios:

1 Point: for a PMO that has no involvement in hiring project management staff and therefore has no say in their promotions or career progressions which are usually in an environment of this type, politically motivated. Favored project managers are always under allocated and the unpopular ones overburdened.

2 Points: can be awarded for a PMO that has limited authority in hiring project management talent but to be awarded 2 points, this PMO must, at a minimum, be able to positively influence the career paths of the project management team. This PMO might not have an *updated* skill list or allocation chart though one may have been created at some point in time and then sporadically updated.

Quality Management, Compliance & Maturity

The Utopian PMO places high reliance on quality and constantly measures its performance against stated baselines using the Quality Management, Compliance & Maturity function. A PMO of this standard that is rated at a score of 3 has:

- A defined list of KPIs for each of its processes. Periodic assessment of the KPIs as well as re-assessment of these metrics at pre-defined intervals.

- An ability to make sure that the captured information on the metrics flow upwards to feed the overall organizational metrics.

- Compliance to processes is audited by itself or by a competent third-party at pre-defined intervals.

- Maturity assessment is done at pre-defined intervals to compare its maturity against itself after a certain period of time has elapsed.

- A clearly defined plan of action exists at all times for items that have been found to be non-compliant as well to improve on the recent maturity assessment results (if required).

A PMO can be graded at less than the maximum points for maturity at the quality management vertical in case of the following scenarios:

1 Point: for a PMO that has no KPIs defined for all of its processes. There is no internal or external check for compliance and maturity assessment is but a pipe dream.

2 Points: can be awarded for a PMO that has KPIs in place for most of its processes. An internal compliance check takes place, though sporadically. Maturity assessments have been attempted but no firm actions have been taken on the identified deficiencies and non-compliances.

Benefits Management

An item of paramount importance for any organization wishing to create a result-oriented, high-impact, project delivery environment is benefits realization or benefits measurement. A Utopian PMO has intrinsically high maturity in the strategic alignment vertical. To be assessed with the maximum scores at this level, this PMO must have business cases clearly linking the project to strategic objective on the top end and expected benefits on the other.

A business case links the strategic objectives for executing a project with the benefits expected from its successful execution

The primary difficulty in practically being able to measure benefits accurately is the long benefits realization cycle that some projects intrinsically have. In fact a BPR project itself is a very good example of a project with long benefit realization cycle. Improvements in reengineered processes often manifest themselves in several non-trivial ways, many of which are seldom measured. For example: adequate, well-defined processes often lead to low employee turn-over due to higher job satisfaction that comes from being in control of daily work but this reduction in employee turnover may sometimes, take several years to surface among the other noise that is generated in any large organization's data.

A PMO with the maximum scores at the benefits realization assessment vertical has:

- A dedicated benefits management team who actively scout purported benefits and have an ability to extrapolate these benefits to unintended ones. For E.g. a customer satisfaction improvement project that also improved employee satisfaction is an unintended benefit.

- An escalation path to highlight projects that have not managed to achieve intended benefits and the resulting recovery plans (if any).

- Reports made for projects that have a fixed benefits realization date. For E.g. A project to add a new server to decrease transaction processing time by 10 minutes within 24hrs of implementation.

A PMO can be graded at less than the maximum points for maturity at the benefits realization vertical in case of the following scenarios:

1 Point: for a PMO, that has no benefits measurement team in place.

2 Points: can be awarded for a PMO, that has a benefits realization team who only work on measuring the benefits for projects that have clearly defined, time-bound benefits established. I.e. no out-of-the box ideas for benefits measurement or lack of benefits measurement for projects with long cycle times.

Reporting

Reporting is one of the most basic functions of any PMO. The Utopian PMO steps up the provision of these services by providing a variety of reporting services using three communication approaches:

- Push
- Pull
- Interactive

A PMO to be assessed at a score of 3 at this vertical must have the following:

Push Reporting capabilities:

- A capability for project managers, at pre-defined intervals, to "push" their status reports using agreed templates to the collaboration portal where it is promptly reviewed for completeness and accuracy by a PMO analyst before presentation at a formal status meeting.

- A capability for the PMO to be able to use these individual project status reports, to collate and produce to an enterprise road map to aid organizational decision making.

- A capability for anyone in the organization is able to raise and assign project risks, while risk owners are able to update mitigation plans.

Pull Reporting capabilities

- A capability for management to be able to "pull" any individual projects' status reports at will and be able to see an organization-wide road-map of the entire portfolio of projects that are:

- Delivered
- In-progress
- In the Pipeline

Interactive capabilities:

- The PMO has the necessary framework and bandwidth to provide any one, wishing further information on the organization wide project management methodology, framework, processes and standard operating procedures.

- The PMO is also able to provide a contact channel, for users to use and be apprised of any project management related information that they may be in need of through customized reports.

A PMO can be graded at less than the maximum points for maturity at the reporting vertical in case of the following scenarios:

1 Point: for a PMO that has no periodic reporting in place but sporadic, ad-hoc information on projects exist. Senior management has no idea where the current portfolio stands and may in some cases directly contact the project manager for project updates, bypassing the PMO entirely.

2 Points: can be awarded for a PMO that has basic push and pull reports in place and understands the need to have an interactive system too. Pull reporting is weaker with senior management often receiving data that is out-of-sync. Outdated reports are characteristic, especially when requested in between report due dates. The publication of a road-map is a fundamental pre-requisite for a PMO to receive a score of 2.

Supplier Management

The delivery of project work packages and sometimes, the delivery of entire projects, in which the organization lacks delivery capability, is often outsourced. Allowing projects to maintain independent relationships with contractors would be akin to a non-centralized effort leading to disparate levels of engagement. Also information about the ability of a vendor (or lack thereof) to deliver will be restricted to the project manager assigned to supervise the engagement. The Utopian PMO which rates at a 3 on this vertical takes care of this by an efficient supplier management function that:

- Has a function within the PMO to manage the relationship with suppliers.

- Represents itself at the vendor selection process and providing key inputs on the vendor's ability to deliver, by assessing the vendor's project management capabilities.

- Appraises the vendor of the internal project management reporting requirements.

- Assists the project manager, in helping the vendor in maintaining compliance to organizational policies or other mandatory requirements.

- Collates information about the engagement from observation and project manager's reports to maintain an organization-wide repository of satisfactory and unsatisfactory vendors.

- Acts as a good-faith intermediary in case of non-contract related disputes and as a medium to escalate to the procurement / legal team in case of contractual disputes.

A PMO can be graded at less than the maximum points for maturity at the supplier management vertical in case of the following scenarios:

1 Point: for a PMO that has no supplier management function and each project manager handles their vendors independently. Project managers are often left to their own discretion to assess if the vendor should be monitored for compliance to processes and policies.

2 Points: can be awarded for a PMO that has a supplier management function that collates information on suppliers at the conclusion of each engagement, purely based on the final report submitted by the project manager. This PMO does not act as an arbitrator and in effect distances itself from the relationship, acting merely as an observer and not as a key stakeholder. It is left to the project manager to ensure the vendor's compliance to the buyer's organizational processes. However, project managers are required to report on the vendor engagement as a non-negotiable line item in their periodic reports.

Business Relationship Management

A PMO is often seen to be an entity that unifies the various departments in an organization. A PMO that operates in isolation can seldom deliver projects that deliver strategic value to an organization. Building key relationships is a very important function of the PMO, one that the Utopian PMO does very well and is rated at the highest score of 3 because this PMO features a business relationship management function that:

- Understands its unique position as a key coordinator of various activities that deliver strategy in an organization.

- Represents itself in meetings with the strategic team in deciding on inclusion of projects in the organization's portfolio as well as on matters pertaining to the measurement of post-project benefits.

- Represent itself in meetings with the procurement team in deciding potential vendors based on their project management capability and as an intermediary throughout the vendor engagement.

- Invites and ensures key representation from stakeholders in project risk meetings.

- Promotes the accomplishments of the PMO by engaging in activities that create awareness and support.

- Maintains an overall cordial relationship with the rest of the organization by providing timely, meaningful information and delivering value to all stakeholders.

A PMO can be graded at less than the maximum points for maturity at the business relationship management vertical, in case of the following scenarios:

1 Point: for a PMO that has no business relationship function and operates independently from the rest of the organization.

2 Points: can be awarded for a PMO that has an "on-call" approach to being present on strategy and procurement meetings and proactive relationship building exercises do not occur.

"As-Is" Study Report & Gap Analysis

Once an assessment of the ten verticals have been completed and the staircase rising from the "as-is" to the "to-be" is drawn, the BPR team gets a fairly comprehensive view of the effort, to be undertaken to bridge this gap. This is a key deliverable of the study phase and forms a precursor to almost all other reengineering related documents.

In a hypothetical PMO reengineering situation, the following scores were assessed at different verticals.

Assessment Vertical	"As-Is" Maturity Score	"To-be" Maturity Score
Governance and Strategic Alignment	2	3
Process Maturity Management	1	3
Delivery Management	3	3
Resource Management	2	3
Quality Mgmt. , Compliance & Maturity	1	3
Benefits Management	1	3
Reporting	3	3
Supplier Management	3	3
Business Relationship Management	2	3

Revisiting the definition of a Utopian PMO given in the first few pages of the book reminds us that reengineering the PMO to anything short of having a maturity score, of less than 3 in each of the verticals would not be sufficient for an organization striving to create the perfect strategic engine.

The BPR team reengineering the PMO is encouraged to align the existing processes with the PMO operating model processes detailed in the next chapter. These 8 highly effective "to-be" processes when implemented correctly and operating to prescribed standards aim to give the reformed PMO a full maturity rating on each of the nine assessment verticals. However, the business relationship management vertical in the PMO is purely subjective and no clear steps can be established to define what it takes to maintain a cordial relationship with the rest of the organization. Therefore improvements for that vertical are highly dynamic and must be suited to the specific needs of the PMO and the environment that it caters to.

It is recommended that the BPR team validate the assessment scores with the stakeholders identified in the previous steps to ensure that a lack of communication has not led to a vertical being assessed at a score, less than what it rightly deserved. In this hypothetical PMO, assuming a score of 2 was awarded on the business relationship vertical, as the BPR team was incorrectly told that PMO only represents itself at strategy meeting only when called for such meetings when in fact, on the contrary, the PMO head actually receives a schedule of meetings from the strategy team, sometimes up to 90 days ahead and proactively plans for representation of the PMO at these meetings.

To avoid erroneous scoring, a template such as the one below is recommended to be created for *each* of the assessment verticals and signed-off before the team proceeds to the next stage of reengineering the PMO.

A template that accurately captures the rationale for the scoring can help the organization understand the reason that influenced the BPR team to assess the PMO at that level for a particular vertical. This information is carefully archived and used for comparison, during later maturity assessment exercises once the reengineered PMO is delivered and is in operational mode.

Assessment Vertical	"As-Is" Maturity Score	Score Validity
Business Relationship Management	1	The PMO under assessment does not recognize BRM as a function and operates independently from the rest of the organization. Other functions make decisions independently and are seldom aware of the activities that this PMO executes.

Quick wins

The 9 step- "As-Is" maturity assessment and other evaluations performed in the study phase will help the BPR team identify organizational pain points and areas where the organization is looking for fixes first. It is recommended that the BPR team create a priority list for implementation, by re-ordering the 9 assessment areas by implementation priority. While considering the implementation priority, the BPR team must weigh between the ease of implementation and creating quick relief. The top two items of the ordered list created as stated can be deemed quick wins for the organization. Quick wins are important to establish credibility of the BPR team as effective change agents. These items must first be approved by the sponsoring organization before being labeled as quick wins and treated as such.

Conclusion

The second phase of the BPR project studies the current state of the PMO by assessing its present maturity against the 9-step maturity assessment model which evaluates the PMO against the following lines of practice called assessment verticals:

- Governance and Strategic Alignment
- Process Maturity Management
- Delivery Management
- Resource Management
- Quality Management , Compliance & Maturity
- Benefits Management
- Reporting
- Supplier Management
- Business Relationship Management

Each of the assessment verticals are scored on a scale of 1 to 3 with 3 being the maximum score. This process helps the BPR team identify those verticals where the PMO is lacking and needs improvement. The results of this evaluation are documented in the "As-Is" report and the next step is to align these deficient processes with those detailed in the next section.

Chapter 6

The Develop Phase, Part 1

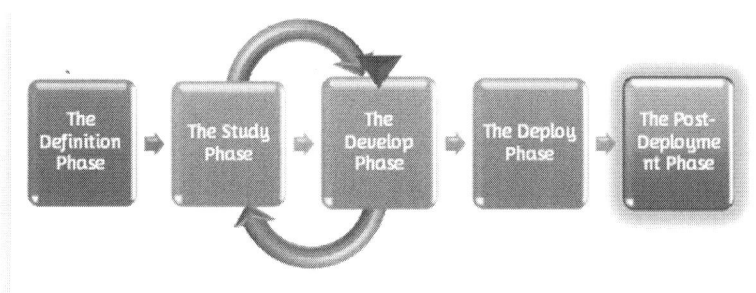

The Utopian PMO Operating Model

The Utopian PMO, is an organizational super structure that rests on exceptional PMO processes for achieving operational excellence. It should be noted that these processes are distinctly different from the project and program management processes that also fall under the remit of the PMO. It has often been the assumption that re-engineering a PMO involves specifically re-working the project and program management processes. This assumption is entirely off track. Re-engineering the PMO involves reworking internal processes that form the very core of the PMO and then aligning the project and program management processes to these core processes.

The BPR team's immediate course of action, once a detailed study phase has been concluded is to design these core processes. The following sections depict how the ideal core processes of a Utopian PMO should operate. The BPR team is encouraged to use these processes, out-of-box, as they come with correspondingly aligned project and program management processes whilst being domain and industry agnostic. They also feature roles and responsibilities detailed in chapters further down the book and in essence provide the framework for a fully reengineered, functional PMO. The BPR team may, depending on the situation, also consider adapting these processes to suit specific needs or to overcome certain implementation constraints.

Key to understanding process maps

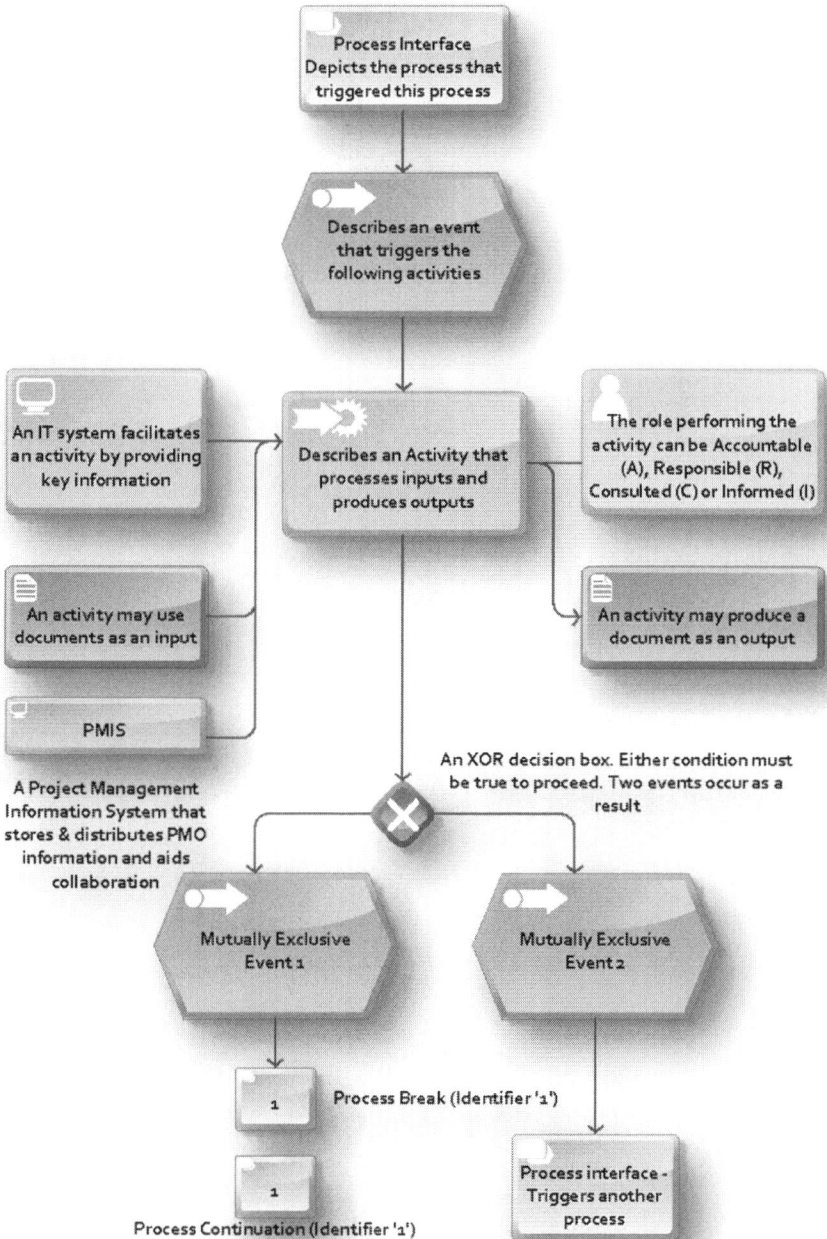

Process Interface
Depicts the process that
triggered this process

Describes an event
that triggers the
following activities

An IT system facilitates
an activity by providing
key information

Describes an Activity that
processes inputs and
produces outputs

The role performing the
activity can be Accountable
(A), Responsible (R),
Consulted (C) or Informed (I)

An activity may use
documents as an input

An activity may produce a
document as an output

PMIS

A Project Management
Information System that
stores & distributes PMO
information and aids
collaboration

An XOR decision box. Either condition must
be true to proceed. Two events occur as a
result

Mutually Exclusive
Event 1

Mutually Exclusive
Event 2

1

Process Break (Identifier '1')

1

Process interface -
Triggers another
process

Process Continuation (Identifier '1')

Governance & Strategic Alignment Process (PMO01GSA)

The PMO01GSA is, without argument, a Utopian PMO's most important core process. This process takes active cognizance of the supreme need to have a robust business case vetting process, before the PMO undertakes any work. Also within the remit of this process, is the need for the PMO to qualify a business case. This is done based on the availability of a feasibility study and the absence of any violation of regulations and conflicts of interest that maybe detrimental to the project further down in its lifecycle. This process is triggered whenever a new business case is received or whenever the Quality Compliance Management Process (PMO05QCM) requires an initiative to fix the root cause of a detected non-compliance or the Benefits Realization Process (PMO08BRM) requires another delivery due to a previous initiative having failed to bring any purported benefits.

Key highlights of this process include:

- A strategic alignment and feasibility check of the submitted business case.

- A check for regulatory violations and potential conflicts of interest.

- An approval / reject step.

- A function that checks for fit into the current portfolio and the availability of resources to support this new initiative.

- A function that checks if this approved strategic element is best run as a strategic project, small project or a program and the methodology the initiative is expected to follow based on its categorization.

The factors for differentiating a project as being small or strategic are multiple in nature. A recommendation is to differentiate projects based on the estimated duration or scope. For example, a project that lasts less than a week or costs less than x dollars can be categorized as a small project.

PMO Process #1 Governance & Strategic Alignment (PMO01GSA)

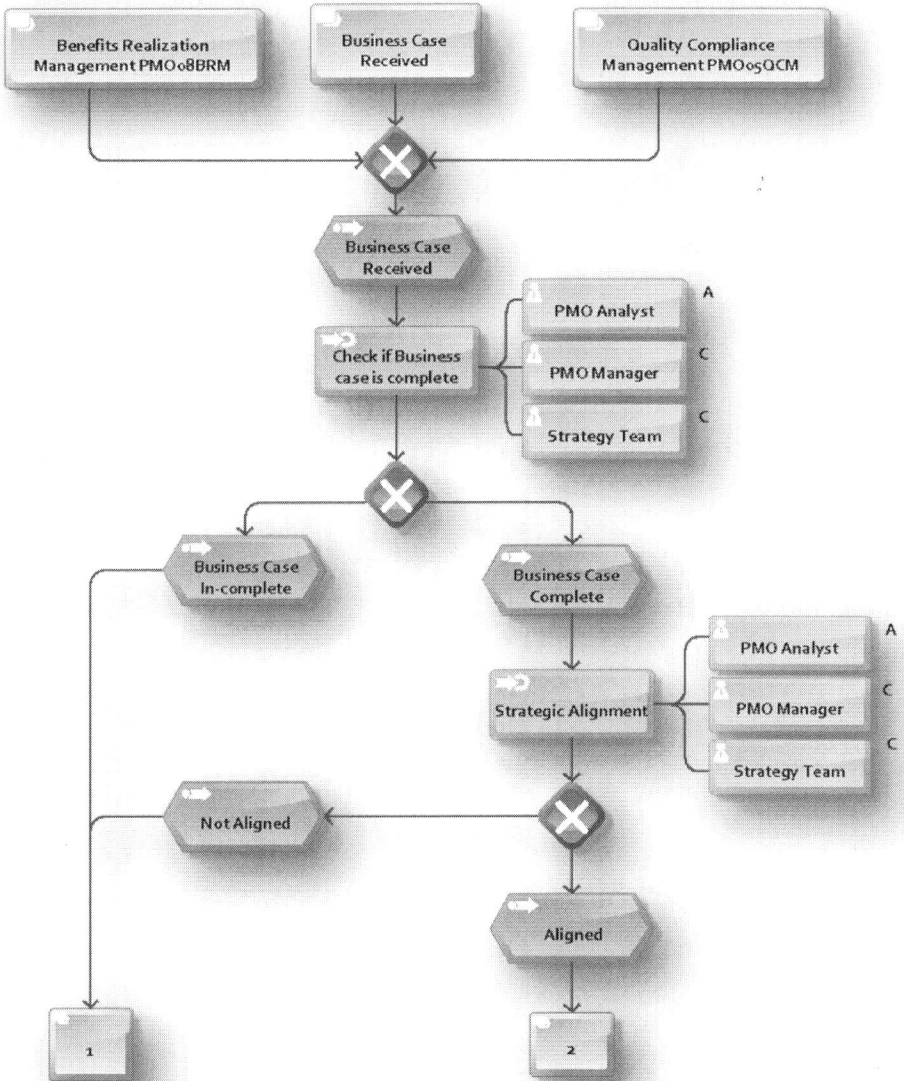

Process #1 Governance & Strategic Alignment (PMO01GSA) Part 2

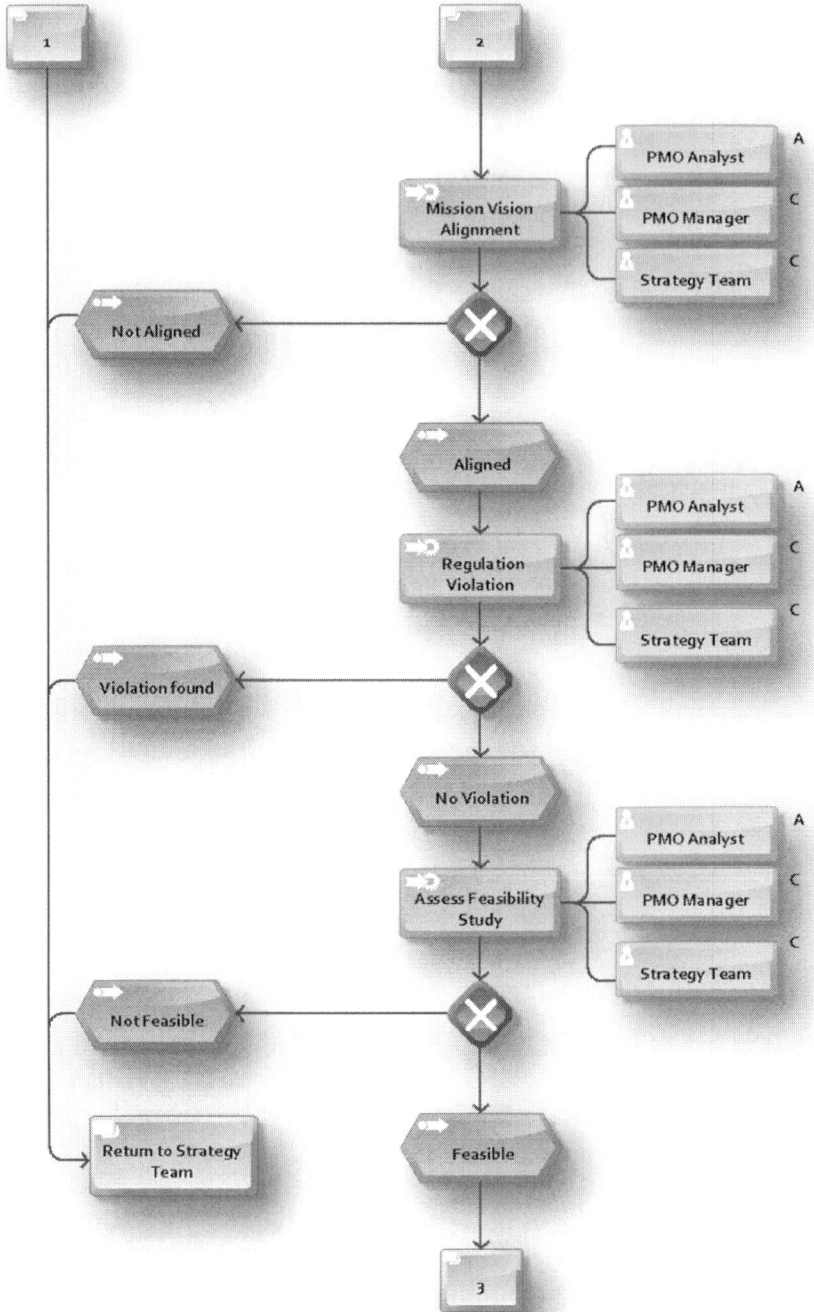

Process #1 Governance & Strategic Alignment (PMO01GSA) Part 3

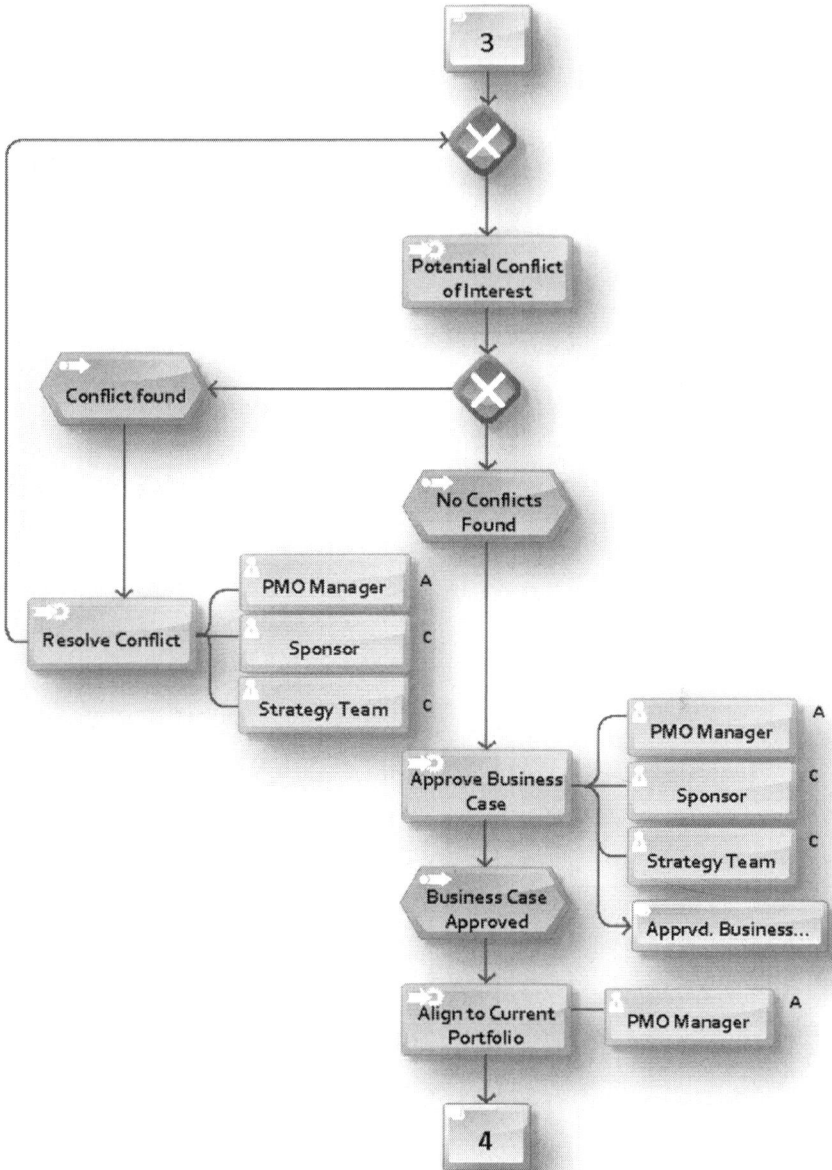

Process #1 Governance & Strategic Alignment (PMO01GSA) Part 4

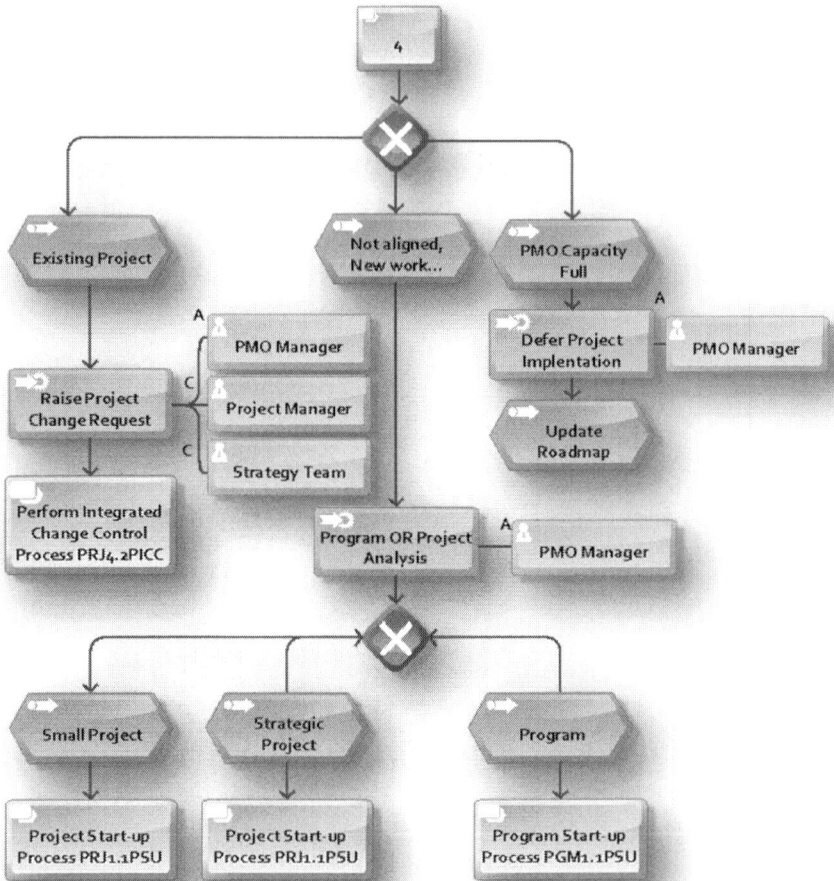

Process Maturity Framework (PMO02PM)

The process that cradles the Utopian PMO's project and program management processes by instituting a framework of scrutiny and alignment to every single new or improved processes introduced into the Utopian PMO's operating environment via any of the following triggers:

- Process updates due to pre-defined review cycles.
- Process updates due to feedback from process practitioners.
- New process introduced into the framework [with a demonstrated business need].

Key highlights of this process include:

- A complete validation of the completeness of the new process including checks for Process Maps, SOPs and review cycles.

- A check for integration points and alignment with the rest of processes currently in use.

- Publishing the new process on the Project Management Information System.

- A process step to continuously look for improvement opportunities to the processes.

PMO Process #2 Process Maturity Framework (PMO02PM)

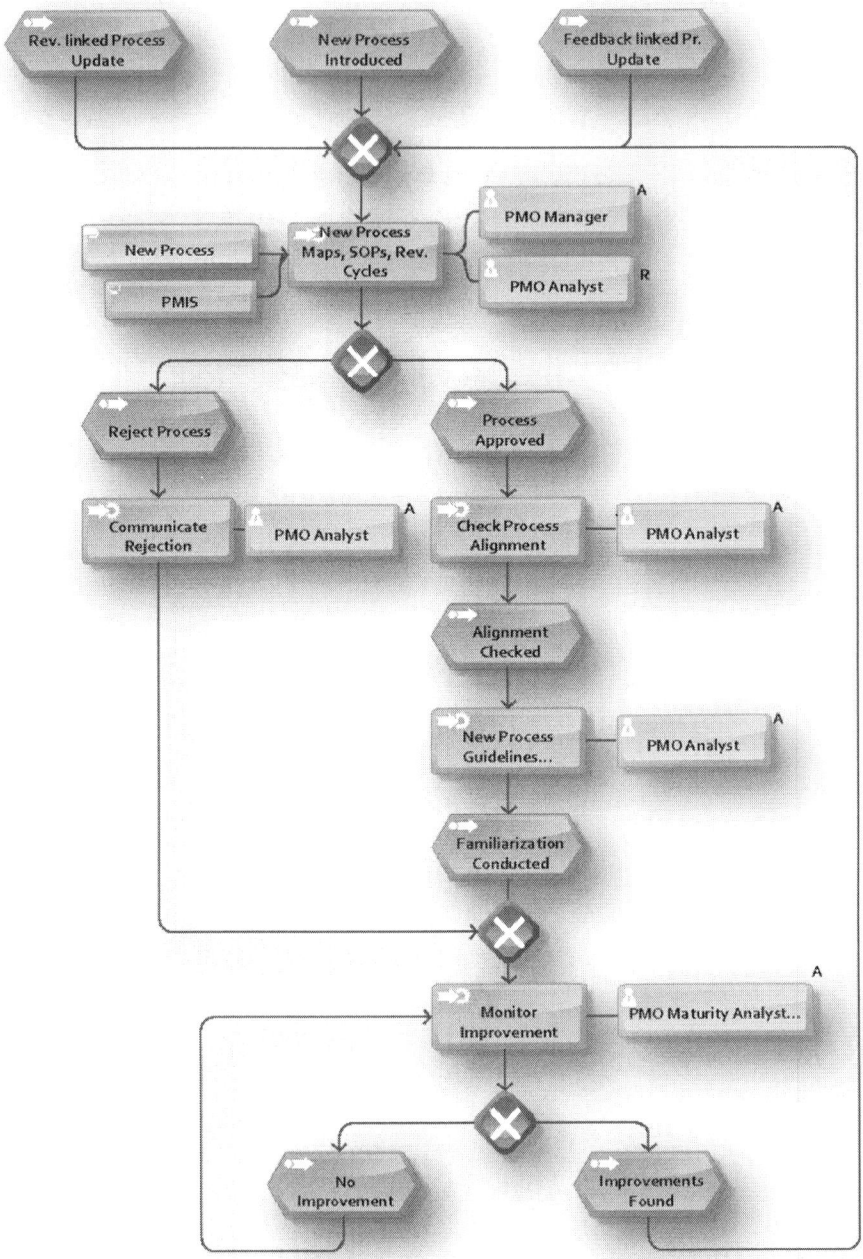

Delivery Management Process (PMO03DM)

This process establishes the PMO as the delivery arm of the organization's strategy. A structural backbone to the entire operations of the PMO, the delivery management process, provides a robust delivery framework for programs and two different kinds of projects, small projects and strategic projects. The PMO process 1: Governance & Strategic Alignment PMO01GSA, helps determine if an initiative is best run as a project or as a program. The process goes on to identify the type of project based on various parameters such as project duration and costs.

For projects classified as a small project, a lighter framework (DF3) which captures all the nuances of an effective project delivery framework and yet keeps the framework practically light for supporting a smaller delivery is recommended. A large strategic project is prescribed a full-blown, project delivery framework, DF2, which is tightly integrated with the Utopian PMO's 8 delivery processes. DF1 is a workable program delivery framework recommended to be used for initiatives classified as programs. Within DF1 and DF2 processes are triggered internally to form an innovative program delivery solution, with built-in management of its constituent projects. PMO03DM keeps track of all initiatives within the PMO, manages an enterprise risk register and escalation procedures. Controls are built into the process at several points and the PMO can appraise project performance when any of the following occur:

- Status reports are submitted.
- The project submits itself voluntarily for checks.
- At the close of each project phase.
- At random, when the PMO wishes to establish ad-hoc status.
- A performing vendor submits report.
- A non-correctable variance or during high-level issues.

Key highlights of this process include:

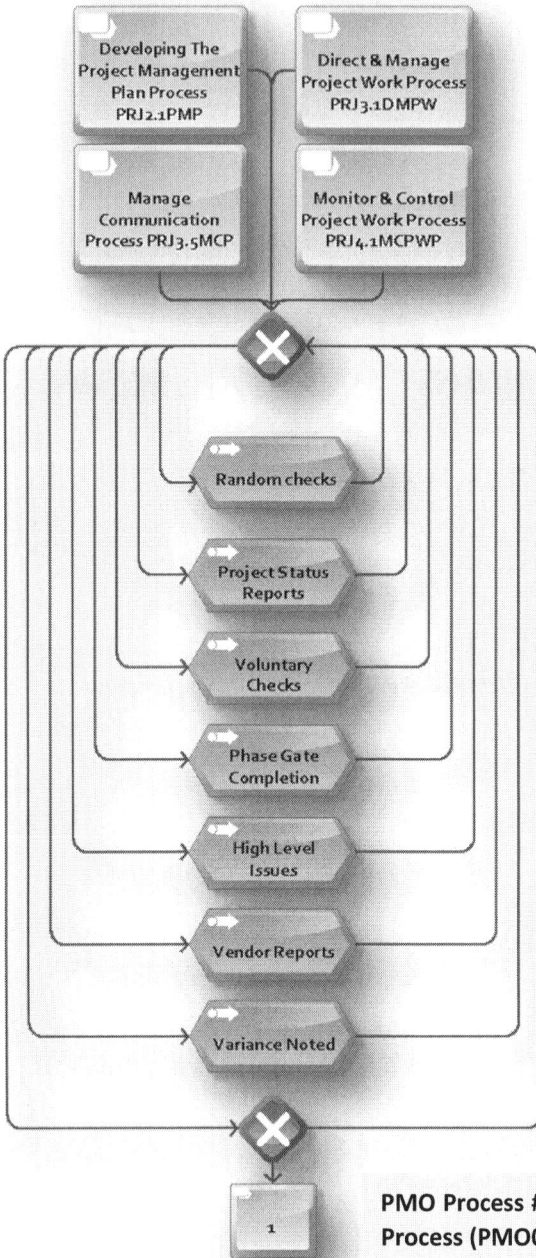

- An assessment check on the performance of all projects in the portfolio by several means detailed above.

- An information archival step to build organizational process assets and a repository of lessons learned.

- An enterprise-level risk assessment process.

- A clear two-step path to escalate unresolved issues.

PMO Process #3 Delivery Management Process (PMO03DM) Part 1

PMO Process #3 Delivery Management Process (PMO03DM) Part 2

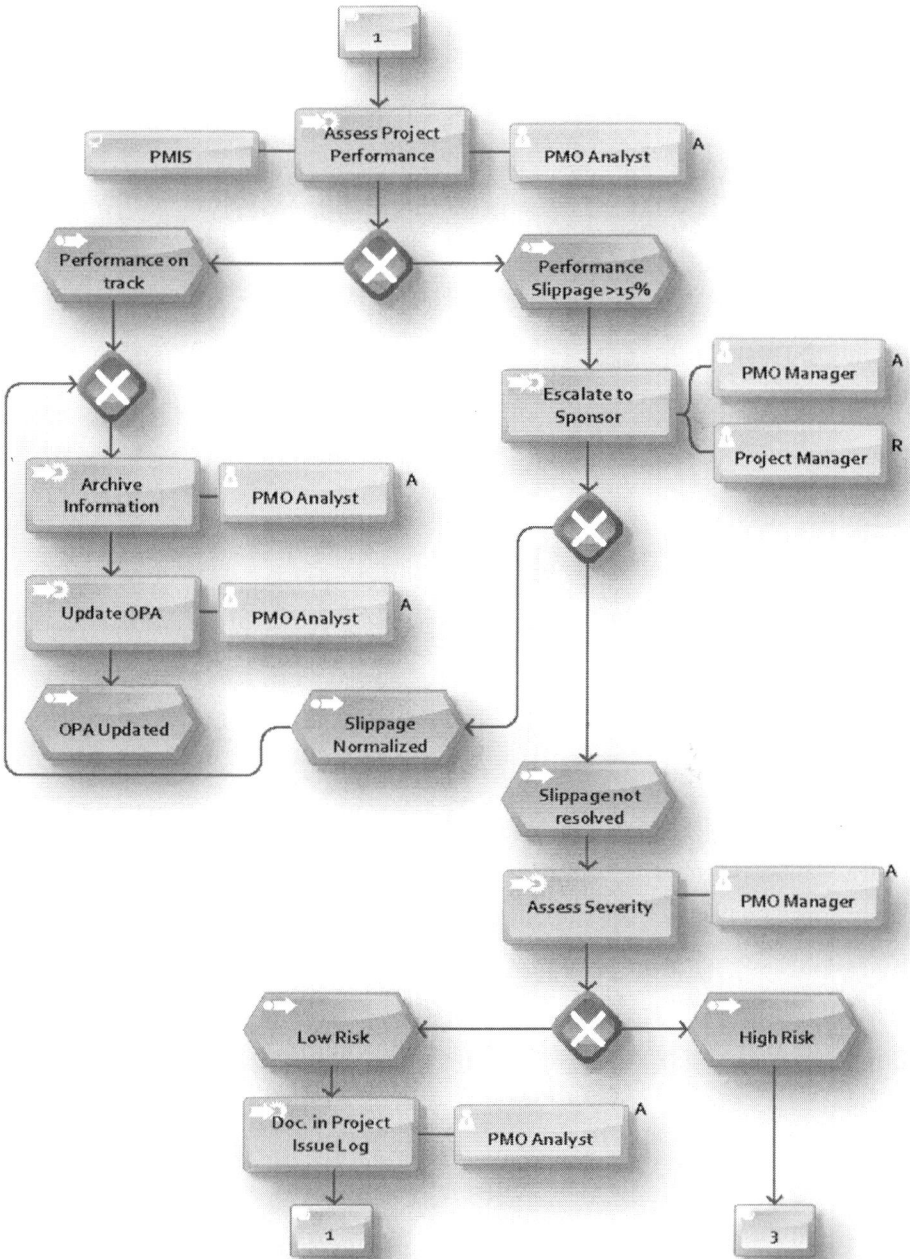

PMO Process #3 Delivery Management Process (PMO03DM) Part 3

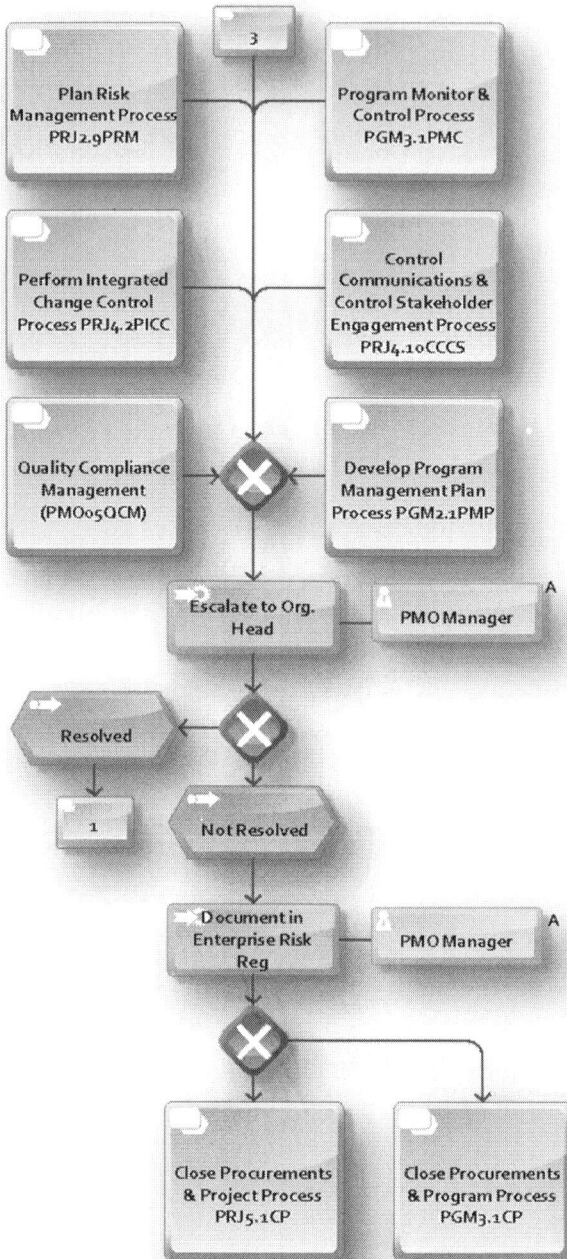

Plan Risk Management Process PRJ2.9PRM

Program Monitor & Control Process PGM3.1PMC

3

Perform Integrated Change Control Process PRJ4.2PICC

Control Communications & Control Stakeholder Engagement Process PRJ4.10CCCS

Quality Compliance Management (PMO05QCM)

Develop Program Management Plan Process PGM2.1PMP

Escalate to Org. Head

PMO Manager

A

Resolved

1

Not Resolved

Document in Enterprise Risk Reg

PMO Manager

A

Close Procurements & Project Process PRJ5.1CP

Close Procurements & Program Process PGM3.1CP

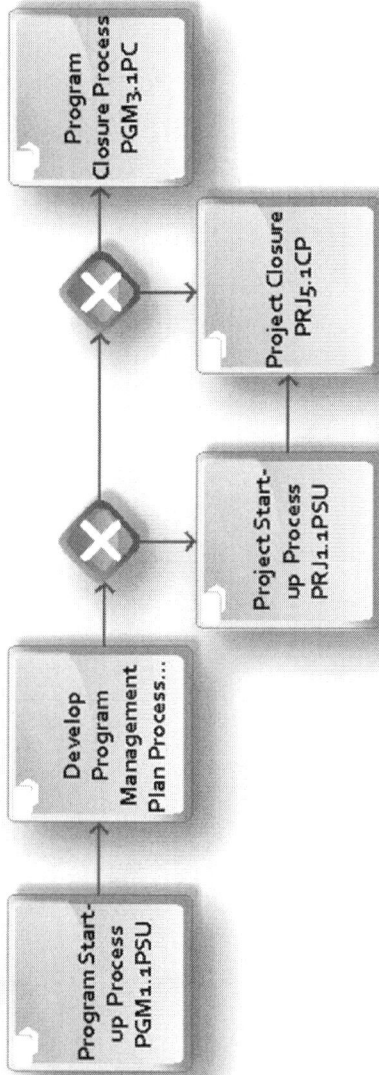

Delivery framework for a program (DF1)

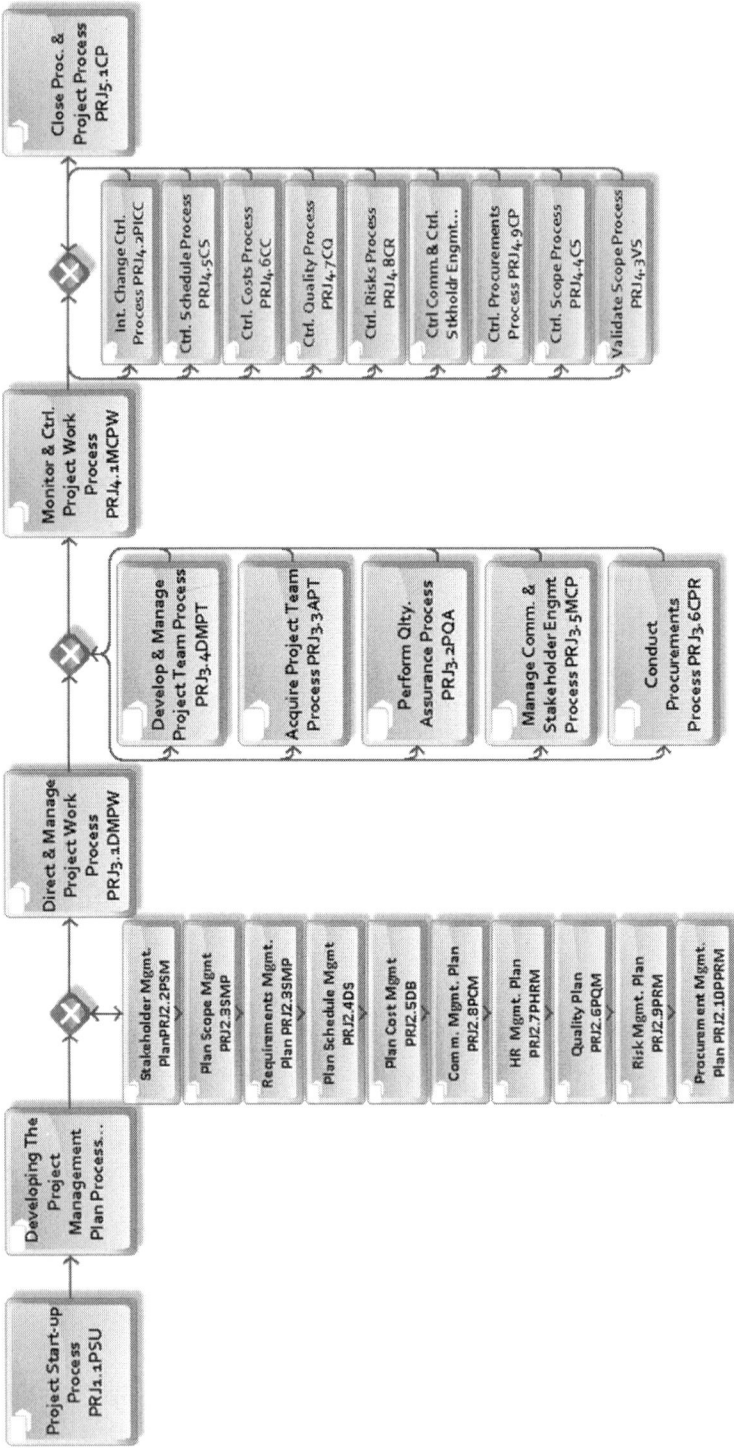

Delivery framework for a strategic project (DF2)

The processes shown in the figure:

- Project Start-up Process PRJ1.1PSU
- Developing The Project Management Plan Process...
- Direct & Manage Project Work Process PRJ3.1DMPW
- Monitor & Ctrl. Project Work Process PRJ4.1MCPW
- Close Proc. & Project Process PRJ5.1CP

- Stakeholder Mgmt. Plan PRJ2.2PSM
- Plan Scope Mgmt PRJ2.3SMP
- Requirements Mgmt. Plan PRJ2.3SMP
- Plan Schedule Mgmt PRJ2.4DS
- Plan Cost Mgmt PRJ2.5DB
- Comm. Mgmt. Plan PRJ2.8PCM
- HR Mgmt. Plan PRJ2.7PHRM
- Quality Plan PRJ2.6PQM
- Risk Mgmt. Plan PRJ2.9PRM
- Procurement Mgmt. Plan PRJ2.10PPRM

- Develop & Manage Project Team Process PRJ3.4DMPT
- Acquire Project Team Process PRJ3.3APT
- Perform Qlty. Assurance Process PRJ3.2PQA
- Manage Comm. & Stakeholder Engmt Process PRJ3.5MCP
- Conduct Procurements Process PRJ3.6CPR

- Int. Change Ctrl. Process PRJ4.2PICC
- Ctrl. Schedule Process PRJ4.5CS
- Ctrl. Costs Process PRJ4.6CC
- Ctrl. Quality Process PRJ4.7CQ
- Ctrl. Risks Process PRJ4.8CR
- Ctrl Comm. & Ctrl. Stkholdr Engmt...
- Ctrl. Procurements Process PRJ4.9CP
- Ctrl. Scope Process PRJ4.4CS
- Validate Scope Process PRJ4.3VS

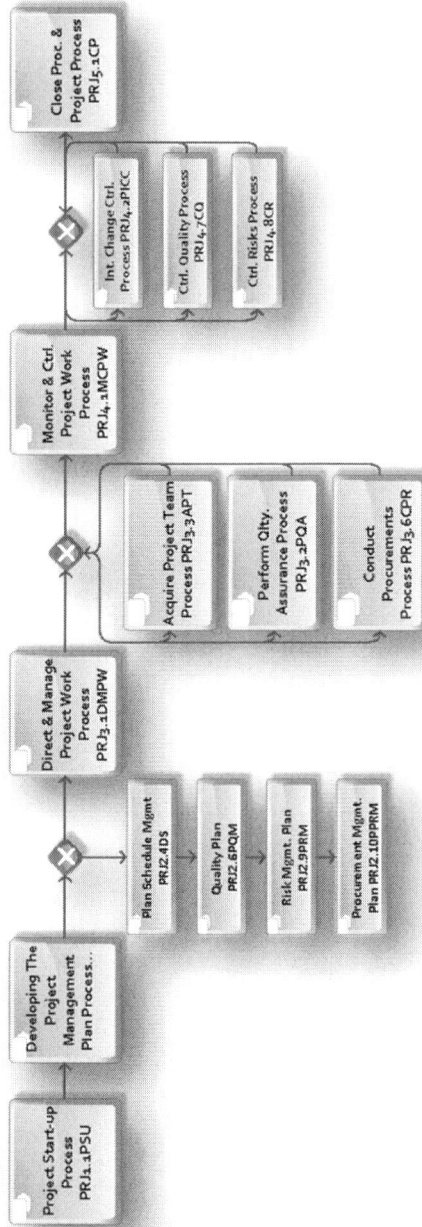

Delivery framework for a small project (DF3)

Resource Management Process (PMO04RM)

This process is used to manage internal PMO resources and helps establish the necessary human resource procedures within the PMO. The PMO maintains an up to date register of the skills of the project management community as well as establishes a personnel performance management process. This process is triggered whenever:

- The Develop & Manage Project Team Process [PRJ3.4DMPT] has completed a performance appraisal for a project's resources.
- New resources for the PMO are hired via the Acquire Project Team Process [PRJ3.3APT].
- PMO resources are released due a PMO sizing exercise.
- An annual appraisal is due.

Key highlights of this process include:

- **A process step to maintain an active, up to date skills register for PMO resources.**

- **A resource-levelling process step to avoid over and under-utilization of resources.**

- **A performance improvement step to assess and improve the skill-set of PMO resources by attempting to analyze the root causes of inadequate performance.**

PMO Process #4 Resource Management Process (PMO04RM) Part 1

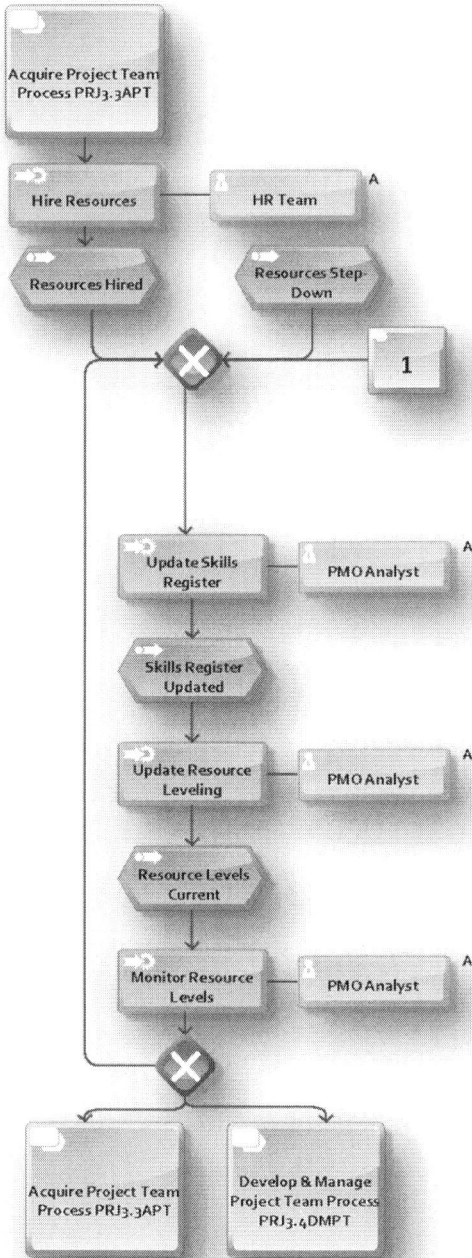

PMO Process #4 Resource Management Process (PMO04RM) Part 2

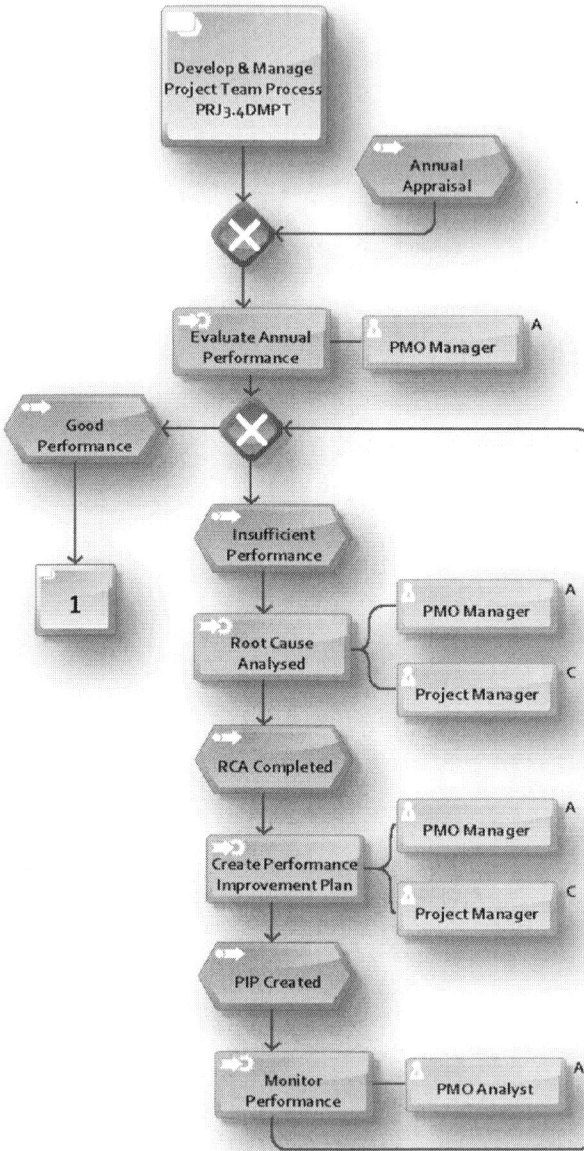

Quality Compliance Management Process (PMO05QCM)

This process is used to manage compliance to the internal PMO processes by actively measuring and comparing process KPIs against the established metrics for each of the PMO processes. Metrics for each of these processes are defined in detail in the following chapters. This process is triggered whenever:

- The PMO's KPIs are assessed

- The PMO subjects itself or is subjected to 3rd party audits

- An annual maturity assessment is due

Key highlights of this process include:

- A process step to assess and measure compliance to established KPIs.

- A process step to analyze root causes of non-compliance.

- Steps to ensure that the root causes of non-compliances are determined and feedback provided to the Governance & Strategic Alignment (PMO01GSA) process to make enterprise level strategic improvements.

PMO Process Map # 5 Quality Compliance Management (PMO05QCM)

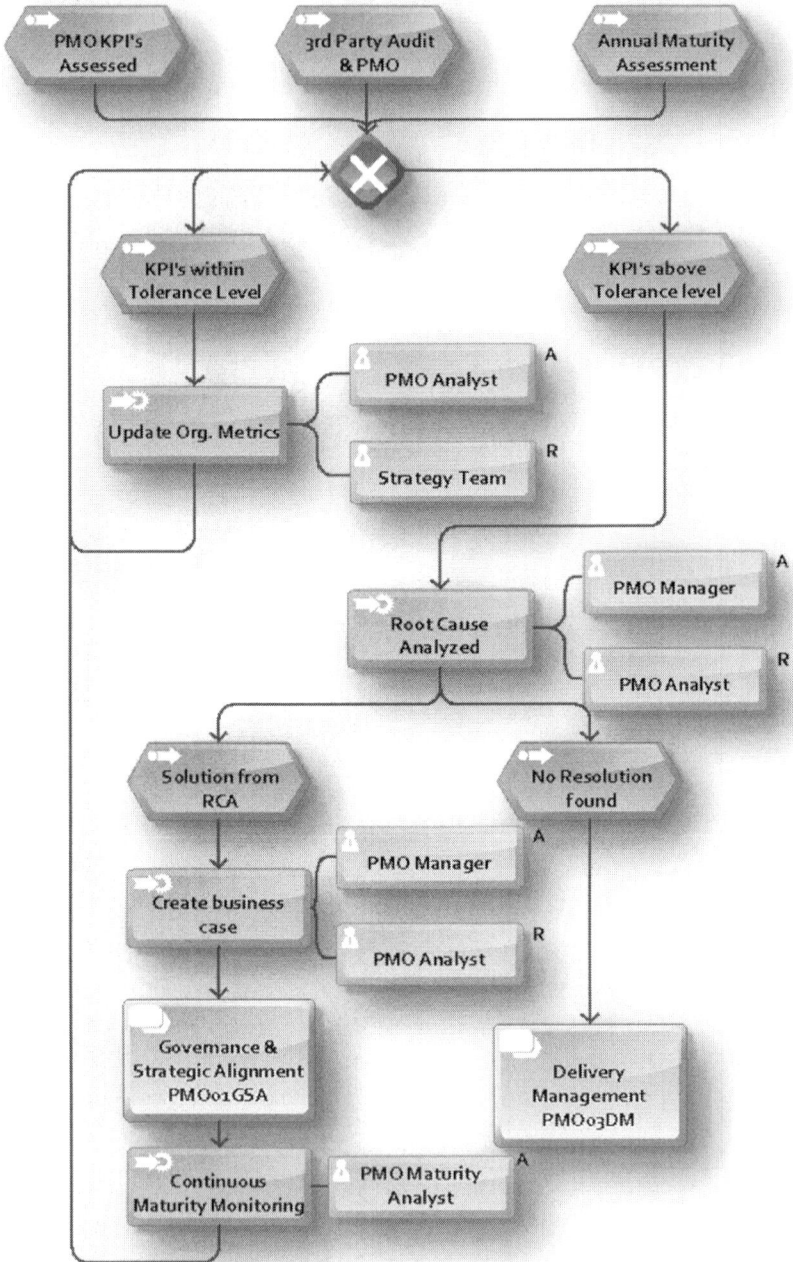

PMO Reporting Process (PMO06R)

One of the most important functions of a Utopian PMO is the organizational-level visibility that this PMO is able to provide into the current portfolio of initiatives and their progress. This mile-high view gives management the necessary visibility to make decisions that would not have been possible without the presence of the enterprise level roadmap. This process is triggered whenever:

- The PMO refreshes the portfolio by the addition or removal of a project from the portfolio.

- PMO has collated and aggregated the individual reports from various initiatives in the organization.

- The Manage Communication Process (PRJ3.5MCP), within the DF2 and DF3 frameworks, triggers this process when an initiative status report is ready to be collated into the enterprise road map.

- A request for an ad-hoc report is received. An analyst from the PMO is assigned to service this request which is received via an advertised communication channel that is used as a single point of contact to reach out to the PMO for any kind of information. This channel can be in the form of a telephone number or the form of a web-based portal for making and servicing requests. The online portal option is better suited to PMOs dealing with a large number of information requests. However, care should be taken to ensure that this ad-hoc reporting process is not misused by the organization. Only when all attempts to source information from the PMIS or published reports have failed, should the requestor use this channel for securing information.

Key highlights of this process include:

- A process step to collate and aggregate individual project reports.
- A process step to push updates from the PMO to the enterprise reporting tool, the PMIS.

- A function to service ad-hoc requests for information.

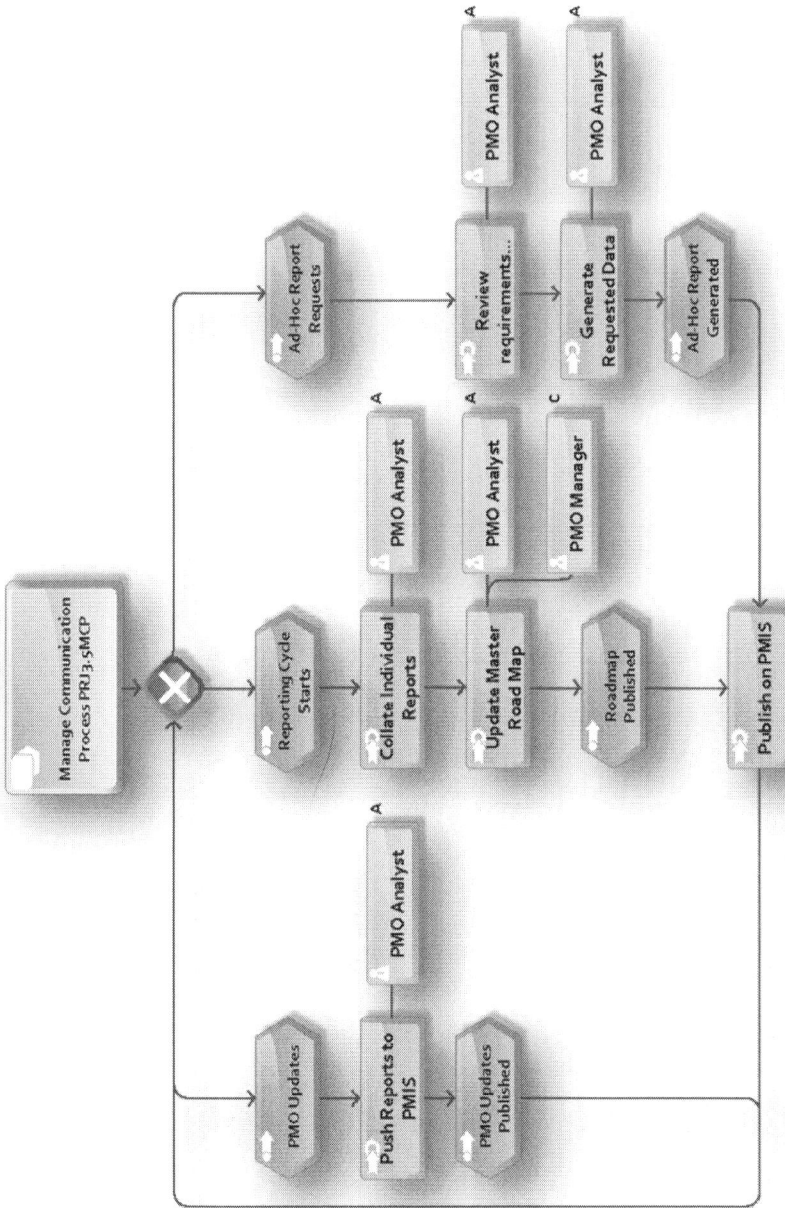

PMO Process Map #6: Reporting Process (PMO06R)

Supplier Management Process (PMO07SM)

A Utopian PMO does not limit its pursuit of project excellence in initiatives that are performed internally by the organization but extends this to vendors who are hired on behalf on the organization to deliver their strategic initiatives. This PMO realizes that to deliver strategy effectively, especially in outsourced projects, effective vendor management is required. A Utopian PMO is also a key stakeholder at vendor status meetings percolating organizational ideals and efficiency into the vendor's delivery.

This process is unique in that it features a 3-pronged approach. The first prong concerns itself with reviewing a proposed vendor's project management capabilities and providing an unbiased opinion. This prong also analyzes vendor reports and publishes the progress on vendor-delivered initiatives on the PMIS.

The second prong concerns itself with building a strong vendor database that can be used by anyone in the organization looking for vendors whose capabilities have already been assessed. The PMO07SM process helps build this database by ensuring that project managers are interviewed and their experience with the vendor captured after the closure of procurement.

The third prong ensures that the project manager has a smooth procurement experience by acting as an arbitrator in case of any legal difficulties in the procurement process.

This process is triggered:

- When a new vendor is on-board triggered by either the conduct procurements process [PRJ3.6CPR] or the Develop Program Management Plan Process [PGM2.1PMP].

- During vendor status meetings.

- Whilst closing contacts after vendor delivery (successful or otherwise).

- When a program-level risk needs to be transferred to a vendor.

- When a change needs to be negotiated with a vendor.

Key highlights of this process include:

Prong 1

- A process step to review the vendor's project management capabilities. Very often vendors are selected based on their technical prowess or because of their ownership of cutting-edge technologies. This process step ensures the vendor possesses the necessary capabilities to deliver projects effectively via application of mature delivery methodologies.

- A process step to help the vendor become accustomed to the reporting requirements prevalent in the organization to help adherence to compliance and a process step to analyze vendor status reports and include progress into roadmaps and other PMO reports.

Prong 2:

- A process step to interview a project manager to establish and document procurement experience.

Prong 3:

- A process step to help manage and negotiate contractual changes on an initiative.

PMO Process Map # 7 Supplier Management Process (PMO07SM) Prong- 1

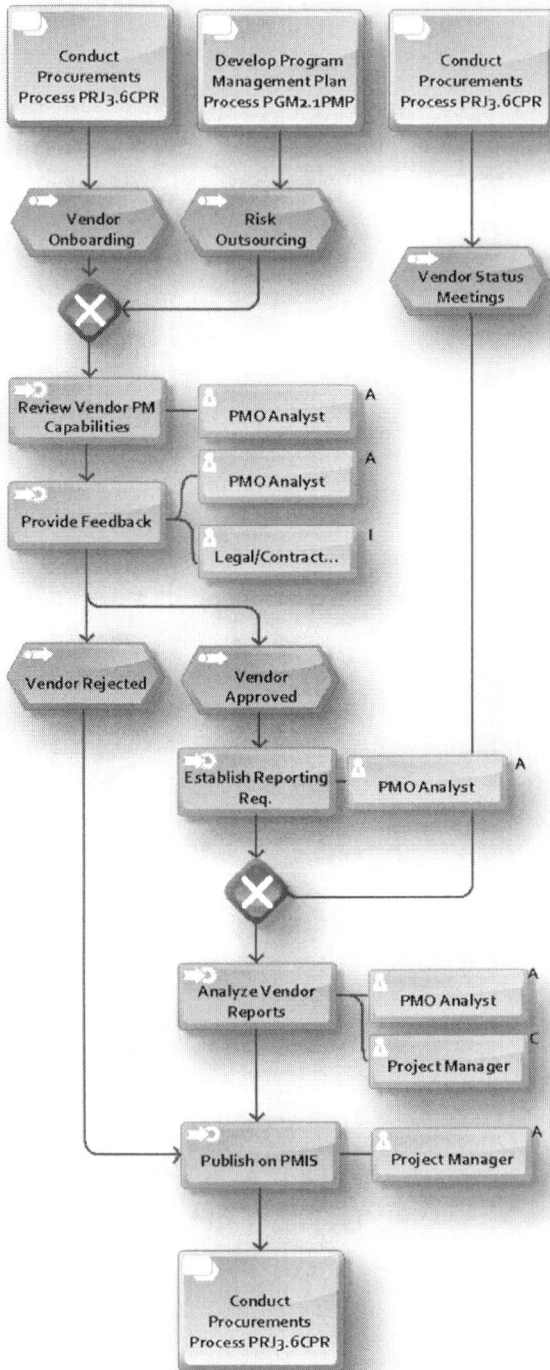

PMO Process Map # 7 Supplier Management Process (PMO07SM) Prong-2

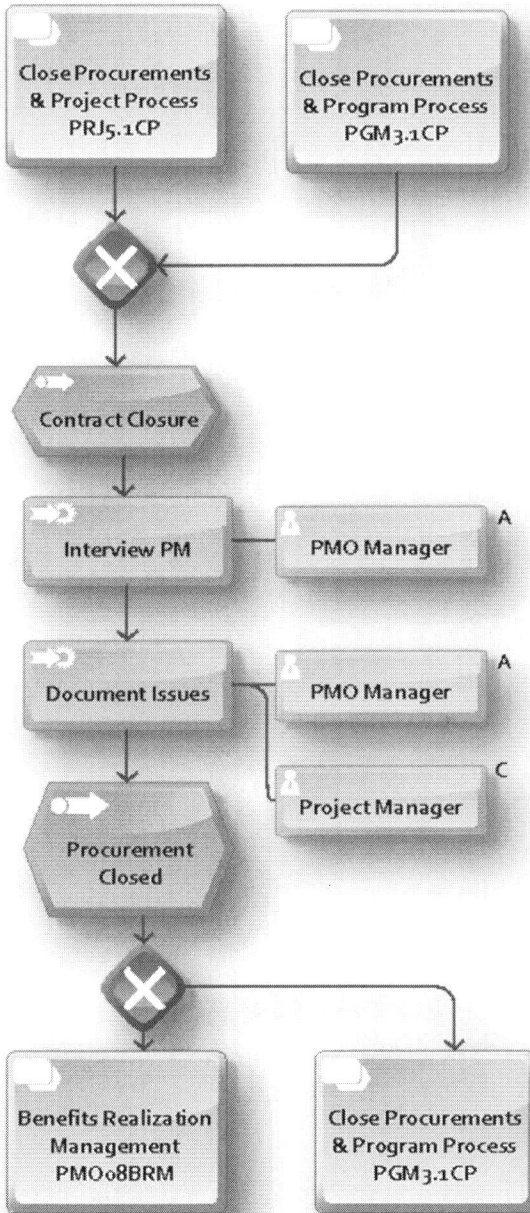

```
┌─────────────────┐         ┌─────────────────┐
│ Close Procurements │       │ Close Procurements │
│ & Project Process │        │ & Program Process │
│     PRJ5.1CP      │        │     PGM3.1CP      │
└─────────────────┘         └─────────────────┘
           │                          │
           └──────► ✕ ◄───────────────┘
                    │
              ┌──────────────┐
              │ Contract Closure │
              └──────────────┘
                    │
              ┌──────────────┐      ┌──────────────┐  A
              │  Interview PM  │─────│  PMO Manager  │
              └──────────────┘      └──────────────┘
                    │
              ┌──────────────┐      ┌──────────────┐  A
              │ Document Issues │────│  PMO Manager  │
              └──────────────┘      └──────────────┘
                    │            │  ┌──────────────┐  C
                    │            └──│ Project Manager │
              ┌──────────────┐      └──────────────┘
              │  Procurement   │
              │    Closed      │
              └──────────────┘
                    │
                    ✕──────────────────┐
                    │                  │
       ┌─────────────────┐    ┌─────────────────┐
       │ Benefits Realization │  │ Close Procurements │
       │    Management     │    │ & Program Process │
       │    PMO08BRM       │    │     PGM3.1CP      │
       └─────────────────┘    └─────────────────┘
```

PMO Process Map # 7 Supplier Management Process (PMO07SM) Prong-3

Benefits Realization Process (PMO08BRM)

The benefits realization process helps realize the value of implementing strategic initiatives, via a dedicated function. The Utopian PMO actively measures the benefits of implementing initiatives, even if the benefits realization cycle is in the magnitude of decades. When the stated waiting period has elapsed, the benefits obtained are compared with those documented in the business case. A value add to this process is the identification of the need to proactively measure benefits by looking at the unintended returns that some projects are intrinsically capable of. This process is triggered:

- When a fixed waiting period for the delivery of predefined benefits has elapsed.

- Whenever the Utopian PMO decides to proactively look for consequences or benefits that were never actually intended when the strategic initiative was originally planned.

- When a project, program or procurement has completed delivery.

Key highlights of this process include:

- **A process step to appraise benefits with the business case.**

- **A process path to create a new strategic initiative if intended benefits have failed realization.**

PMO Process Map # 8 Benefits Realization Process (PMO08BR)

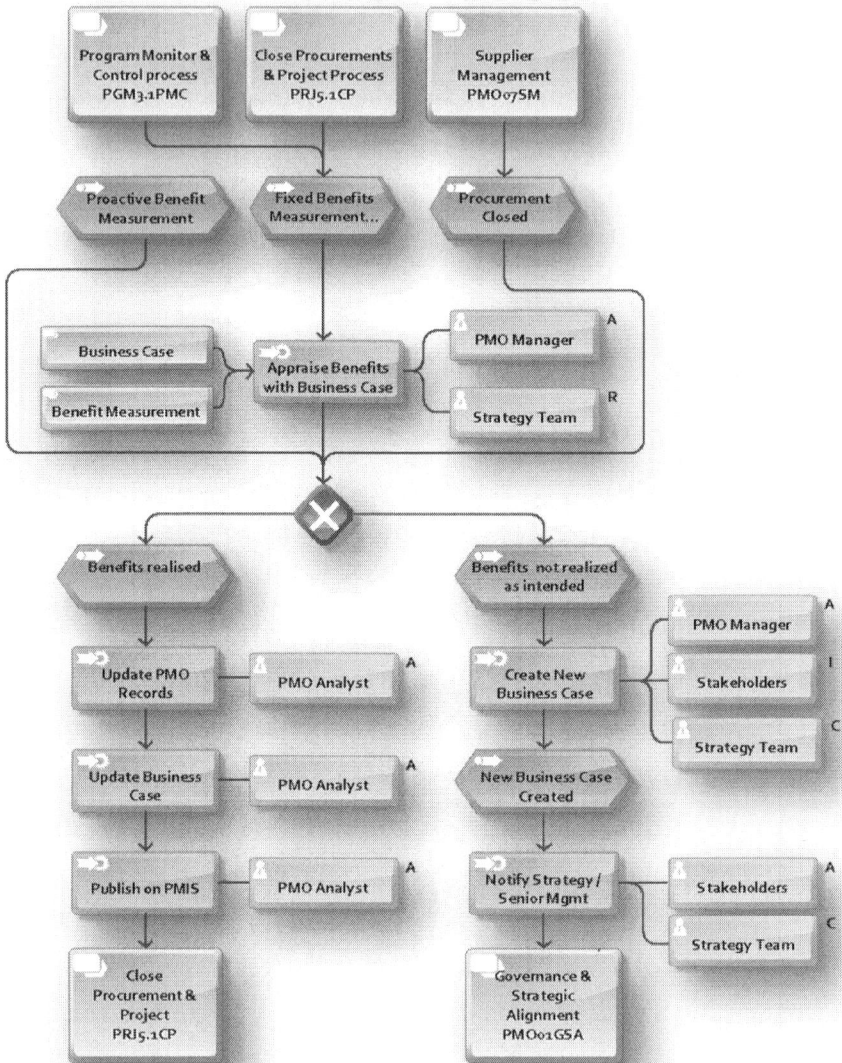

Chapter 6.1
The Develop Phase, Part 2

Project Management Processes for the Utopian PMO

This section of the book provides a robust framework for project management comprising of 29 well-designed processes encompassing the entire project management lifecycle. The Utopian PMO's DF2 and DF3 are reliable, domain-agnostic frameworks, for project delivery and management, fully aligned to the leading standard for project management, the PMBoK®.

The terminology used in this chapter does not conflict with PMBoK® definitions. However, the scope of this book is different than that of the PMBoK®, so not every topic found in either book can be referenced to the other.

The processes in this section feature:

- A defined PMO function that has PMO management processes which integrate seamlessly into the delivery frameworks.

- Defined PMO roles within the delivery framework (who, what, when)

- A selection of delivery frameworks to choose from based on the nature and complexity of the initiatives instead of a one-size-fits-all approach.

- A homogenous framework for organizational delivery that acutely interweaves the following into a cohesive whole providing for the most effective and efficient realization of an organization's strengths.
    - Strategy
    - Business case
    - Project management
    - Benefits management

- Active involvement of the PMO at all key interfaces that feed-back into the PMO operational processes. Key actors, roles and responsibilities for each process clearly defined.

- Checks and controls built into each process to ensure maximum effectiveness and compliance.

Initiation Phase Processes

The Utopian PMO's project initiation process provides the necessary bridge between the PMO's Governance and Strategic Alignment Process (PMO01GSA) and project delivery. Any and all work executed by the Utopian PMO is necessarily in alignment with the organization's overall strategy. Once the PMO01GSA process confirms and checks for this essential alignment, a decision is made to decide if the proposed initiative is best delivered as a strategic project, small project or as a program. If it is determined that the initiative is best run as a project, then Project Start-up Process (PR1.1PSU) is triggered.

Project Start-up Processes (PR1.1PSU)

Once, the approved and strategically validated business case is received, the first course of action for the head of the PMO, the PMO manager, is to assign a PMO Analyst to the project. A PMO analyst, one of the most important, of all resources working within the PMO, is dedicated to one or more projects and acts as a point of liaison between the PMO and the project, throughout its entire lifecycle. Acting on behalf of the PMO, the PMO analyst mentors and monitors the project, keeping the delivery in strict alignment with the accepted practices of the Utopian PMO.

Once a PMO analyst is assigned, the PMO manager then checks if the project business case comes with a preferred project manager pre-assigned to the project by the project sponsor. If not, the PMO manager assigns a competent project manager whose skills set suits the requirements outlined in the business case. The assignment of the project manager is confirmed after agreement with the project sponsor. The first remit of the newly assigned project manager is to create the project charter using the approved business case and project statement of work as inputs. The newly created project charter is taken through an approval process and upon final approval, is published to the Project Management Information System (PMIS).

The PMIS is a generic project management software that aids in collaborating, storing and disseminating project management related data including but not limited to project reports, project documents, schedules, program level reports, PMO reports, historical data and roadmaps. In short, the PMIS forms the information backbone of all the operations the PMO is involved in.

After the successful approval of the project charter, the project manager produces the next critical project management deliverable, the stakeholder register. The stakeholder register identifies all positive and negative stakeholders associated with the project. The project manager collects the information for the stakeholder register via a number of information gathering techniques including but not limited to looking at historical information as well as by interviewing key contacts at the organization. The completion of the stakeholder register signals the end of the project initiation phase. The project manager notifies the PMO and the project then passes through a phase gate test. The PMO analyst is primarily tasked with conducting the phase gate test. Any non-compliance detected is worked out with the project manager and an opportunity is provided to bring the project back on track.

The project manager, then documents the lessons learned by the project in this particular phase including what they (the project team) did right and would like to repeat and what they did wrong. An end of phase report is made collectively by the project manager and the PMO analyst and is submitted to the PMO to archive as a part of the PMO database also known as organizational process assets. The project, then moves to the next phase of the lifecycle.

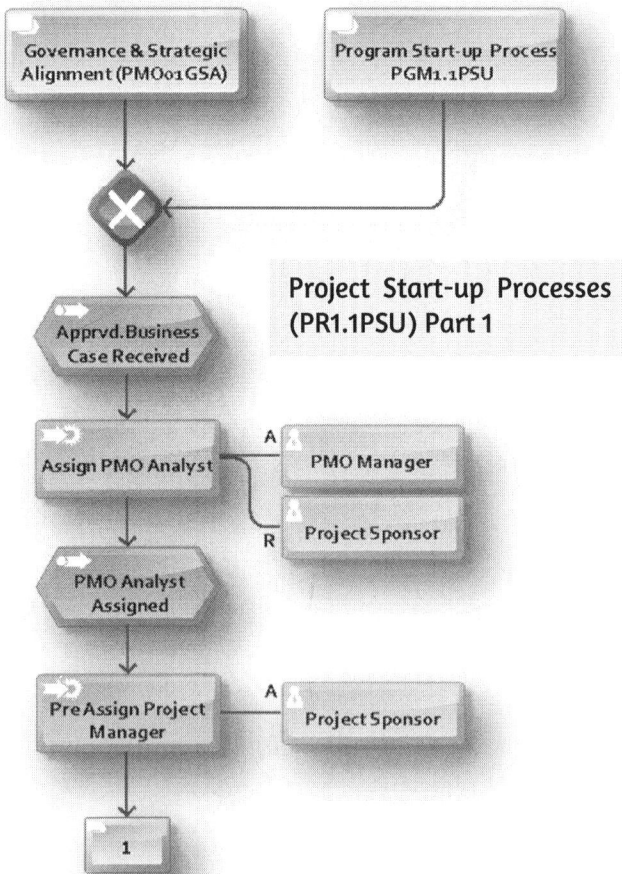

Project Start-up Processes (PR1.1PSU) Part 1

Project Start-up Processes (PR1.1PSU) Part 2

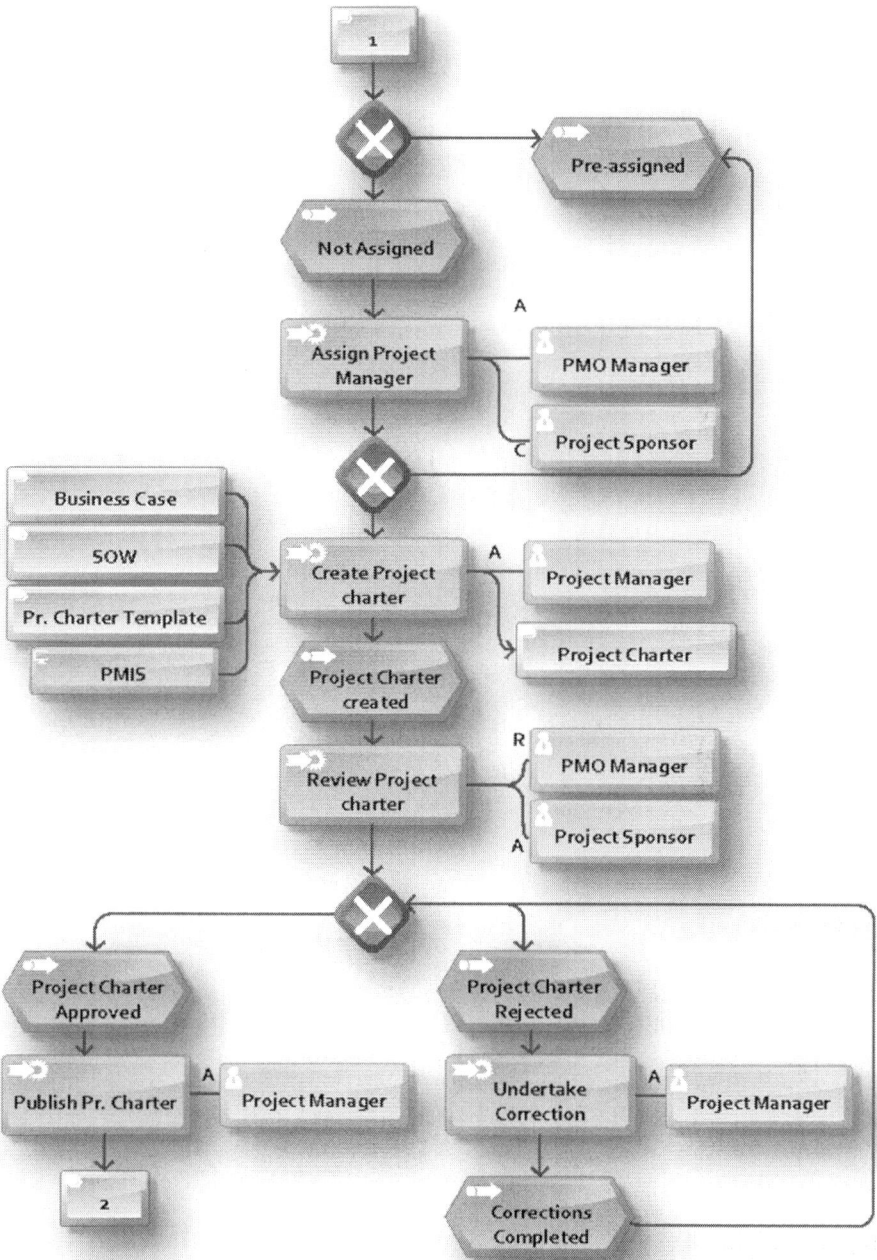

1

Pre-assigned

Not Assigned

A

Assign Project Manager — PMO Manager

Project Sponsor

C

Business Case

SOW

Pr. Charter Template

PMIS

Create Project charter — A — Project Manager

Project Charter

Project Charter created

Review Project charter — R — PMO Manager

A — Project Sponsor

Project Charter Approved

Publish Pr. Charter — A — Project Manager

2

Project Charter Rejected

Undertake Correction — A — Project Manager

Corrections Completed

Project Start-up Processes (PR1.1PSU) Part 3

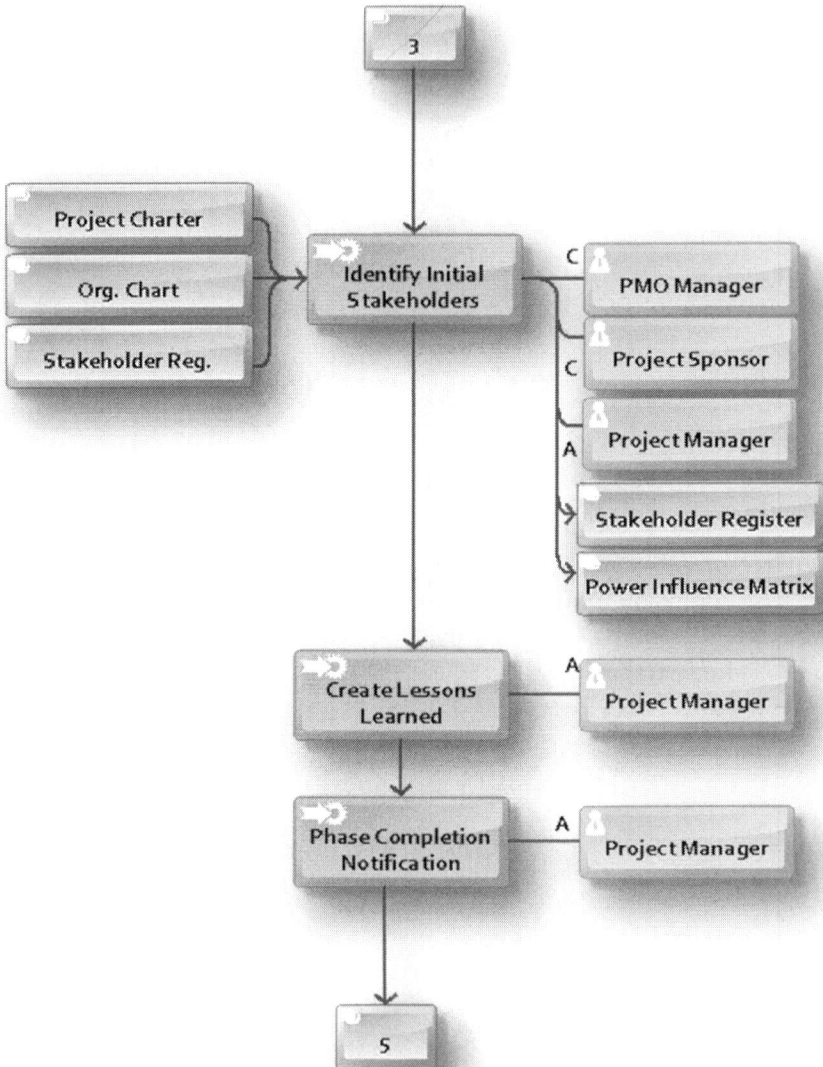

Project Start-up Processes (PR1.1PSdU) Part 4

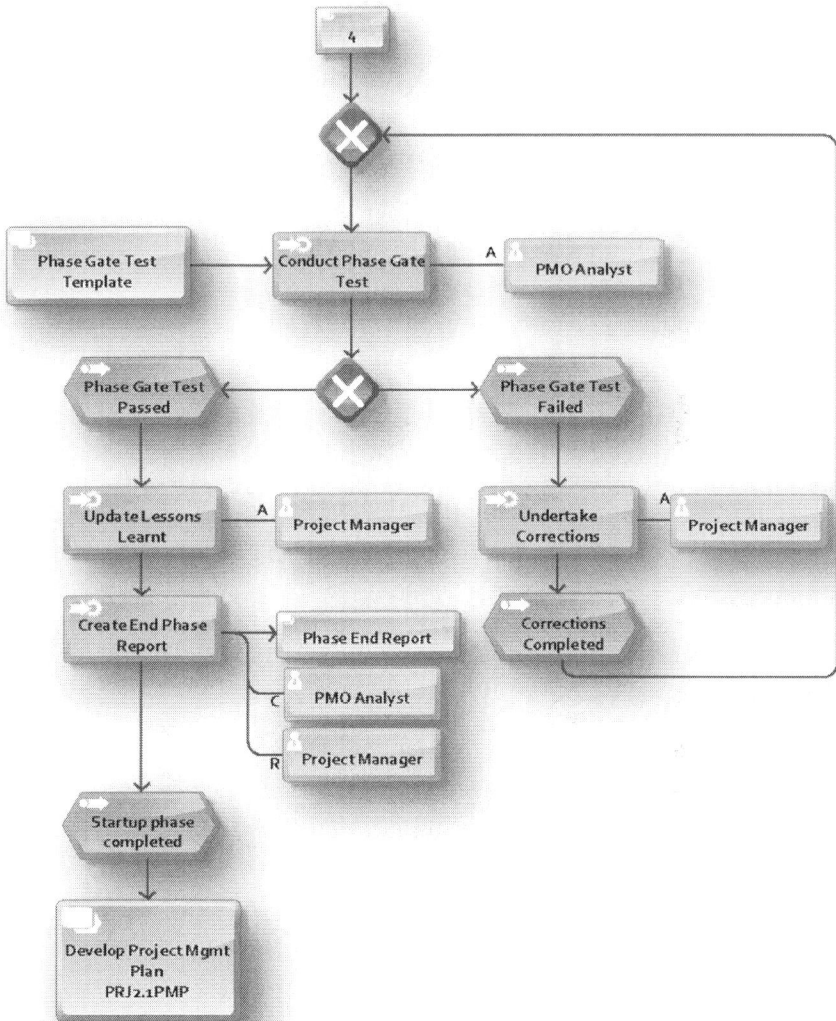

The phase gate test is a formal assessment of the project conducted by the PMO. This assessment checks if the project has complied with the organizationally mandated project management framework and if all deliverables due for the completed phase have indeed been delivered according to the prescribed specifications.

Planning Phase Processes

The Utopian PMO's planning processes help create the planning backbone of the project, the project management plan. The total effort of the planning process aims to develop a clear, articulate and efficient planning tool that'll help a project manager deliver a project that falls within its scope, time and cost boundaries.

Developing the Project Management Plan Process (PR2.1PMP)

The successful completion of a phase gate test concludes the project start-up process (PR1.1PSU) and Developing the project management plan (PR2.1PMP) is triggered

The PR2.1PMP process can be construed as a "home process" which holds the sub-processes of planning within its remit. The PR2.1PMP process triggers Plan Stakeholder Mgmt. Process (PRJ2.2PSM) and then from there on, control is handed over from process to process till all the sub-plans that make up the project management plan is created. Once the procurement management plan is created through the Plan Procurement Mgmt. Process (PRJ2.10PPRM), flow is returned to the "home process" to put together the various sub-plans to make the completed project management plan for the project.

The PR2.1PMP process hands over to the sub-process in the following order before taking over in the final steps to consolidate the various elements of the project management plan:

- Developing The Project Management Plan Process
- Plan Stakeholder Mgmt. Process
- Collect Requirements, Plan scope management & Define Scope Process
- Creating the WBS & Developing the Schedule Process

- Cost Estimation & Determining Budget Process
- Plan Quality Management Process
- Plan HR Management Process
- Plan Communication Management Process
- Plan Risk Management Process
- Plan Procurement Management Process

Once the final sub-plan, i.e. the procurement management plan is received, the completed project management plan is taken through a review and approval process with the project sponsor playing a key role. The PMO analyst facilitates the process and the approved project management plan is published on the PMIS for organizational review. The publishing of the project management plan signals the end of the planning phase and the project manager notifies the PMO of the completion of the phase. The PMO analyst then undertakes a phase gate test to ascertain if the project has followed the methodology in its entirety and if all recommended deliverables have in fact been produced and approved. On the successful passage of a phase gate test, the project manager updates the lessons learned by the project in this particular phase including what they (the project team) did right and would like to repeat and what they did wrong. An end of phase report is collectively made by the project manager and the PMO analyst and is submitted to the PMO to archive as a part of the historical information database also known as the organizational process assets.

Completion of the planning phase triggers the next phase in the lifecycle, i.e. execution via the Direct & Manage Project Work Process [PRJ3.1DMPW] while concurrently triggering the PMO's core Delivery Management process [PMO03DM] to enable the PMO to begin monitoring delivery of the project and to ramp up support. Triggering PMO03DM also enables the project to start getting visibility on the organizational level roadmaps to help draw management's attention and support for this strategic initiative. The presence of a new initiative on the roadmap is also a trigger for the human resources function in the organization to expect requests for new resources to help staff the project.

Developing the Project Management Plan Process (PRJ2.1PMP) Part 1

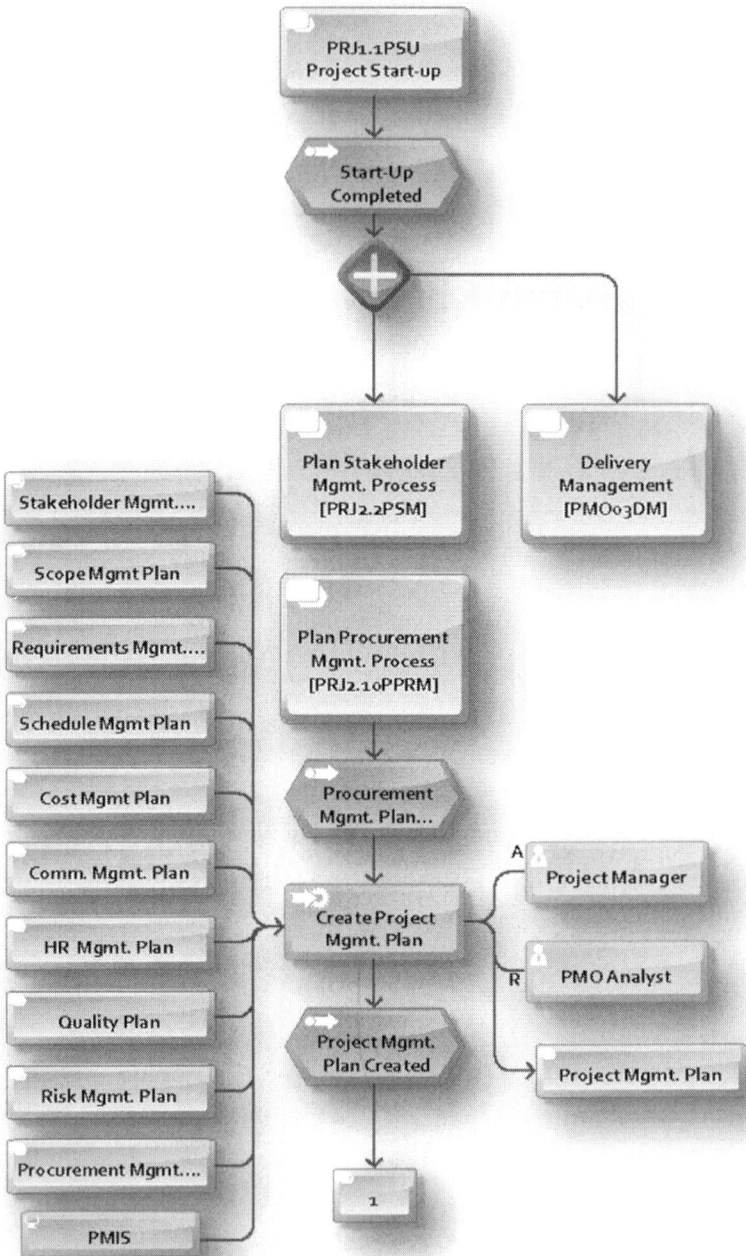

Developing the Project Management Plan Process (PRJ2.1PMP) Part 2

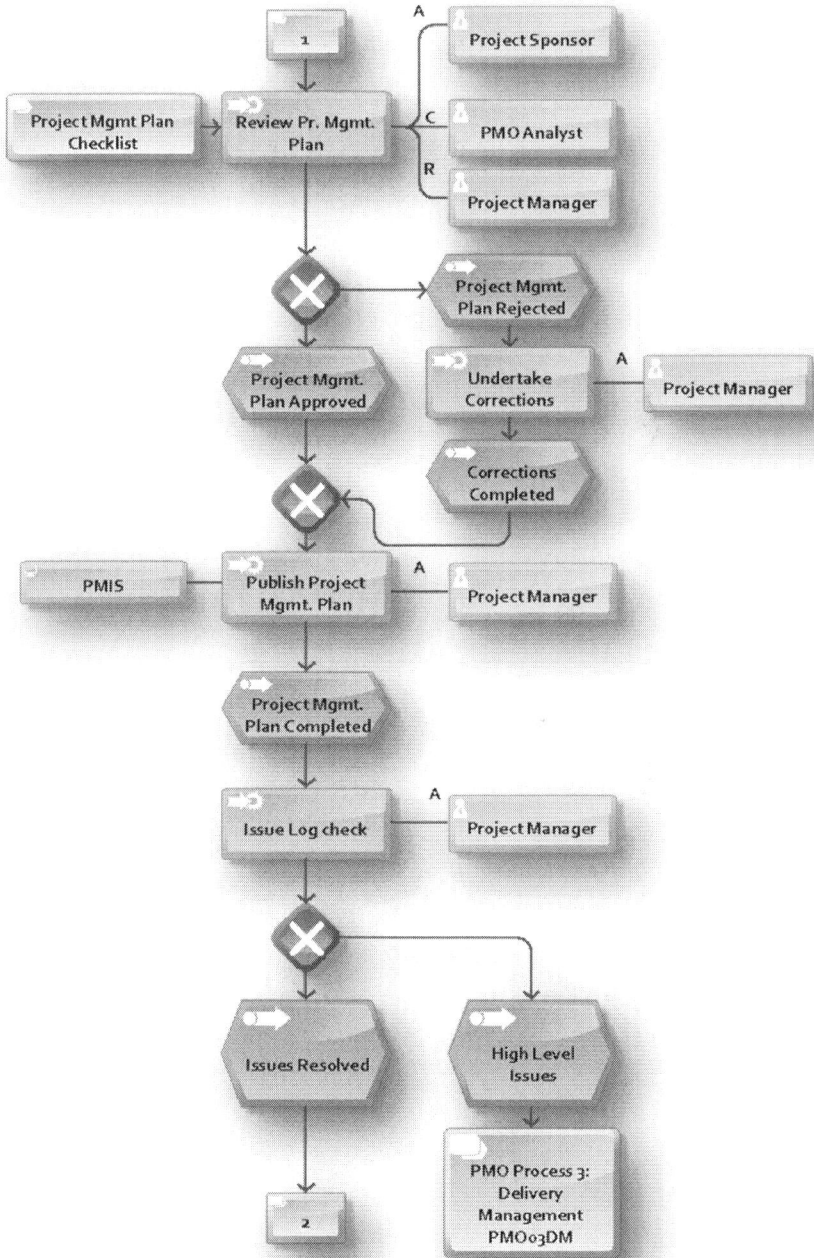

Developing the Project Management Plan Process (PRJ2.1PMP) Part 3

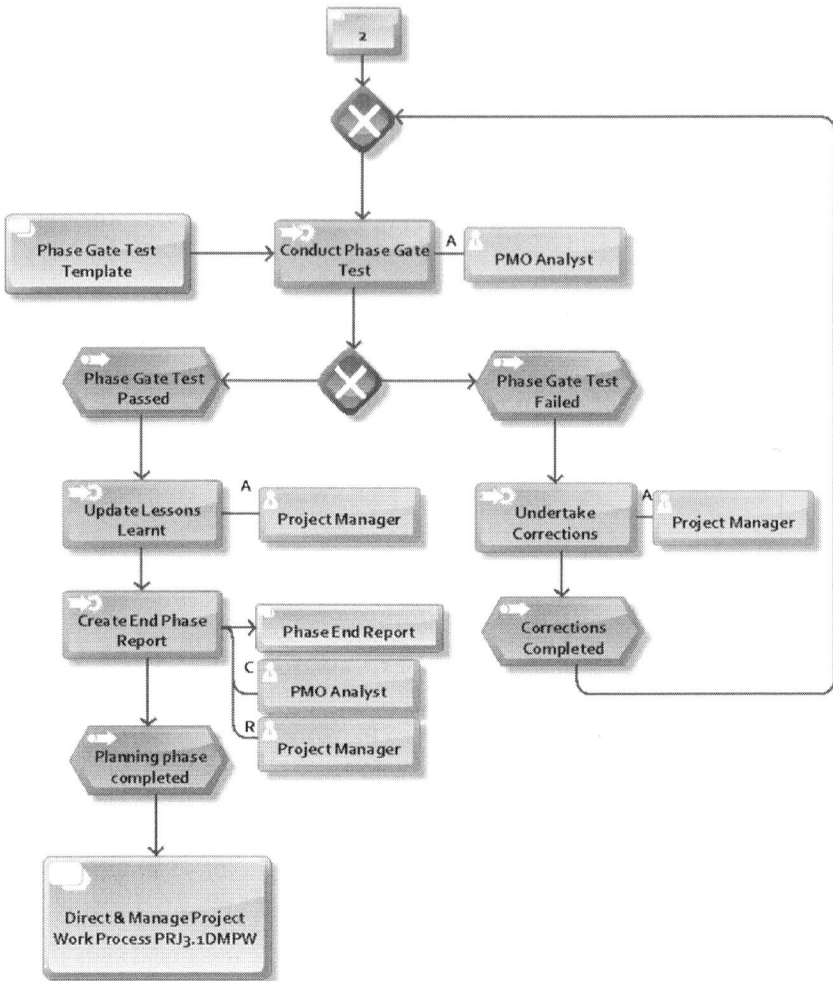

2

Phase Gate Test Template → Conduct Phase Gate Test — A — PMO Analyst

Phase Gate Test Passed ← → Phase Gate Test Failed

Update Lessons Learnt — A — Project Manager

Undertake Corrections — A — Project Manager

Create End Phase Report → Phase End Report

C — PMO Analyst

R — Project Manager

Corrections Completed

Planning phase completed

Direct & Manage Project Work Process PRJ3.1DMPW

Plan Stakeholder Management Process (PR2.2PSM)

Once the project manager has begun to start planning for the project, one of the first and most important things that need to be done is an exhaustive plan to manage the stakeholders involved in the project. It may be helpful to remember that the bulk of the identification of the stakeholders involved was completed in the initiation phase of the project itself.

This process is more specific to defining a plan to manage the identified stakeholders and ascertaining whether a qualitative or quantitative measurement model is to be used. A recommended technique for effective stakeholder management is to score each stakeholder based on their power and influence on the project and then multiplying the two gives each stakeholder a score that helps the project manager determine the approach to take whilst managing their expectations. It must be noted that all signed contracts must be taken into account whilst creating a stakeholder management plan due to contractual obligations that give rise to a whole new set of stakeholders for a project.

The completed stakeholder management plan is taken through a review with the project sponsor who gives necessary inputs and changes. The completed and approved stakeholder management plan is published on the PMIS for purposes of information recording, dissemination and collaboration.

Should the project manager wish, a voluntary check on the plan is requested from the PMO and any issues with completeness, alignment to best practices and prescribed methodology is fixed. A sufficiently competent and experienced project manager may alternatively not wish to proceed with a voluntary check, in which case this step is skipped. Any lessons learned whilst preparing the stakeholder management plan are documented, published on the PMIS and the next process, viz. Collect Requirements, Plan Scope Management & Define Scope Process [PRJ2.3SMP] is triggered.

Plan Stakeholder Management Process (PRJ2.2PSM) Complete

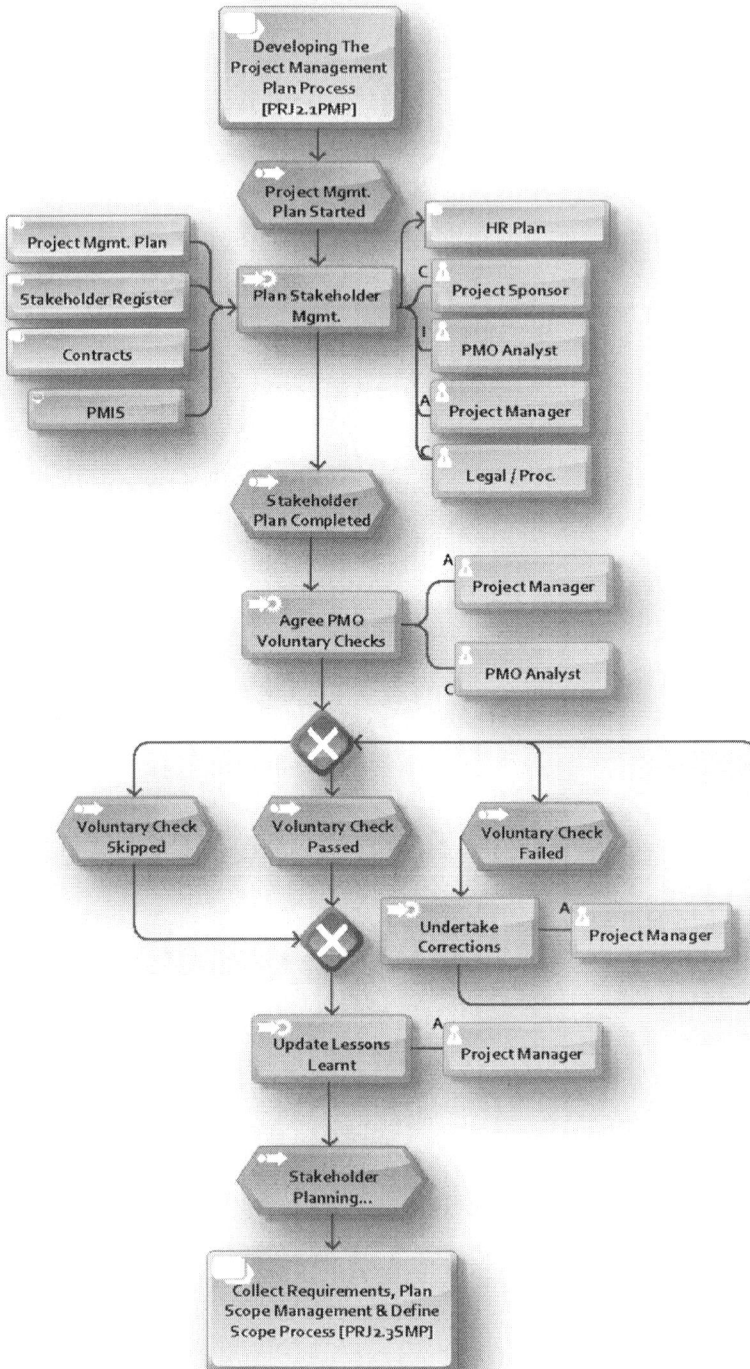

Collect Requirements, Plan scope management & Define Scope Process (PRJ2.3SMP)

Once the stakeholder management plan is finalized, work begins on the next part of the project management plan, i.e. collecting the requirements and solidifying everything into a base lined scope, which then forms the precursor to all the other planning activities in the project.

PRJ2.3SMP concerns itself with first creating a requirements management plan that details a methodology for collecting the requirements for the deliverables of the project. Once a requirements plan is put together, the project manager then begins work on collecting the actual requirements. The stakeholder register and sub-plans created during the previous processes [Viz. PRJ1.1PSU & PRJ2.1PMP] help provide guidance on who and how to approach for the project deliverable's requirements.

A consolidation of the collected requirements, with conflicting items nullified, helps produce the next output of this process, the scope management plan. This plan elucidates a methodology to manage scope on the project. During the last step in this process, the final, agreed, work, the project is expected to accomplish, is put together in the form of the scope statement. The project is expected to deliver the scope detailed in this document, nothing more and certainly nothing less. The detailed scope document is put through a rigorous validation and approval process and the scope is base lined.

Collect Requirements, Plan scope management & Define Scope Process (PRJ2.3SMP) Part 1

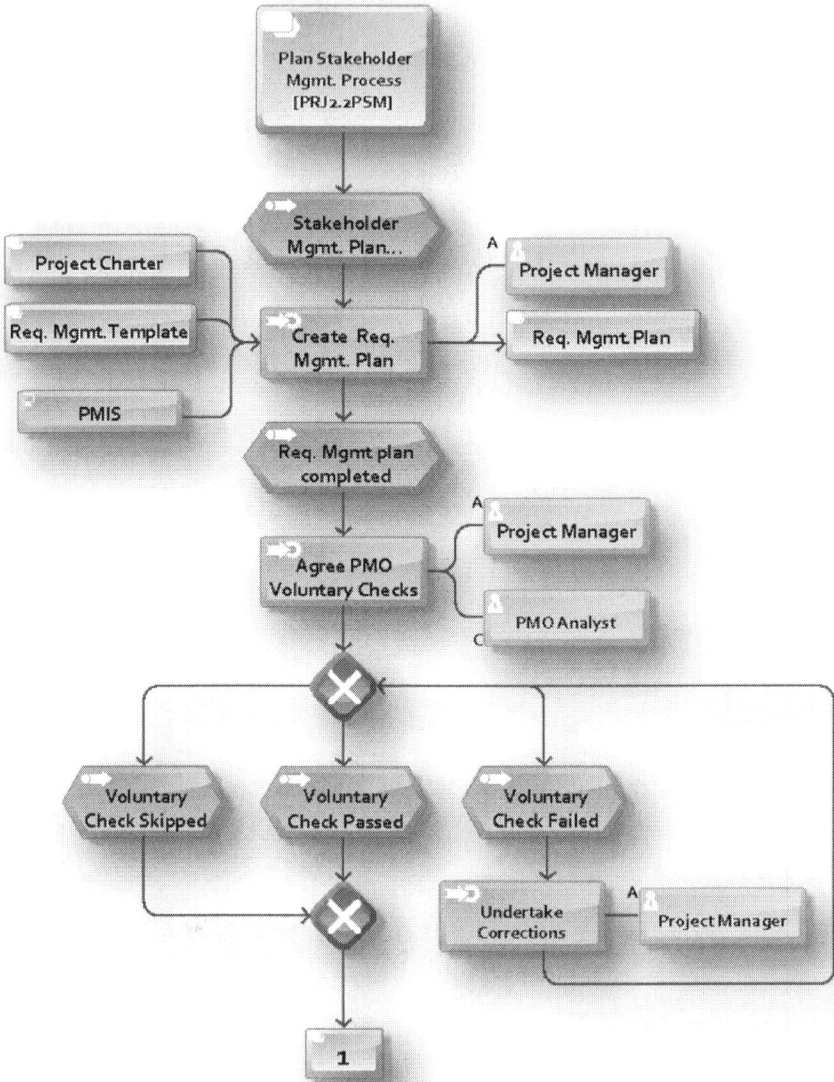

Collect Requirements, Plan scope management & Define Scope Process (PRJ2.3SMP) Part 2

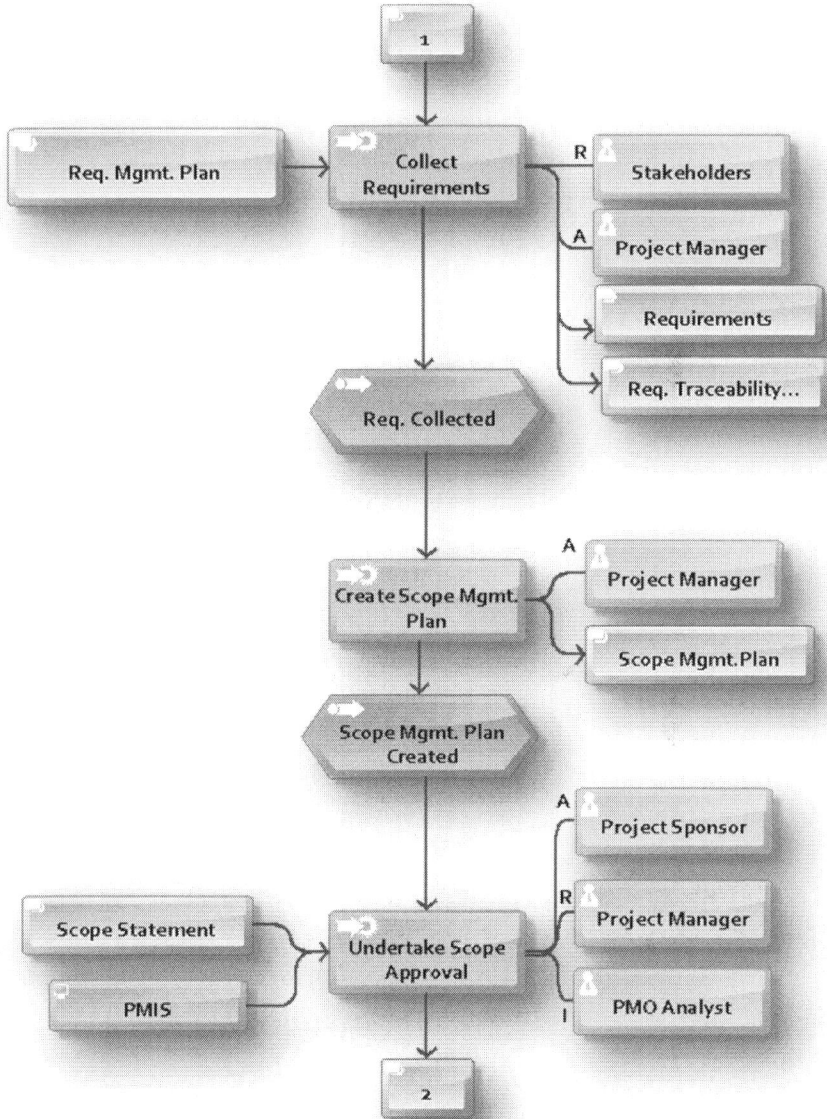

Collect Requirements, Plan scope management & Define Scope Process (PRJ2.3SMP) Part 3

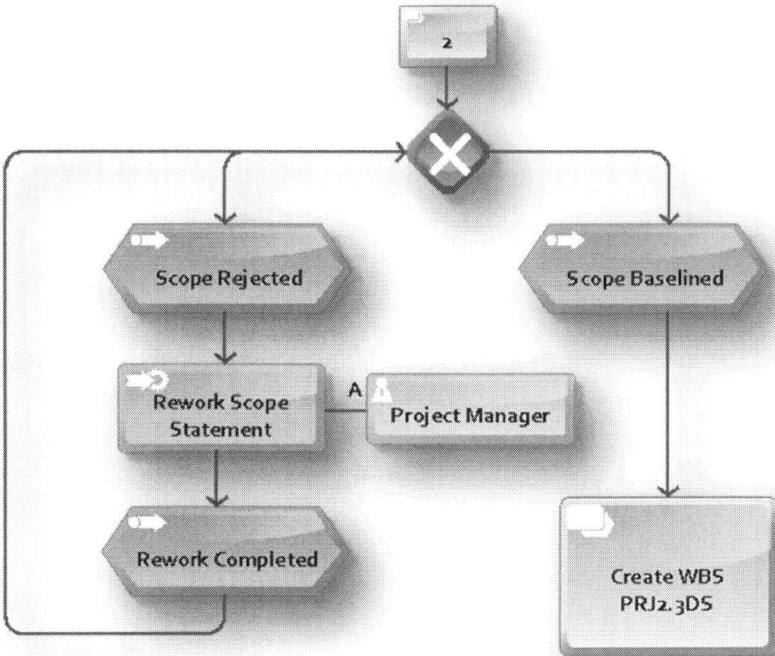

Baselining is the act of taking a "snap-shot" of the current state of any item, usually a document, with the intent of noting and freezing its current state. Any changes to a baselined document can only be accomplished via a rigorous change management process involving an explicit review and approval of the proposed changes. Once approved changes are made, the document is re-baselined and resumes its protected existence once again.

Creating the WBS & Developing the Schedule Process (PRJ2.4DS)

The creation of the scope statement and getting the agreement of all stakeholders puts the project manager in a much better position to truly understand the project and the expected deliverables. The project manager is now able to make concrete plans with the assurance of having a baselined scope in hand and the development of a very critical planning tool, the WBS (Work Break-down Structure) begins.

The WBS is a hierarchical decomposition of the project scope broken down into smaller elements. At the lowest level, the elements of a WBS are called work packages. The act of breaking down the project scope into work packages is called decomposition. The level to which to decompose a project's scope depends on the complexity and specific needs of a project. Too less and it doesn't aid in planning and conversely too much decomposition can make the management of the WBS very difficult. However, used correctly, the WBS is immensely invaluable as a planning tool.

Once the scope is broken down meaningfully into work packages, the activities required to accomplish each work package can be defined. Before this can be done, a plan describing how the schedule will be managed is put together. This plan should detail methodologies, responsibilities and other specifics pertaining to the schedule.

The activities, required to deliver each work package, can now be ordered in the sequence in which they can potentially be executed. Activities, in an ideal world, can be executed in linearly but in the real world, various constraints define the order of execution. An estimation of the effort required is carried out through any known qualitative and quantitative methods. Estimated resources are assigned to the re-ordered activities with the involvement of the organization's HR representatives to avoid over allocation of shared resources. Once activities are listed, ordered and allocated resources, the expected duration of each activity can be assessed, again using both qualitative and quantitative methods.

At this stage, the project manager essentially has an ordered list of activities, with estimated durations and resources, preferably on a project scheduling tool, to help monitor progress against recorded tasks. The schedule is baselined and published on the PMIS.

Should the project manager wish, a voluntary check on the plan is requested from the PMO and any issues with completeness, alignment to best practices and prescribed methodology is fixed. A sufficiently competent and experienced project manager may alternatively not wish to proceed with a voluntary check, in which case this step is skipped. Any lessons learned whilst preparing the schedule management plan, the WBS or the project schedule are documented, published on the PMIS and the next process, viz. Cost Estimation & Determining Budget Process [PRJ2.5DB] is triggered to enable the completion of the next part of the project management plan.

Creating the WBS & Developing the Schedule Pr. (PRJ2.4DS) Pt. 1

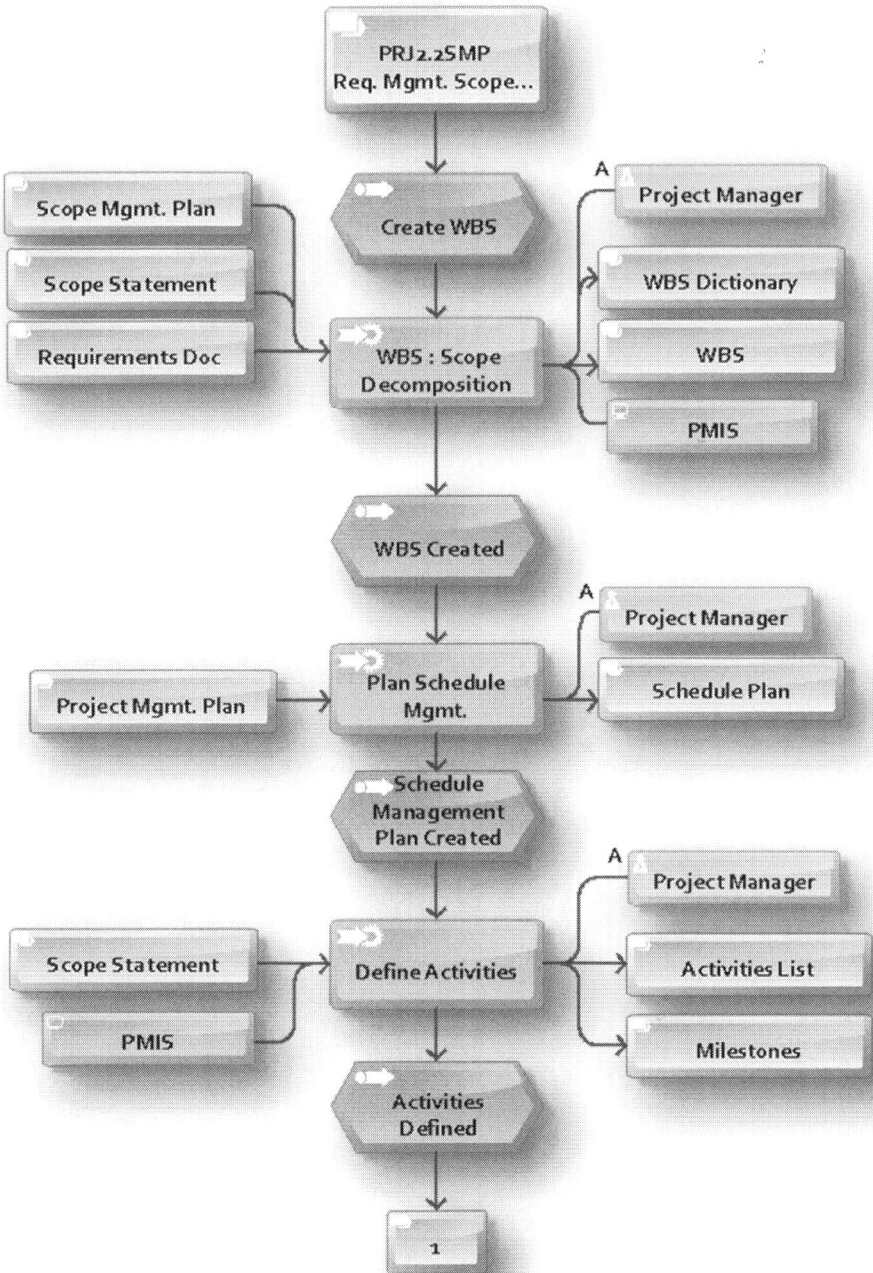

PRJ2.2SMP
Req. Mgmt. Scope...

Scope Mgmt. Plan

Scope Statement

Requirements Doc

Create WBS

WBS : Scope
Decomposition

A

Project Manager

WBS Dictionary

WBS

PMIS

WBS Created

Project Mgmt. Plan

Plan Schedule
Mgmt.

A

Project Manager

Schedule Plan

Schedule
Management
Plan Created

Scope Statement

PMIS

Define Activities

A

Project Manager

Activities List

Milestones

Activities
Defined

1

Creating the WBS & Developing the Schedule Pr. (PRJ2.4DS) Pt. 2

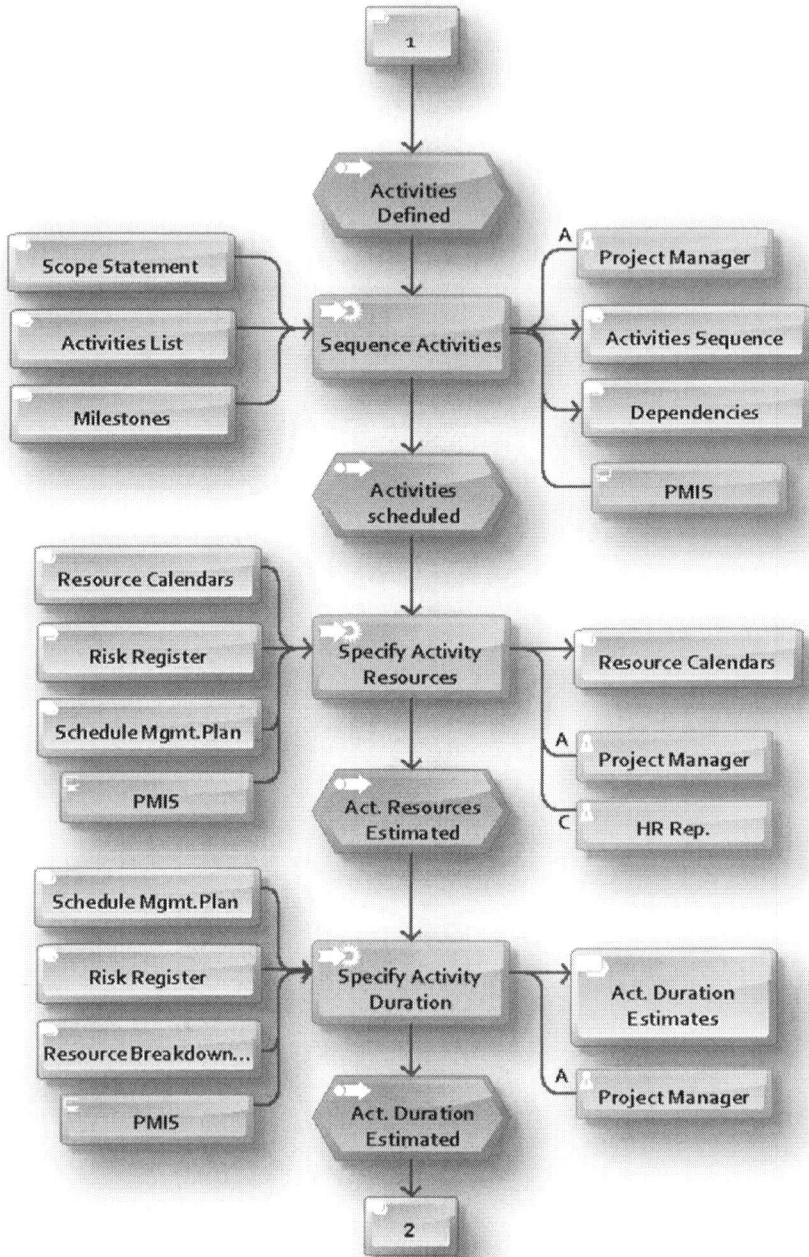

Creating the WBS & Developing the Schedule Pr. (PRJ2.4DS) Pt. 3

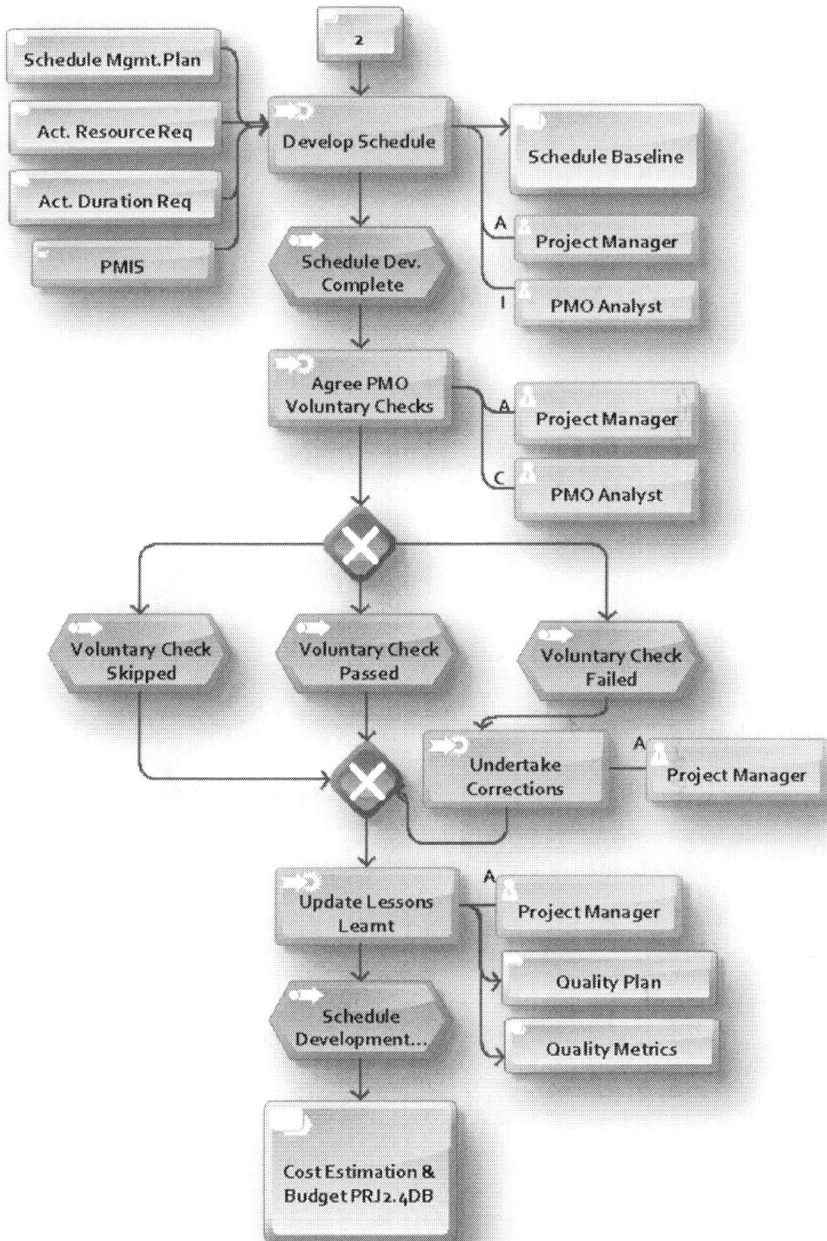

Schedule Mgmt. Plan	
Act. Resource Req	**2**
Act. Duration Req	Develop Schedule
PMIS	Schedule Baseline

A Project Manager

I PMO Analyst

Schedule Dev. Complete

Agree PMO Voluntary Checks

A Project Manager

C PMO Analyst

Voluntary Check Skipped — Voluntary Check Passed — Voluntary Check Failed

Undertake Corrections **A** Project Manager

Update Lessons Learnt **A** Project Manager

Quality Plan

Schedule Development...

Quality Metrics

Cost Estimation & Budget PRJ2.4DB

Cost Estimation & Determining Budget Process (PRJ2.5DB)

One of the key advantages of having the PMO01GSA process is the ability to have a high level estimate of the initiative at the business case level itself. The financial case section of the business case contains this information and by approving the business case for an initiative, an organization implies that it understands the costs involved in executing the initiative.

However, at this stage, the project has undergone further elaboration and the creation of a complete schedule with resource and time estimates puts the project manager in a better position to review the initial estimates provided in the business case to check if they still possess merits. The PRJ2.5DB process is triggered by a completed schedule being published on the PMIS. A detailed cost management plan is drafted, elucidating the strategies planned to be used to manage and control costs on the project. The project manager then begins to assess the cost associated with performing each activity detailed in the project schedule. An estimation of the costs involved is carried out through any known qualitative and quantitative methods. This estimate is then compared against the initial estimates provided in the business case. In an ideal scenario, the business case estimates and the activity level estimates must not have significant deviation from each other. The level of deviation acceptable is usually mandated by the organization. It is usually set to be about ± 15%. If the two estimates are within the prescribed tolerances, then the new budget for the project is revised, the sponsor provides the necessary approvals, the project manager updates the lessons learned and the process moves to the next part of the planning lifecycle, i.e. Plan Quality Management Process [PRJ2.6PQM]

However, if the variation between the two estimates are outside allowable limits then the PMO Process #3 Delivery Management [PMO03DM] is triggered which then undertakes the necessary activities to provide organizational visibility to bring this conundrum to a conclusion.

Cost Estimation & Determining Budget Process (PRJ2.5DB) Part 1

```
                          WBS & Developing
                          Schedule PRJ2.3DS

                              Schedule
                          Development...

WBS

Schedule Mgmt. Plan

HR Mgmt. Plan          Develop Cost Mgmt.      C    PMO Analyst
                             Plan
                                               A    Project Manager
Risk Mgmt. Plan

PMIS                      Cost Plan                 Cost Mgmt. Plan
                          Complete


                          Estimate Costs        A    Project Sponsor

                                                C    PMO Analyst

                                                R    Project Manager

                          Estimation                 Activity Cost
                          Complete                    Estimates


                               1
```

Cost Estimation & Determining Budget Process (PRJ2.5DB) Part 2

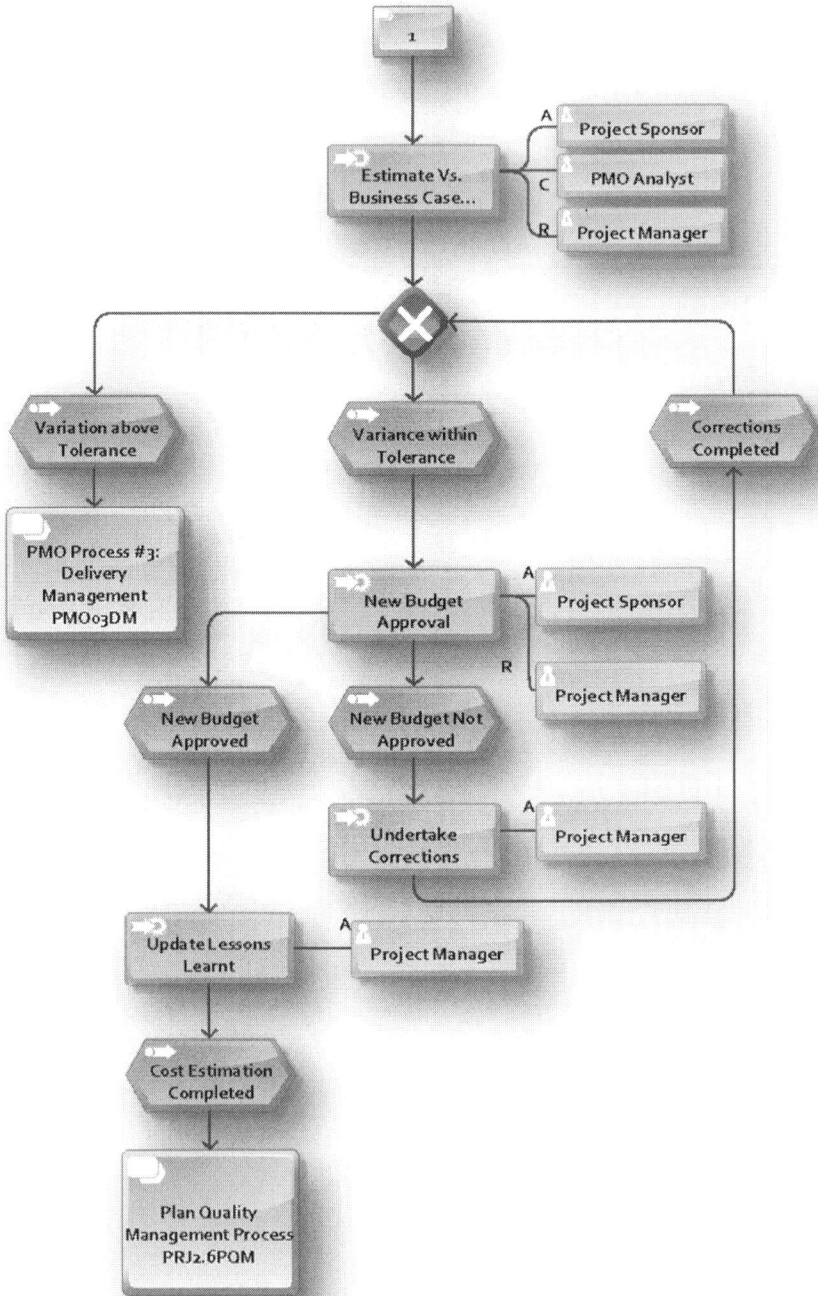

Plan Quality Management Process (PRJ2.6PQM)

The completion of the cost estimation activities triggers the next process in the planning lifecycle, i.e. the plan quality management process [PRJ2.6PQM]. This process is also triggered by Perform Quality Assurance Process [PRJ3.2PQA], if the initial quality plans fail to meet stated quality requirements. This process creates a detailed plan to manage the activities pertaining to quality assurance and quality control on the project. The specifics of the plan include the acceptable level of quality, which is typically defined by the customer, and describes how the project will ensure this level of quality in its deliverables and work processes. Quality management ensures that the project deliverables meet stated or prescribed requirements and that work processes are performed efficiently and as documented. The plan also ensures that both preventive and corrective actions are taken to ensure quality is consistent

Also included in the plan are methodologies, responsibilities, budgets, metrics and other tools including checklists. The project manager uses the parameters stated in the requirements documentation to determine final quality requirements for the product. This plan that facilitates meeting the defined quality criteria, encompassing all of the above is then created. The project manager may also avail the expertise of a quality management SME, in matters that require a detailed quality analysis. The completed quality management plan is published on the PMIS.

Should the project manager wish, a voluntary check on the plan is requested from the PMO and any issues with completeness, alignment to best practices and prescribed methodology is fixed. A sufficiently competent and experienced project manager may alternatively not wish to proceed with a voluntary check, in which case this step is skipped. Any lessons learned whilst preparing the quality management plan is published on the PMIS and the next process, viz. Plan HR Management Process [PRJ2.7PHRM] is triggered to enable the completion of the next part of the project management plan.

Plan Quality Management Process (PRJ2.6PQM) Part 1

Plan Quality Management Process (PRJ2.6PQM) Part 2

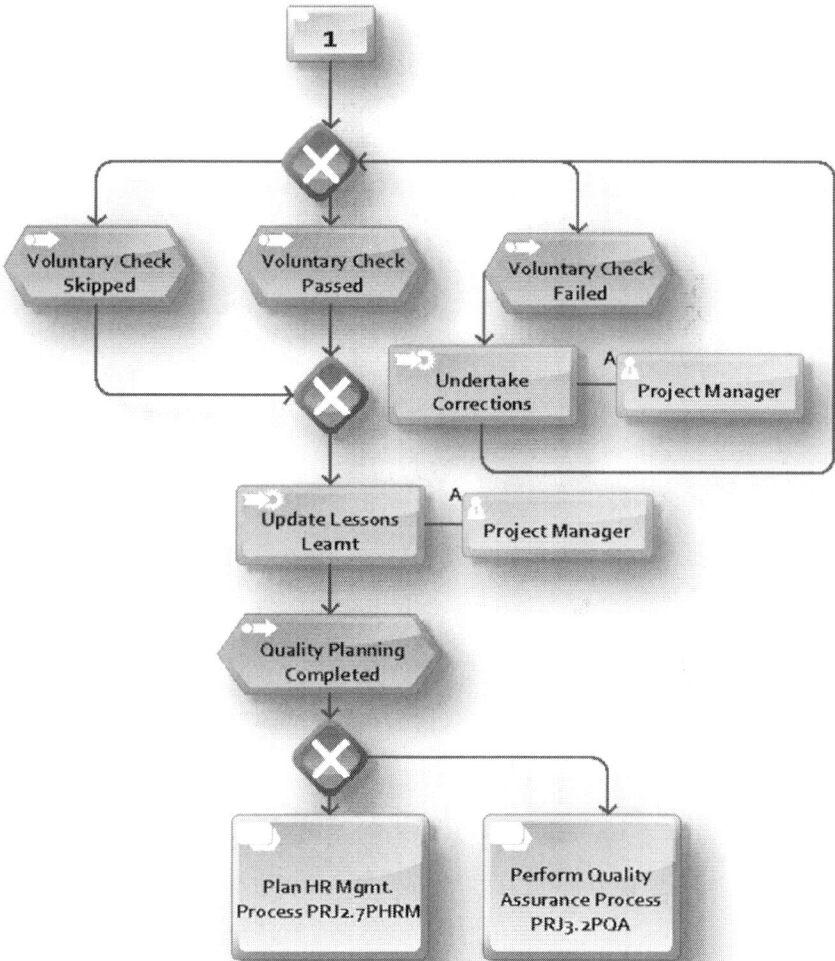

Plan HR Management Process (PRJ2.7PHRM)

After establishing the quality management protocols on the project, the project manager's next course of action is to establish a solid base for management of the human resources assigned to the project. The project manager then determines how to acquire resources identified in Creating the WBS & Developing the Schedule Process (PRJ2.4DS). Key project roles and responsibilities are defined and documented in the plan, including the creation of a RACI matrix for all identified project tasks

A RACI matrix is a layout depicting tasks on the left column and resource names on the top row. Each task is mapped to a resource who is Accountable, Responsible, Consulted or Informed (R,A,C,I) for /on/ about each listed task. Good practices dictate having at least one resource accountable for a task and no more than one to avoid finger-pointing.

To effectively manage resources working on the project, organizational charts and reporting hierarchies are created and documented in the HR management plan. It would also serve in the best interests of the project manager to study and understand various organizational behavior and motivational theories to help define an approach to managing resources. The management of resources is a subjective topic and hence must be tailored to meet the unique requirements of each project. Also, any limitations arising out of the physical location of the project team members is analyzed for any potential conflicts. For e.g.: virtually located key project resources. Care must be taken to avoid limiting planning for only the human resource aspect and all other resources such as materials and equipment must also be taken into account too. A hierarchical decomposition of resources by type can be used and such a diagram is known as a Resource Breakdown Structure (RBS). An elaborate rewards and recognition system is also developed as a part of this plan, to influence and promote team performance. The completed HR management plan which considers all potential HR management aspects such as the ones discussed above, is published on the PMIS.

Should the project manager wish, a voluntary check on the plan is requested from the PMO and any issues with completeness, alignment to best practices and prescribed methodology is fixed. A sufficiently competent and experienced project manager may alternatively not wish to proceed with a voluntary check, in which case this step is skipped. Any lessons learned whilst preparing the quality management plan are published on the PMIS and the next process, viz. Plan Communication Management. Process [PRJ2.8PCM] is triggered to enable the completion of the next part of the project management plan.

Plan HR Management Process (PRJ2.7PHRM)

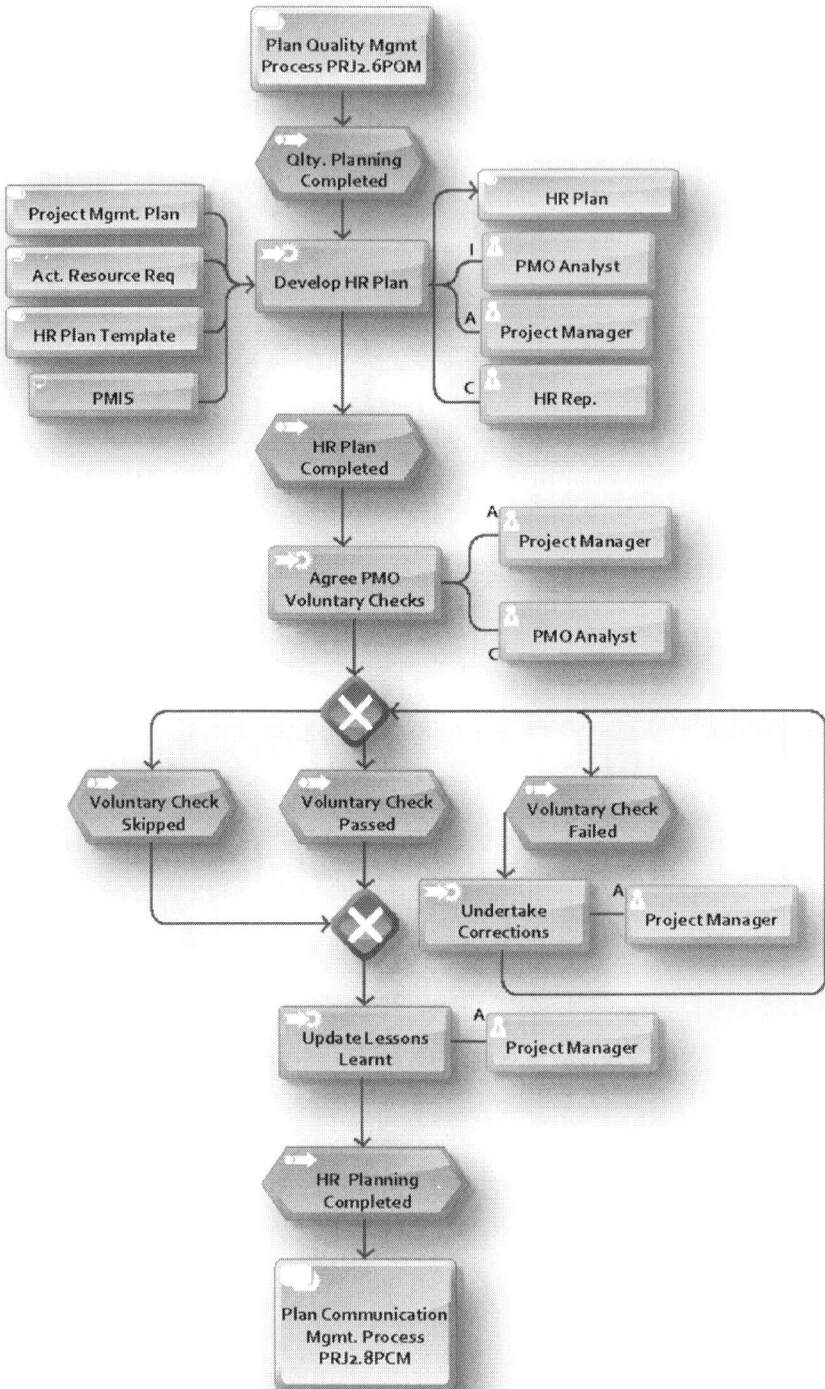

```
                    ┌─────────────────┐
                    │ Plan Quality Mgmt│
                    │ Process PRJ2.6PQM│
                    └─────────────────┘
                             │
                    ┌─────────────────┐
                    │ Qlty. Planning   │
                    │ Completed        │
                    └─────────────────┘
```

- Plan Quality Mgmt Process PRJ2.6PQM
- Qlty. Planning Completed

Inputs	Develop HR Plan	Outputs
Project Mgmt. Plan		HR Plan
Act. Resource Req		PMO Analyst
HR Plan Template		Project Manager
PMIS		HR Rep.

- HR Plan Completed

Agree PMO Voluntary Checks	
	Project Manager
	PMO Analyst

- Voluntary Check Skipped
- Voluntary Check Passed
- Voluntary Check Failed

Undertake Corrections	Project Manager

Update Lessons Learnt	Project Manager

- HR Planning Completed

- Plan Communication Mgmt. Process PRJ2.8PCM

Plan Communication Management Process (PRJ2.8PCM)

One of the key responsibilities of a project manager is to maintain effective communications with the team and with all stakeholders. To do this, an effective communications management plan is pertinent. An effective communications management plan must document, in detail, how the project manager intends to communicate with the identified stakeholders of the project. This involves identifying the information needs for each of the stakeholders, their reason for wanting this information, and the preferred medium of communication. Also important is the requirement to document the information needs of the project and the project manager itself. This includes the various pieces of information that the project needs from the stakeholders to make timely decisions. The completed communications management plan which considers all potential communication management aspects such as the ones discussed above, is published on the PMIS.

Should the project manager wish, a voluntary check on the plan is requested from the PMO and any issues with completeness, alignment to best practices and prescribed methodology is fixed. A sufficiently competent and experienced project manager may alternatively not wish to proceed with a voluntary check, in which case this step is skipped. Any lessons learned whilst preparing the quality management plan is published on the PMIS and the next gargantuan process, viz. Plan Risk Management Process [PRJ2.9PRM] is triggered to enable the completion of the next part of the project management plan.

Plan Communication Management Process (PRJ2.8PCM)

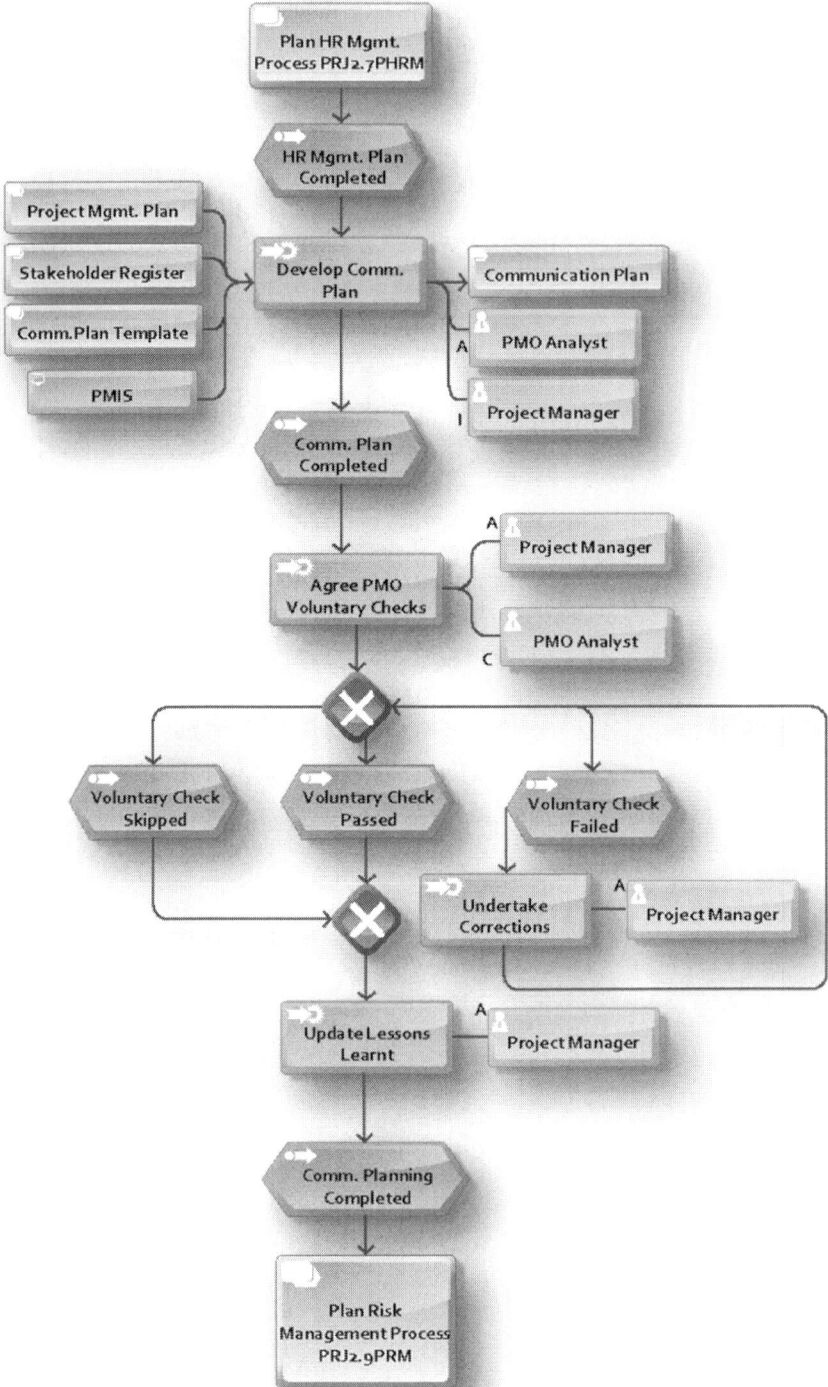

Plan Risk Management Process (PRJ2.9PRM)

The gargantuan plan risk management process (PRJ2.9PRM) is enormous in its scope and covers the entire gamut of risk management activities on a project, from the identification of risks to qualitative and quantitative assessments and culminating in developing mitigation plans for the identified risks.

The first step of the process is the creation of a risk management plan detailing the methodology, roles, and categories of risk, definitions and most importantly the risk tolerances of the organization. A start-up company will have a significantly higher risk appetite than an older traditionally-run organization. The risk management plan will also include, a high-level initial assessment of risks on the project. Since this plan provides the entire framework for managing risk on the project, impetus exists for creating an all-encompassing risk management plan. The completed risk management plan and list of initial risks is put through a review cycle and is signed-off by the PMO. If the initial list of risks is deemed excessive to what the organization considers as acceptable, the PMO Process 3: Delivery Management [PMO03DM] is triggered to decide whether to move ahead with the project or not. If both the plan and the initial list of risks is acceptable then stakeholders are notified, lessons learned are documented and the process moves to the next step.

The next step in the risk management process is the identification of risks. Several techniques exist to undertake a detailed identification of risks including but not limited to simple methods such as interviewing and brainstorming, to more in depth ones such as the Delphi technique. Care is taken to ensure that the identification of opportunities is not missed. A detailed risk / opportunity register is produced with a list of risks / opportunities and includes various categories under which to categorize the identified risks. Risks / opportunities can also be identified by individuals/ teams, in which case the individual/ team fills in the risk identification form and is vetted for validity during risk meetings and considered for inclusion into the project's risk register, if the risk is approved as having merit. The risk / opportunity register is then published on the PMIS for purposes of information dissemination and storage.

The next step of the risk management process assigns a probability and impact rating to each identified risk based on pre-established rating scales. The rating scales are established based on the risk appetite of the organization ascertained in the risk management planning phase. Risks having a high risk score is taken through quantitative risk assessment process while risks having a low score bypass this step of the process. During quantitative analysis, risks are analyzed using a variety of advanced risk management techniques such as Monte Carlo and decision trees. Risks which have been found to have a highest value are reviewed with the project sponsor for acceptability. If the risk poses a threat greater than which the organization is willing to endure, it is handed over to PMO Process 3: Delivery Management [PMO03DM] where a decision is made whether to continue or close the project. Risks with an acceptable impact value are documented in the risk register and then a plan for each identified risk / opportunity is determined.

Each risk or opportunity as segregated and treated according to commonly accepted strategies for dealing with risks and opportunities. Risks are avoided, transferred or mitigated while opportunities are shared, enhanced or exploited. A passive strategy for both risks and opportunities is to simply accept the risk, a decision that requires no process to accomplish. The identified treatment is formulated into mitigation plan and is either implemented straight away or slated for implementation when a risk or it's triggers surface. The new risk score is calculated after mitigation is implemented. In certain cases, a mitigation activity might sufficiently reduce a risk to a point where it longer poses a threat in its present form. Such risks are placed on a watch list and monitored for changes. Other risks are updated with their new scores and the risk register is re-ordered. The project management plans are updated on the PMIS and the project can proceed to the next planning process albeit with a robust risk management framework now in place.

Plan Risk Management Process (PRJ2.9PRM) Part 1

```
Plan Communication          Develop Program
Mgmt. Process               Management Plan
PRJ2.8PCM                    Process PGM2.1PMP
```

Comm. Planning
Completed

Project Level
Risk

Risk Mgmt. Plan

Project Mgmt. Plan

Stakeholder Register

Risk Mgmt. Plan...

PMIS

Create Risk Mgmt.
Plan

PMO Analyst   I

Project Manager   A

Stakeholders   I

Strategy Team   C

Risk Mgmt. Plan
Created

PMIS

Create Initial
Risks/Opportunities

PMO Analyst   I

Project Manager   A

Validate with
Stakeholders

Project Manager   A

Validation
Completed

Stakeholders   C

1

Plan Risk Management Process (PRJ2.9PRM) Part 2

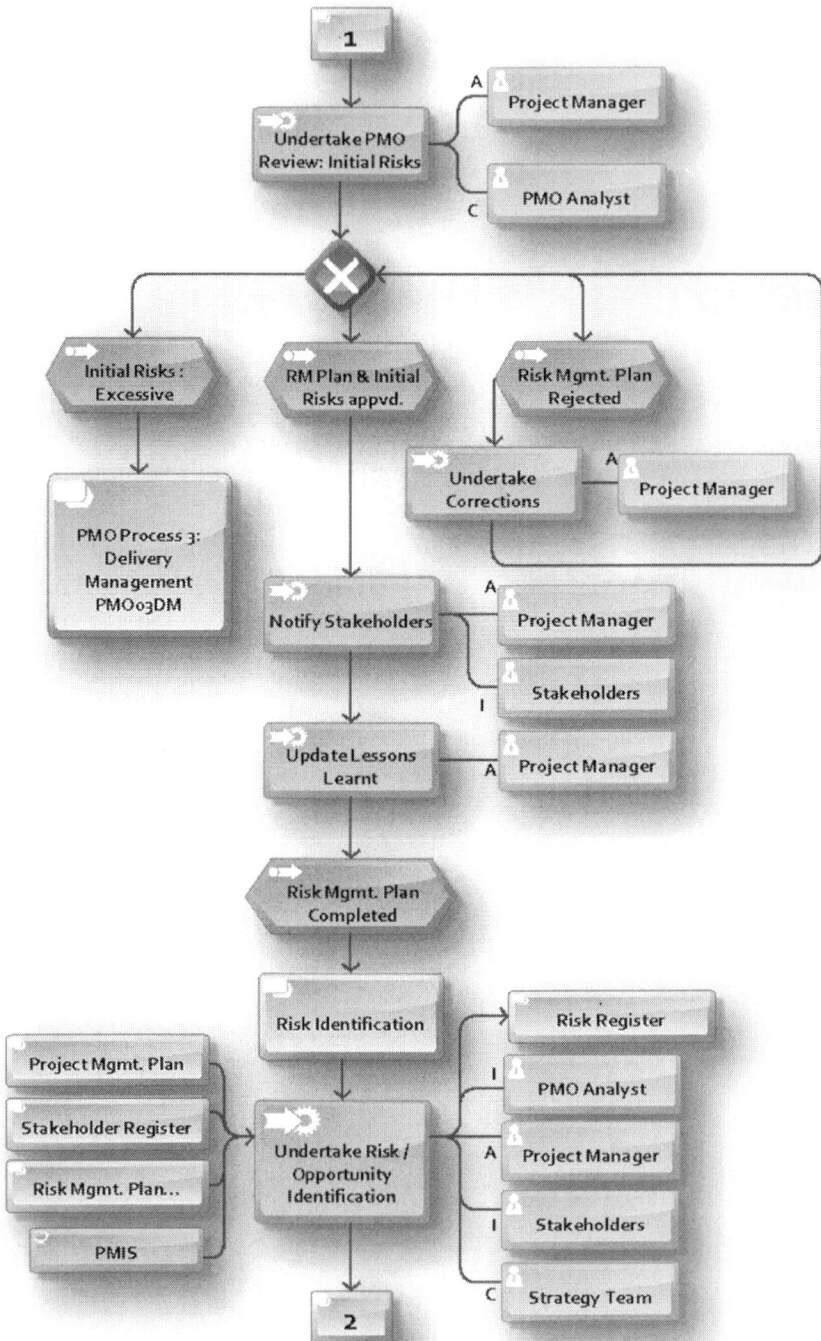

Plan Risk Management Process (PRJ2.9PRM) Part 3

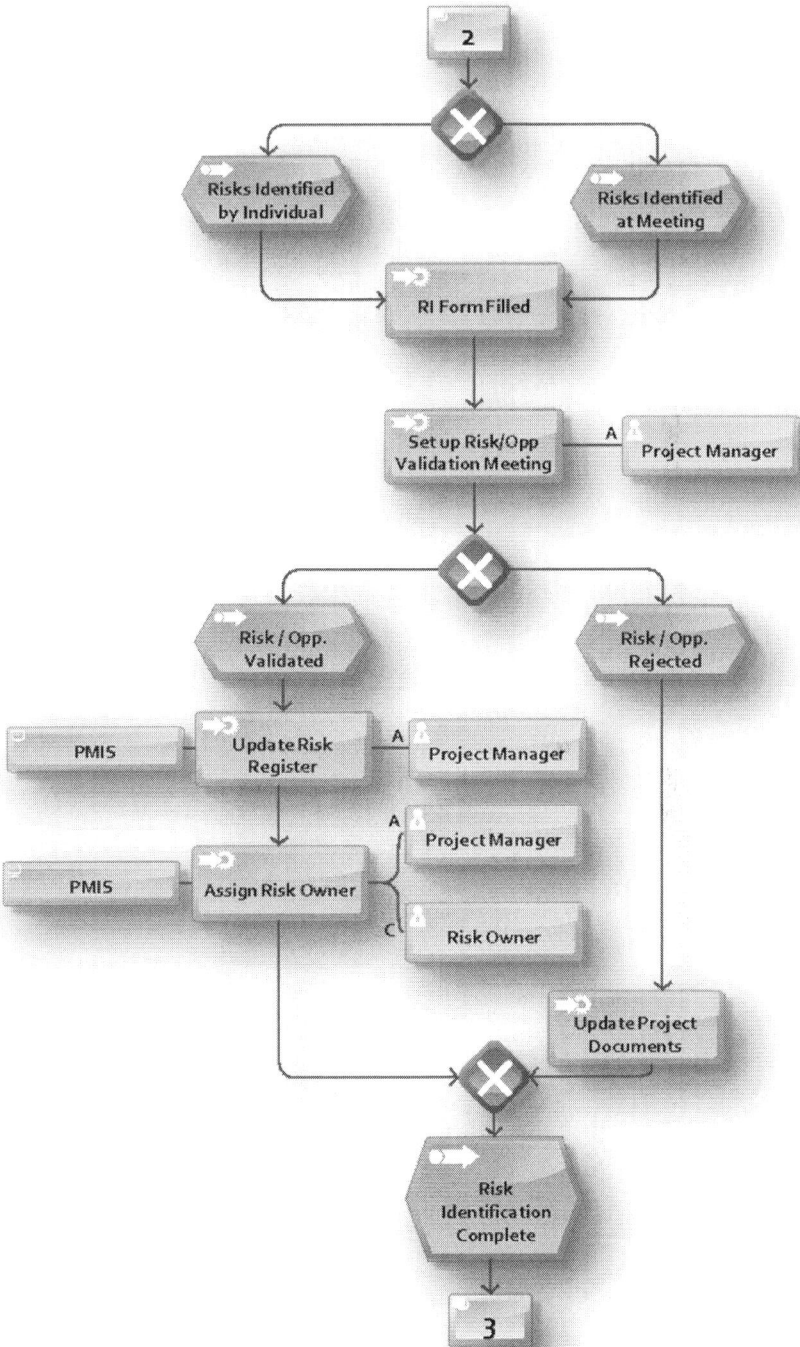

Plan Risk Management Process (PRJ2.9PRM) Part 4

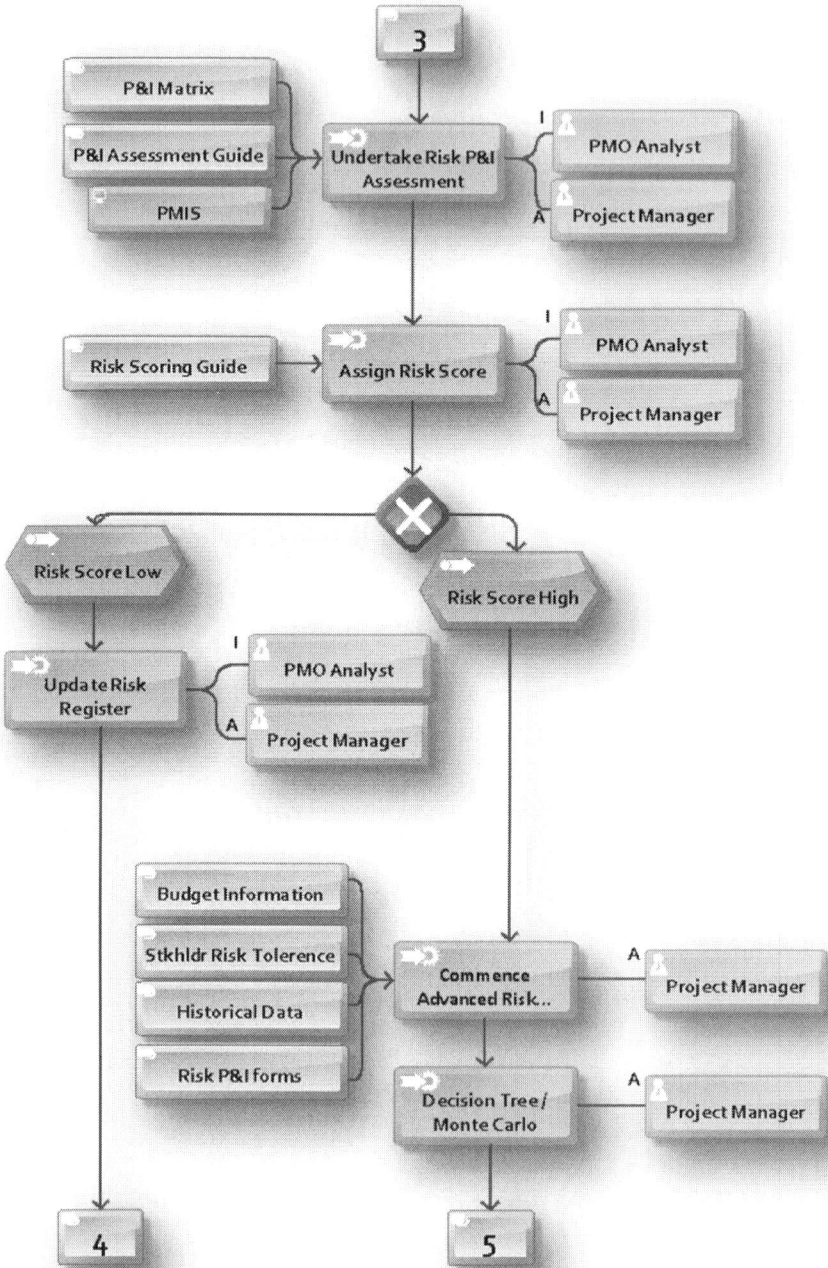

Plan Risk Management Process (PRJ2.9PRM) Part 5

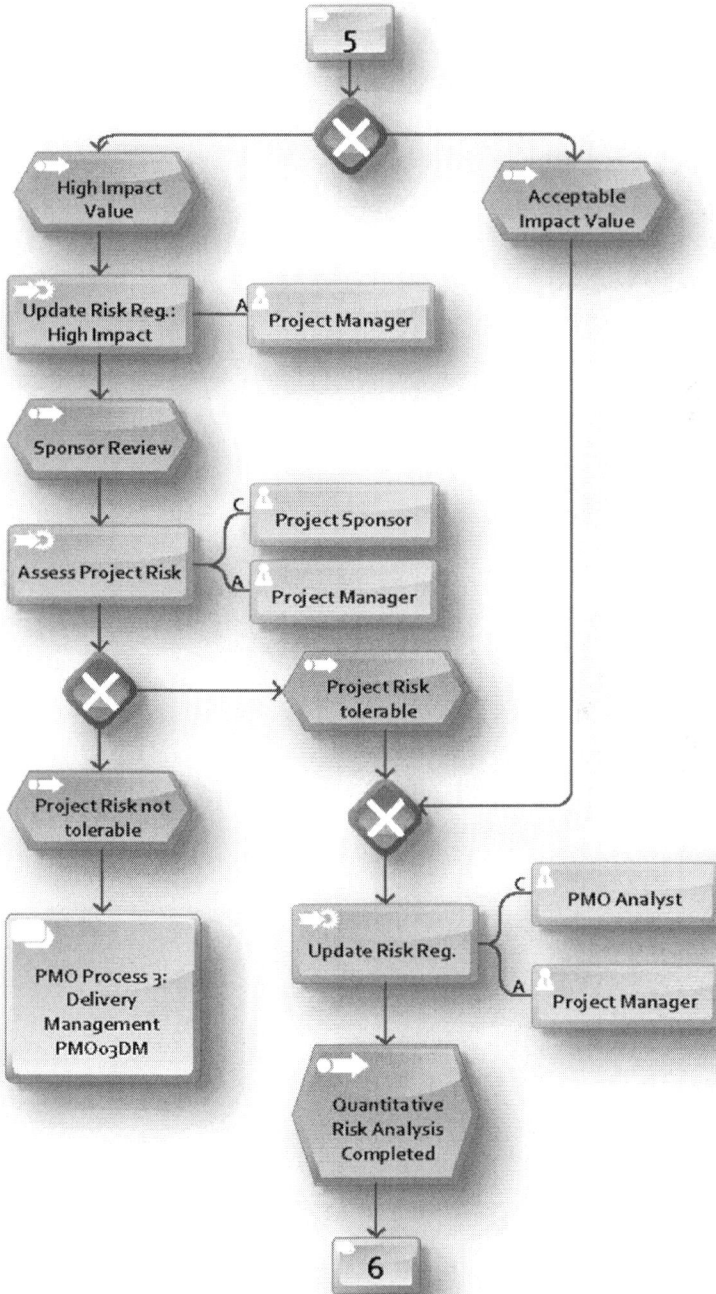

```
                        ┌─────┐
                        │  5  │
                        └──┬──┘
                           ▼
                         ╳
        ┌──────────────────────────────────┐
        ▼                                   ▼
   High Impact                        Acceptable
     Value                          Impact Value
        │                                   │
        ▼                                   │
  Update Risk Reg.: ──A── Project Manager   │
    High Impact                             │
        │                                   │
        ▼                                   │
  Sponsor Review                            │
        │                                   │
        ▼                                   │
  Assess Project Risk ──C── Project Sponsor │
                       ──A── Project Manager │
        │                                   │
        ▼                                   │
      ╳ ─────────────► Project Risk         │
        │                 tolerable         │
        ▼                    │              │
  Project Risk not           ▼              │
    tolerable              ╳ ───────────────┘
        │                    │
        ▼                    ▼
  PMO Process 3:       Update Risk Reg. ──C── PMO Analyst
    Delivery                │          ──A── Project Manager
   Management               ▼
   PMOo3DM            Quantitative
                      Risk Analysis
                       Completed
                           │
                           ▼
                        ┌─────┐
                        │  6  │
                        └─────┘
```

Plan Risk Management Process (PRJ2.9PRM) Part 6

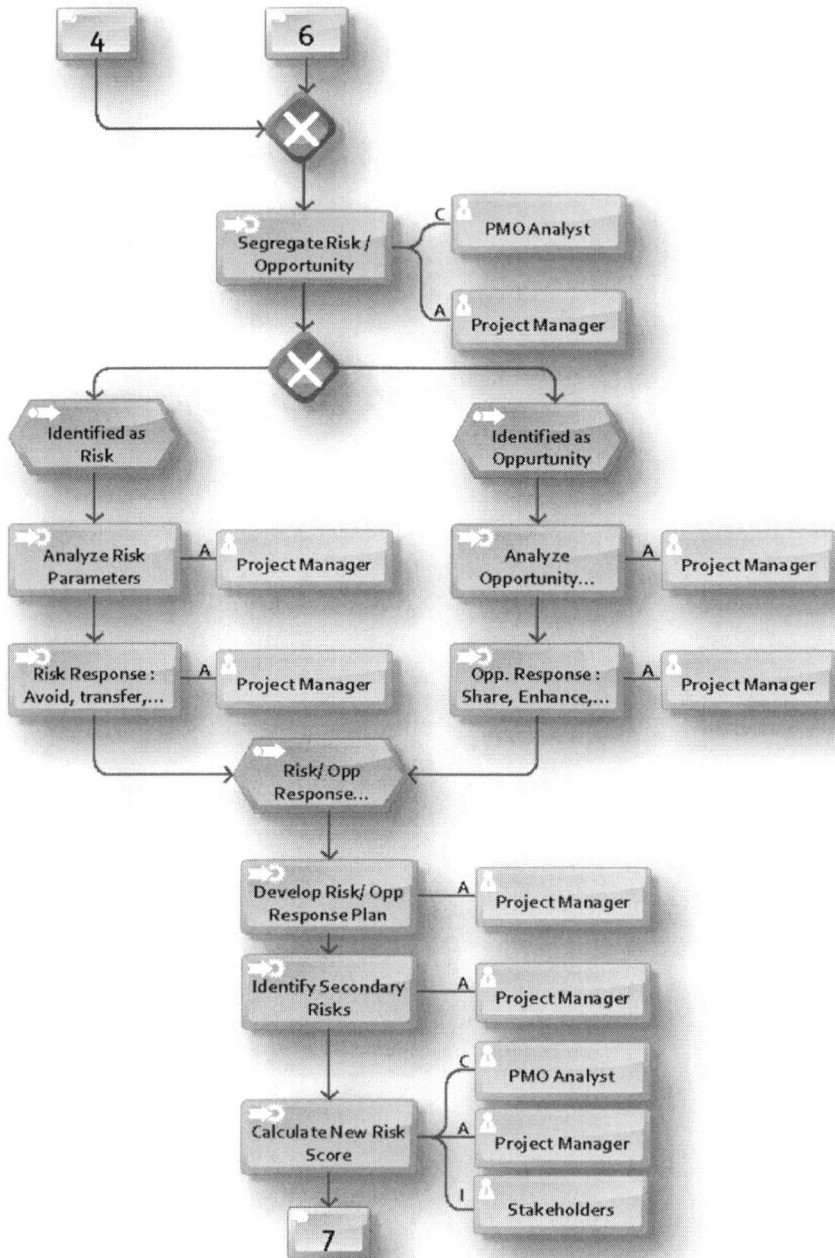

Plan Risk Management Process (PRJ2.9PRM) Part 7

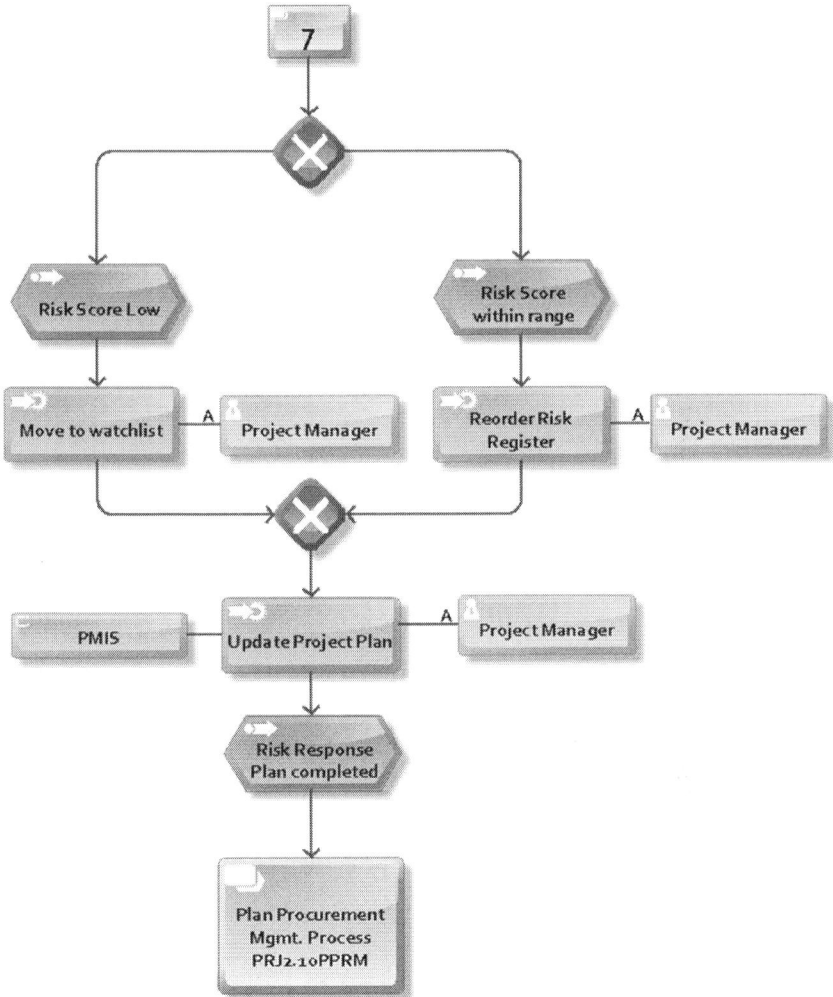

Plan Procurement Mgmt. Process (PRJ2.10PPRM)

The final sub-plan of the project management plan is the procurement management plan and this is created by the Plan Procurement Mgmt. Process (PRJ2.10PPRM). The procurement management plan is only created if any of the project work is outsourced. The project manager need not be concerned with this process is all of the project work is accomplished internally.

The PRJ2.10PRM process produces a procurement management plan that will subsequently be used by the Conduct Procurements Process (PRJ3.6CPR) and PMO Process 7: Supplier Management [PMO07SM] to manage outsourced work on the project. The plan concerns itself with creating a statement of work for each of the items planned to be procured, the types of contracts, the criteria for evaluating potential vendors and other procurement related documents. The completed procurement management plan which considers all potential procurement management aspects such as the ones discussed above, is published on the PMIS.

Should the project manager wish, a voluntary check on the plan is requested from the PMO and any issues with completeness, alignment to best practices and prescribed methodology is fixed. A sufficiently competent and experienced project manager may alternatively not wish to proceed with a voluntary check, in which case this step is skipped. Any lessons learned whilst preparing the quality management plan are published on the PMIS and the project proceeds to the next phase of the project lifecycle. Viz. executing the project.

Plan Procurement Mgmt. Process (PRJ2.10PPRM)

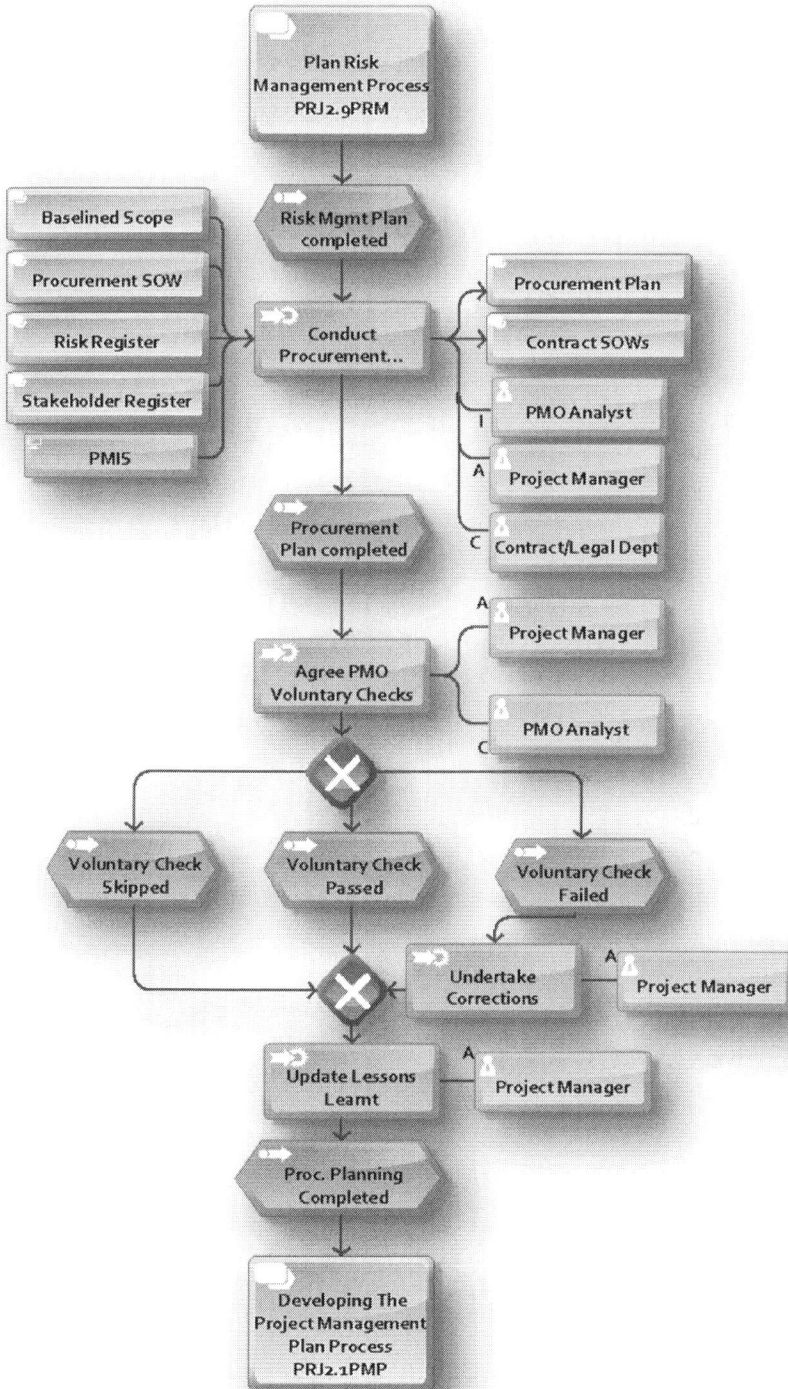

```
                    Plan Risk
              Management Process
                   PRJ2.9PRM
                        |
                        v
                  Risk Mgmt Plan
                    completed
                        |
Baselined Scope         v                    Procurement Plan
                    Conduct
Procurement SOW     Procurement...           Contract SOWs

Risk Register                            I   PMO Analyst

Stakeholder Register                     A   Project Manager
                    Procurement
PMIS                Plan completed        C  Contract/Legal Dept

                                         A   Project Manager
                    Agree PMO
                    Voluntary Checks          PMO Analyst
                                         C
                         X
        |                |                    |
Voluntary Check    Voluntary Check       Voluntary Check
   Skipped            Passed                 Failed
        |                |                    |
                         X  <----  Undertake    A  Project Manager
                                   Corrections
                    Update Lessons    A  Project Manager
                    Learnt
                         |
                    Proc. Planning
                    Completed
                         |
                    Developing The
                    Project Management
                    Plan Process
                    PRJ2.1PMP
```

Executing Phase Processes

The Utopian PMO's planning processes, helped create the planning backbone of the project, the project management plan, which provides executive guidance during the next phase of the project to:

- Perform activities to accomplish project objectives.

- Manage and use resources to create project deliverables of agreed quality standards.

- Implement the planned sub-project management plans.

- Mitigate risks that hinder the achievement of project objectives.

- Communicate with stakeholders and manage their expectations.

- Manage vendors.

- Periodically measure work performance data.

- Document lessons learned.

Direct & Manage Project Work Process (PRJ3.1DMPW)

Similar to Developing The Project Management Plan Process (PRJ2.1PMP), the Direct & Manage Project Work Process (PRJ3.1DMPW) is a holding process but unlike PRJ2.1PMP, the internal processes are not executed in a sequential fashion but rather in parallel and whenever required. The execution of a project is not a set of sequential steps but a mix of various processes that are performed many times over, in several iterations. Once the project manager triggers a process and performs its activities, the project manager returns back to this home process to execute the next execution process activity as the situation may warrant. The sub-processes of execution are, in no particular order:

- Perform Quality Assurance Process (PRJ3.2PQA)

- Acquire Project Team Process (PRJ3.3APT)

- Develop & Manage Project Team Process (PRJ3.4DMPT)

- Manage Communication & Stakeholder Engagement Process (PRJ3.5MCP)

- Conduct Procurements Process (PRJ3.6CPR)

When all the deliverables are complete and signed off, usually via the Validate Scope Process (PRJ4.3VS) of the Monitoring & Control phase (triggered internally), the project is deemed to have been completed and the PMO analyst then, undertakes a phase gate test to ascertain if the project has followed the methodology and if all recommended deliverables have in fact been produced and approved. On the successful passage of a phase gate test, the project manager updates the lessons learned by the project in this particular phase including what they (the project team) did right and would like to repeat and what they did wrong. An end of phase report is collectively made by the project manager and the PMO analyst and is submitted to the PMO to archive as a part of the historical information database also known as the organizational process assets.

The completion of the executing phase effectively concludes project execution and the project manager may now begin work on the closure activities. The project then moves on to the last and final part of its lifecycle which is represented by a single process, Close Procurements & Project Process (PRJ5.1CP).

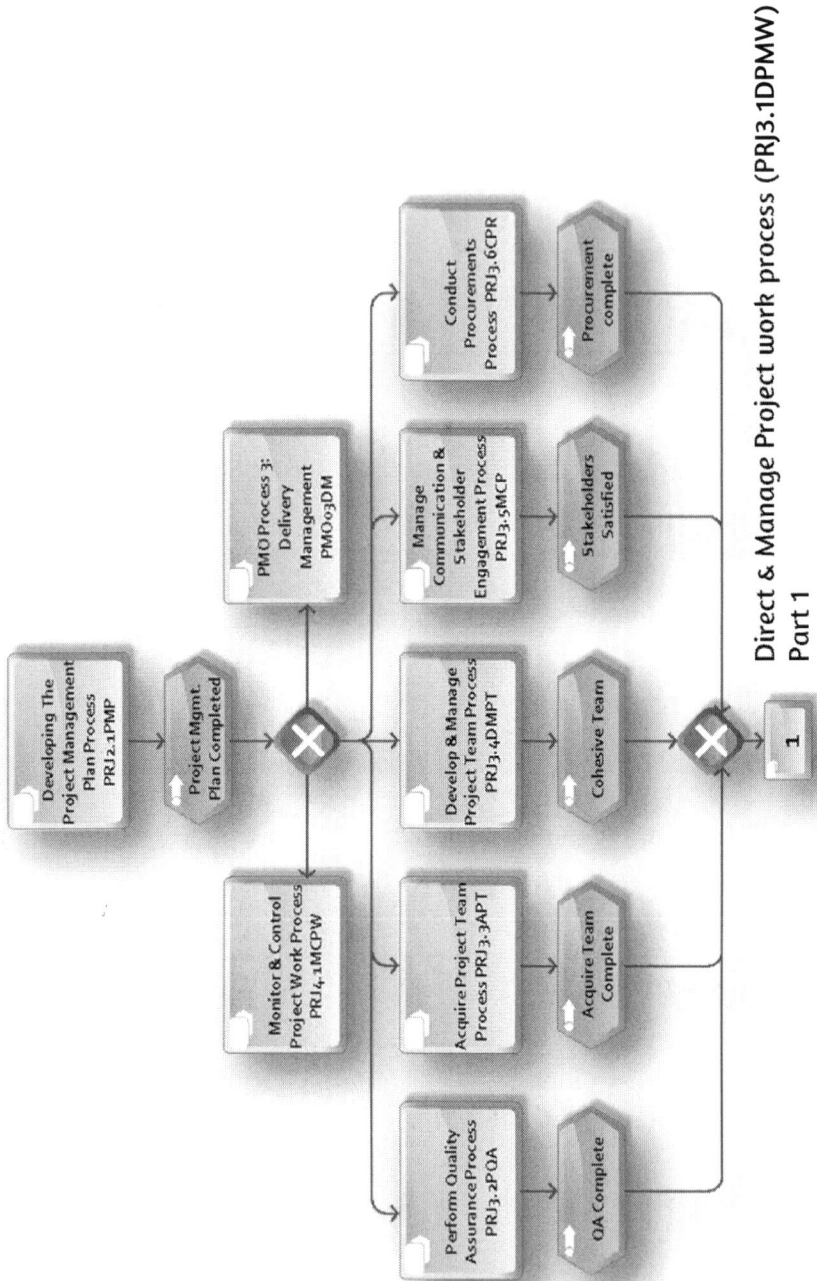

Direct & Manage Project work process (PRJ3.1DPMW)
Part 1

The flowchart contains the following elements:

- Developing The Project Management Plan Process PRJ2.1PMP
- Project Mgmt. Plan Completed
- PMO Process 3: Delivery Management PMO.o3DM
- Monitor & Control Project Work Process PRJ4.1MCPW
- Conduct Procurements Process PRJ3.6CPR
- Procurement complete
- Manage Communication & Stakeholder Engagement Process PRJ3.5MCP
- Stakeholders Satisfied
- Develop & Manage Project Team Process PRJ3.4DMPT
- Cohesive Team
- Acquire Project Team Process PRJ3.3APT
- Acquire Team Complete
- Perform Quality Assurance Process PRJ3.2PQA
- QA Complete
- 1

Direct & Manage Project Work Process (PRJ3.1DMPW) Part 2

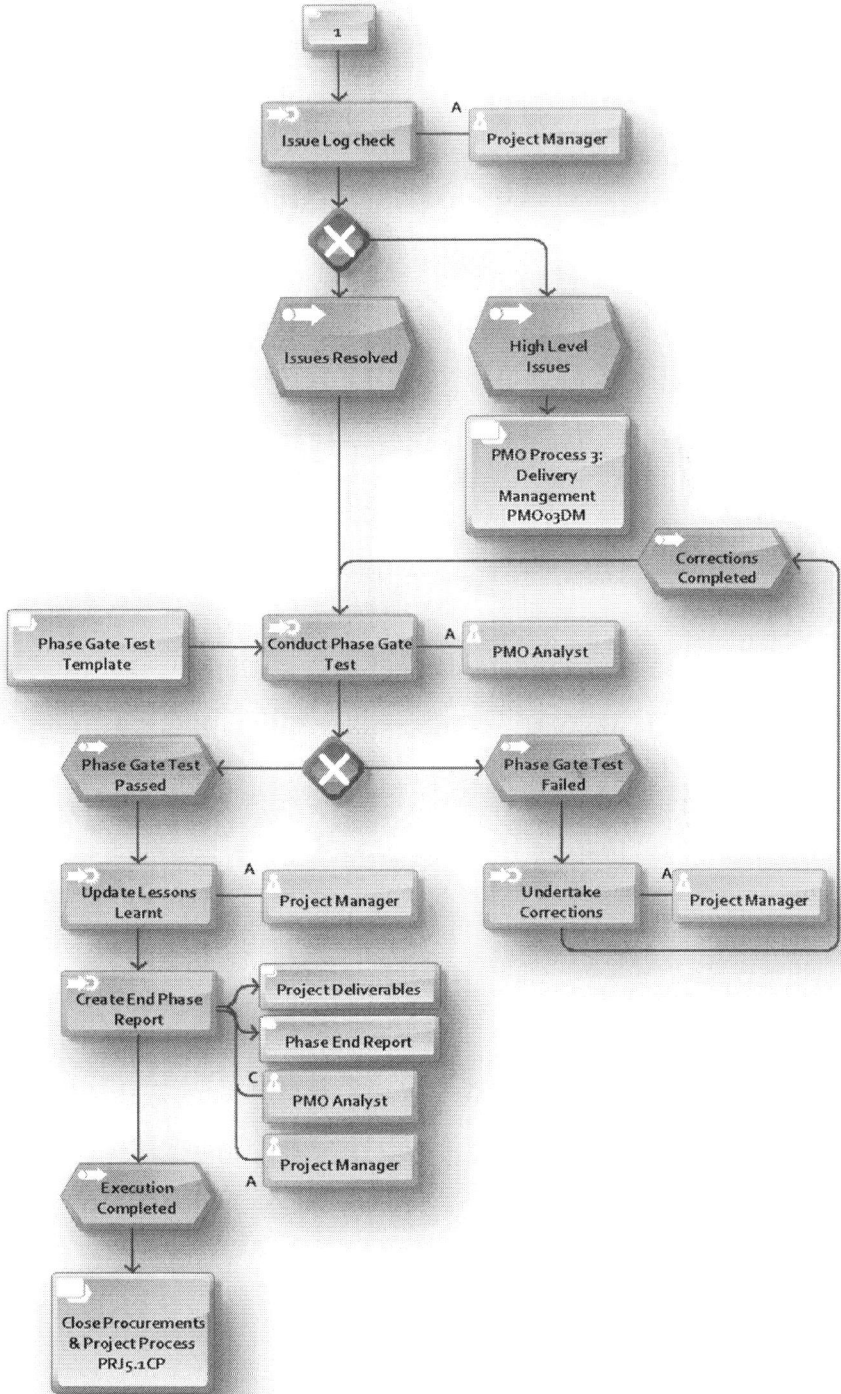

Perform Quality Assurance Process (PRJ3.2PQA)

The perform quality assurance process ensures that the quality processes in the project are sufficient to meet stated requirements. The process does this by undertaking periodic quality measurements of the final products to ensure that the quality metrics indicate good quality. It is recommended that the project manager avail the expertise of a quality management SME to help with interpreting quality management data and other statistical concepts. Should an appreciable variation exist in the quality measurements, the project manager raises a change request and simultaneously re-triggers the Plan Quality Management Process [PRJ2.6PQM] to re-plan quality on the project. The PRJ3.2PQA process can be thought of as being autonomous in its ability to correct any process related deficiencies within itself. This is accomplished whenever an out-of-tolerance, quality control measurement triggers this process and a re-evaluation of the QA processes in place, occurs.

On completion of this process, the project manager returns to the Direct & Manage Project Work Process (PRJ3.1DMPW) to proceed with executing the project and to trigger any sub-process, within PRJ3.1DMPW as the situation may call for.

Perform Quality Assurance Process (PRJ3.2PQA)

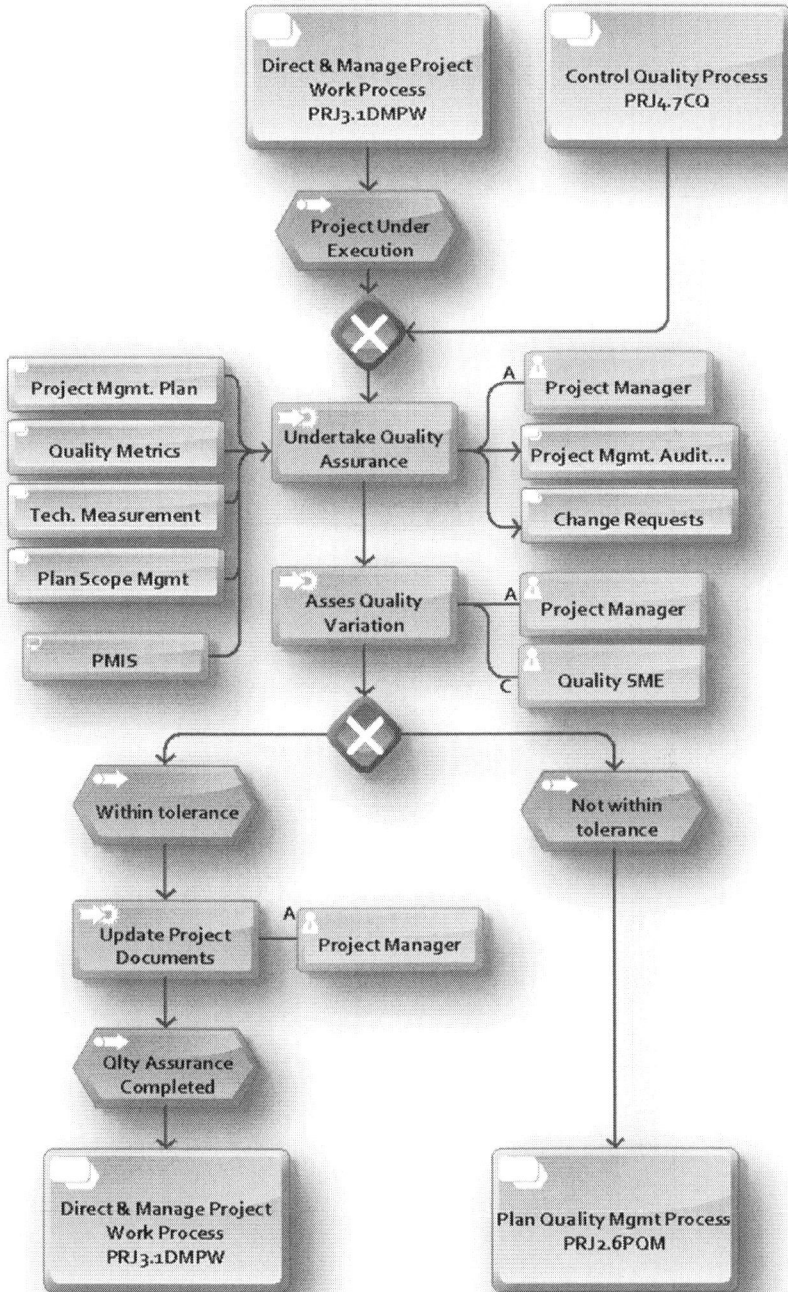

Acquire Project Team Process (PRJ3.3APT)

The Acquire Project Team Process (PRJ3.3APT) helps put together the core team that will accomplish the work that the project encompasses.

Acquire Project Team Process (PRJ3.3APT)

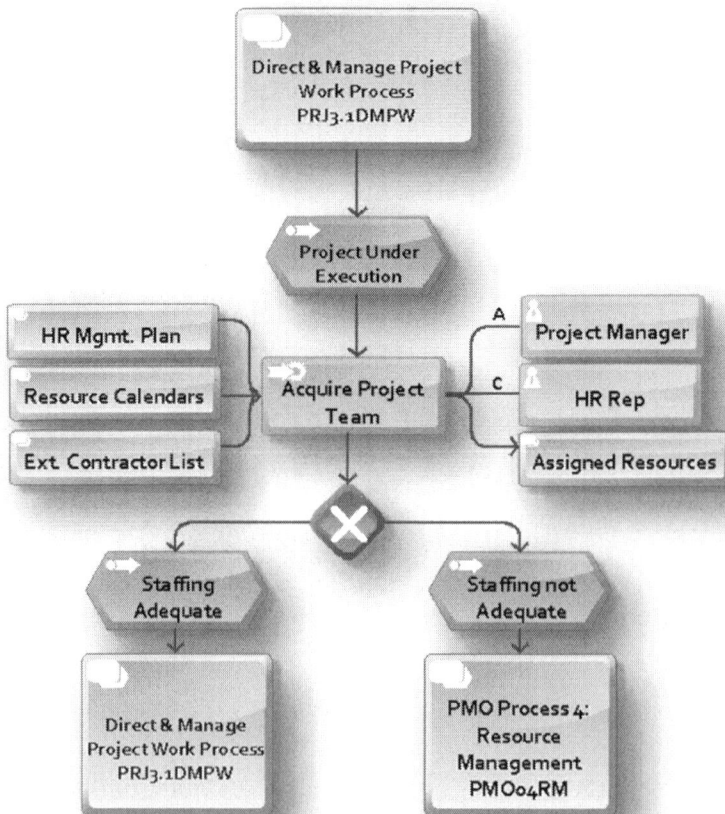

The project manager with the help of the HR function in the organization identifies various team members for various roles in the project. For work that is of the kind that requires specialized expertise, the project manager could also consider outsourced resources. At the end of the acquisition step, the project manager must have all project roles filled with named resources.

If the project manager is unable to completely meet his staffing needs, then PMO process 4: Resource Management [PMO04RM] is triggered to enable new recruitments to commence. On completion of this process, the project manager returns to the Direct & Manage Project Work Process (PRJ3.1DMPW) to proceed with executing the project and to trigger any sub-process, within PRJ3.1DMPW, as the situation calls for.

Develop & Manage Project Team Process (PRJ3.4DMPT)

The Develop & Manage Project Team Process (PRJ3.4DMPT) works closely with PMO Process 4: Resource Management [PMO04RM] in creating a cohesive, functional and most importantly an effective team that delivers. Every team member's performance is periodically assessed for efficiency. Team dynamics and synergetic ability to deliver are also focused upon, by ensuring that the incentive and rewards scheme detailed in the HR management plan, by the Plan HR Management Process (PRJ2.7PHRM) is implemented. Any training requirements that may benefit the team are also identified and independent steps undertaken, under the auspices of the project sponsor, to ensure that this training in provisioned.

Once a performance appraisal is done, the PMO04RM process ensures that the team's performance is in alignment with organizational requirements and seeks to understand the root cause, if not. A detailed performance improvement plan is created to ensure any deficiencies identified in the team's performance are fixed.

Develop & Manage Project Team Process (PRJ3.4DMPT)

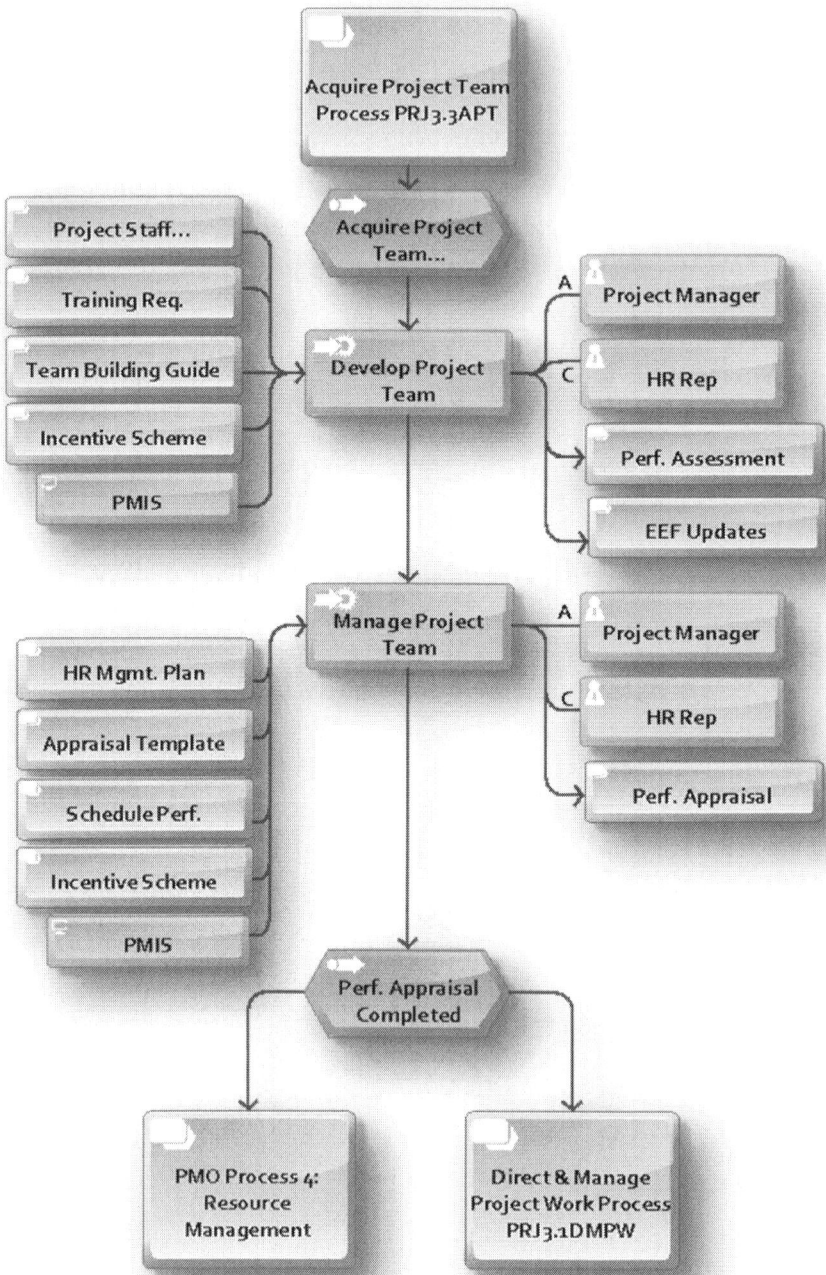

Acquire Project Team Process PRJ3.3APT

Acquire Project Team...

Project Staff...

Training Req.

Team Building Guide

Incentive Scheme

PMIS

Develop Project Team

A   Project Manager

C   HR Rep

Perf. Assessment

EEF Updates

HR Mgmt. Plan

Appraisal Template

Schedule Perf.

Incentive Scheme

PMIS

Manage Project Team

A   Project Manager

C   HR Rep

Perf. Appraisal

Perf. Appraisal Completed

PMO Process 4: Resource Management

Direct & Manage Project Work Process PRJ3.1DMPW

Manage Communication & Stakeholder Engagement Process (PRJ3.5MCP)

The Manage Communication Process (PRJ3.5MCP) primarily ensures that stakeholders are sent timely communication about the status on the progress of the project (or lack thereof). The communication management plan provides guidance on to whom, what and in which format to address communications. This process also ensures that the project manager publishes reports on the project's status on the PMIS for effective dissemination of project related information. This method also benefits anybody not identified as recipients in the stakeholder register, but yet wishes to be updated on the progress of the project.

The reports submitted by the project manager also feed into the overall organization-level reports. This is ensured by feeding the project-level reports into the PMO level reporting process PMO Process 6: Reporting [PMO06R] for inclusion into any and all high level reports that the PMO produces for strategic decision making.

Conduct Procurements Process (PRJ3.6CPR)

If all of the project's delivery is internal and no deliverables are planned to be procured, then the Conduct Procurements Process (PRJ3.6CPR) can be bypassed. In this case, the precursor planning process Viz. Plan Procurement Management Process (PRJ2.10PPRM) would have also been bypassed and as a result, this process is automatically invalidated.

However, if work is outsourced then, the PRJ3.6CPR process provides guidance on conducting an enhanced procurement experience. Depending on the procurement scenario, PRJ3.6CPR, provides two distinct routes for the project manager to take: A process flow to be used in the case of a competitive procurement and one to be used in case only a sole or a single preferred vendor exists. In case of a competitive procurement, the project manager decides on the type of procurement Viz. quote, proposal or information and then issues a public notice. On receiving responses, the project manager evaluates the same, documents the decision and then triggers PMO Process 7: Supplier Management [PMO07SM], to take advantage of the PMO's competences to review and approve vendors, based on their ability to deliver, by virtue of having a solid internal project management framework. Based on these judgments, a decision is made to award the contract or reject the vendor. The PMO07SM process also provides value by ensuring that the PMO is present at vendor status meetings to ensure that contractual obligations are satisfied by both parties and no violations and consequential litigations occur. PMO07SM is also triggered whenever a contractual change has been identified. In this situation too, the PMO acts as an arbitrator to ensure that changes are made in a manner benefiting both parties.

Conduct Procurements Process (PRJ3.6CPR) Part 1

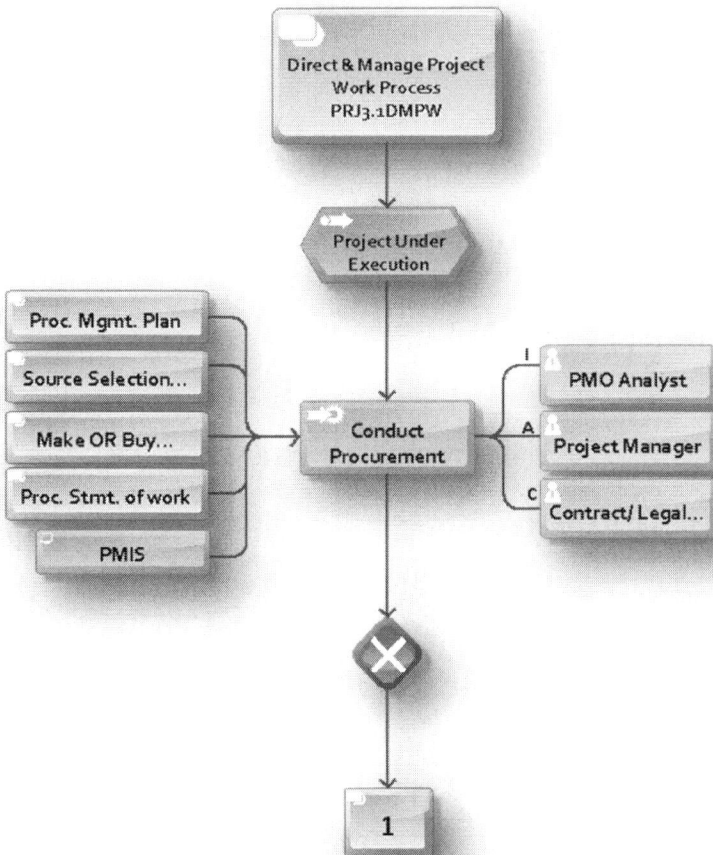

Conduct Procurements Process (PRJ3.6CPR) Part 2

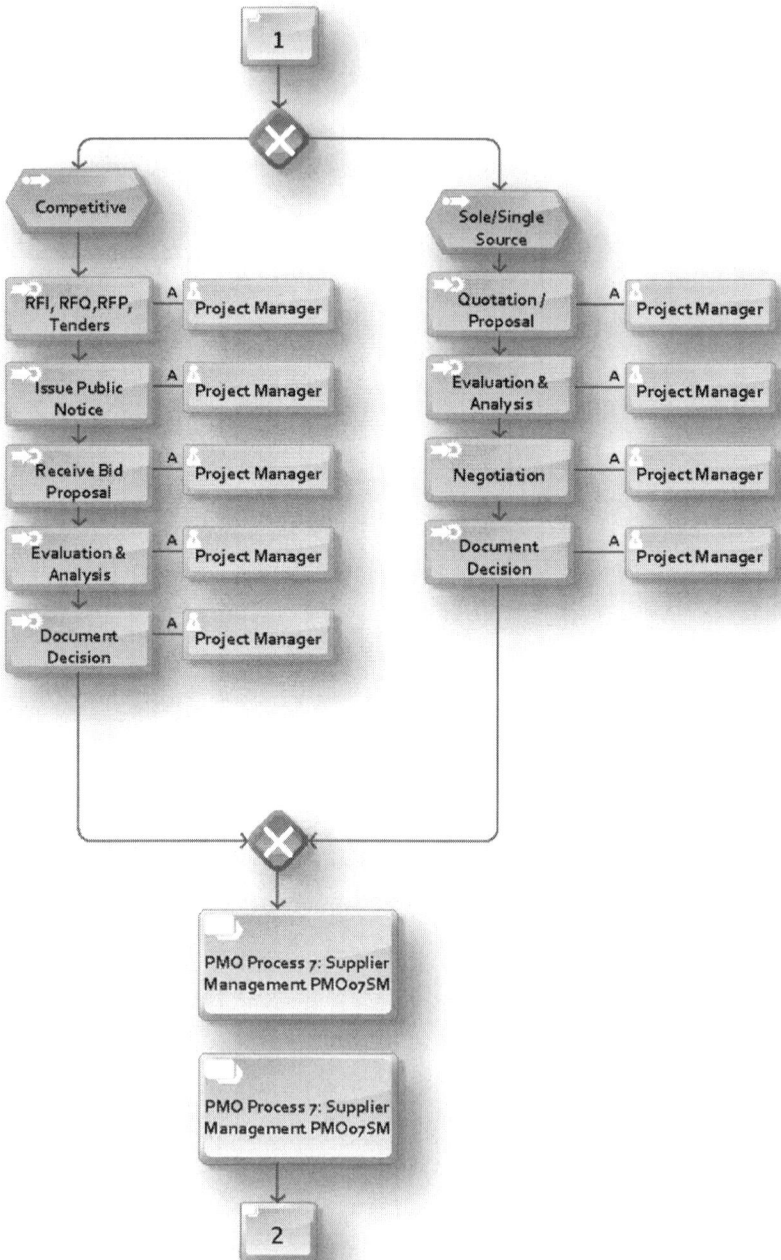

```
                          ┌─────┐
                          │  1  │
                          └──┬──┘
                           ╳
        ┌──────────────────┴──────────────────┐
   ┌─────────┐                            ┌──────────┐
   │Competitive│                          │Sole/Single│
   └────┬────┘                            │  Source  │
                                          └────┬─────┘
```

Competitive		Sole/Single Source	
RFI, RFQ,RFP, Tenders	A Project Manager	Quotation / Proposal	A Project Manager
Issue Public Notice	A Project Manager	Evaluation & Analysis	A Project Manager
Receive Bid Proposal	A Project Manager	Negotiation	A Project Manager
Evaluation & Analysis	A Project Manager	Document Decision	A Project Manager
Document Decision	A Project Manager		

PMO Process 7: Supplier Management PMO07SM

PMO Process 7: Supplier Management PMO07SM

```
┌─────┐
│  2  │
└─────┘
```

Conduct Procurements Process (PRJ3.6CPR) Part 3

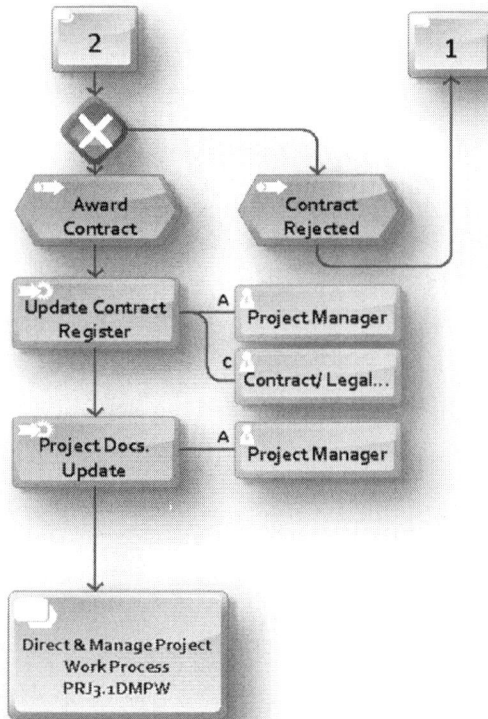

Monitoring & Control Phase Processes

The monitoring and control phase processes of the Utopian PMO help the project manager review progress on the project and make necessary corrections to bring any deviations back on track. Other activities of the monitor and control phase include:

- Measuring performance on the project to ensure that the integrity of project baselines is not compromised by unnecessary changes.

- Corrective and preventive action to alleviate any present and future deviations and to bring the project back on track.

- Inspecting, reviewing, verifying and signing off on project deliverables.

- Evaluating the impact of proposed changes and approving those that meet established criteria.

- Generating data on the progress of the project for purposes of measurement and decision-making.

- Monitoring of risks for changes and adjusting mitigation plans accordingly.

Monitor & Control Project Work Process (PRJ4.1MCPW)

The Monitor & Control Project Work Process (PRJ4.1MCPW) is a holding process similar to the Direct & Manage Project Work Process (PRJ3.1DMPW). Throughout execution and whenever control is required on the project delivery, PRJ4.1MCPW is triggered, inherently meaning that any of its sub-processes are triggered. This process can be thought of as a stand-by or on-call process that is invoked during execution whenever the project needs a proactive or reactive push to correct deviations. The sub-processes of the PRJ4.1MCPW are, in no particular order:

- Perform Integrated Change Control Process (PRJ4.2PICC)
- Validate Scope Process (PRJ4.3VS)
- Control Scope Process (PRJ4.4CS)
- Control Schedule Process (PRJ4.5CS)
- Control Costs Process (PRJ4.6CC)
- Control Quality Process (PRJ4.7CQ)

- Control Risks Process (PRJ4.8CR)
- Control Procurements Process (PRJ4.9CP)
- Control Communications & Control Stakeholder Engagement Process (PRJ4.10CCCS)

After a sub-process is used to perform the activities required to bring a particular aspect of a the project back on track, the project manager returns to the Direct & Manage Project Work Process (PRJ3.1DMPW) to continue delivering the project deliverables until they are each checked for compliance by the Control Quality Process (PRJ4.7CQ) and then subsequently validated by the Validate Scope Process (PRJ4.3VS). After verification of the final deliverables, the project manager moves on to closure activities via Close Procurements & Project Process (PRJ5.1CP).

Monitor & Control Project Work Process (PRJ4.1MCPW) Part 1

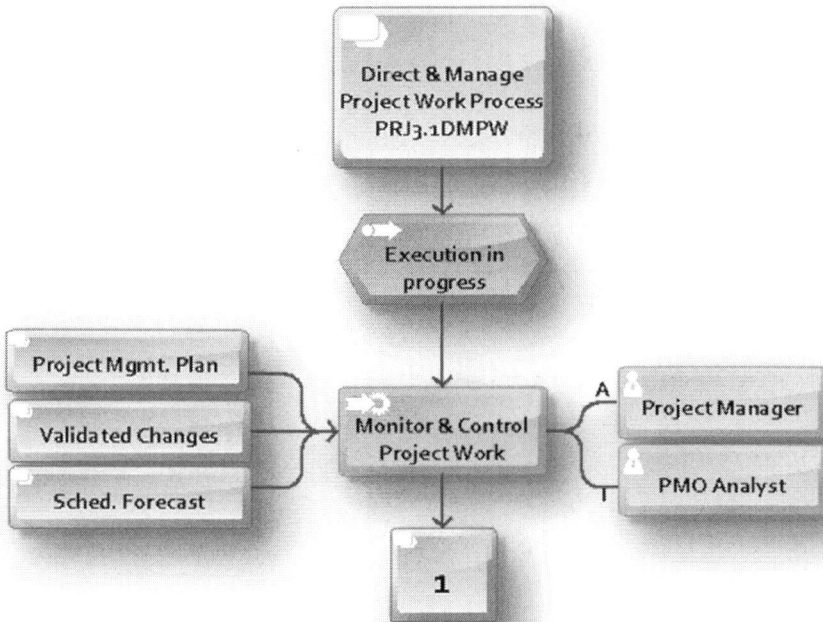

Monitor & Control Project Work Process (PRJ4.1MCPW) Part 2

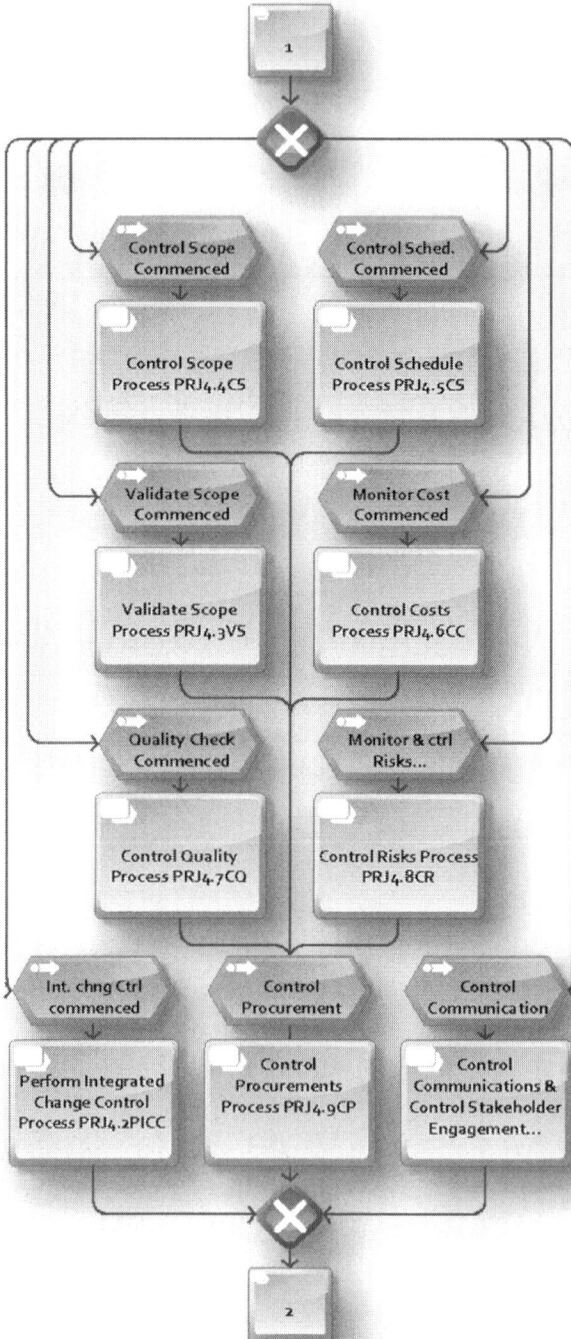

Monitor & Control Project Work Process (PRJ4.1MCPW) Part 3

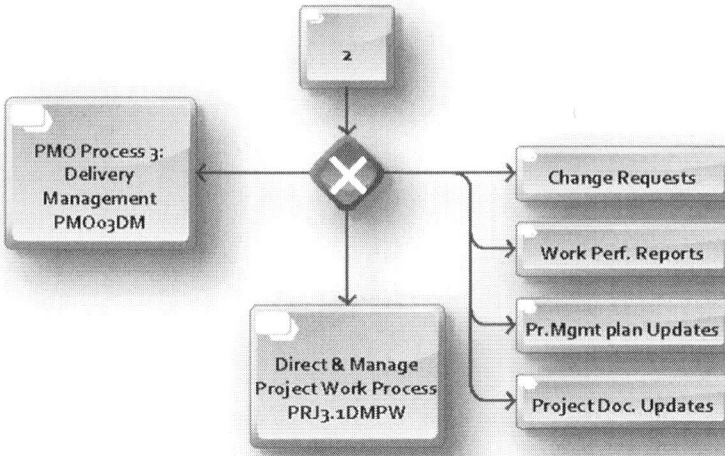

Perform Integrated Change Control Process (PRJ4.2PICC)

Change control is one of the most important responsibilities of a project manager. Precariously balancing delivery against change requests will frequently test the resolve of the practicing project manager. Having a change control process that is robust, in being easy enough to allow required changes to pass through, but at the same time formidable enough to prevent whimsical and unnecessary changes from affecting the project, will greatly help the project manager in achieving project success.

The first steps of the PRJ4.2PICC process is concerned with receiving the change request from the individual / team/ entity raising the request. A preliminary assessment is done by the project manager to determine the nature of the change, i.e. a normal change or an expedited / emergency change. The organization must have an agreed categorization for determining when a change is to be categorized as normal and when it can be considered an urgent change. It is prudent to have exhaustive vetting criteria in place before a change can be categorized as an emergency change to avoid misuse of the process. A normal change is first assessed by the project manager and the team and may receive preliminary approval. A rejected change is documented in the lessons learned and abandoned.

Next, both the emergency changes (that bypassed the preliminary approval stage) and the changes with preliminary approval are checked to see if any of them warrant organization level escalation. I.e. the change being requested is so large that it is beyond the powers of the project manager to decide, which is usually in the case of strategic changes. If escalation is required, the process hands over to PMO Process 3: Delivery Management [PMO03DM]. The change may also be rejected at this stage. However, if the change doesn't require escalation and is also not rejected, then a detailed consultation takes place with subject matter experts to obtain an in-depth understanding of the impact of implementing the

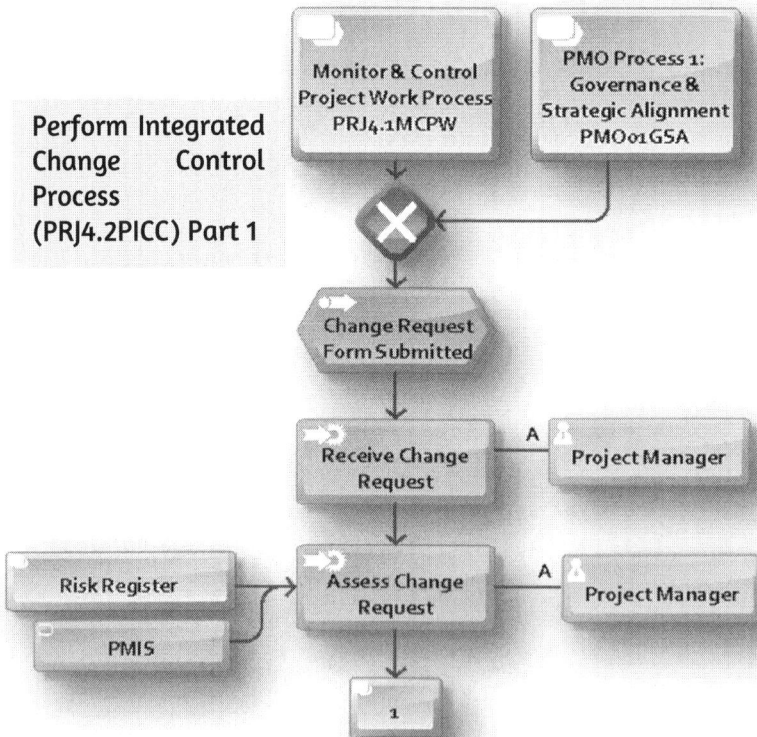

requested change. The change is then approved or rejected based on the project's tolerance of the assessed impact.

The next step in the process determines if the requested change is to a deliverable being produced internally or by a vendor. If the piece of work is being accomplished internally, then the project manager makes the required changes to the delivery approach and plans, documents the lessons learned whilst processing this change, and returns to executing the project, with updated plans.

If the change being requested is to an activity that is presently being performed by a vendor then the 3rd prong of PMO Process 7: Supplier Management [PMO07SM] is triggered, enabling a contractual change to be processed including the legal procedures involved.

Perform Integrated Change Control Process (PRJ4.2PICC) Part 2

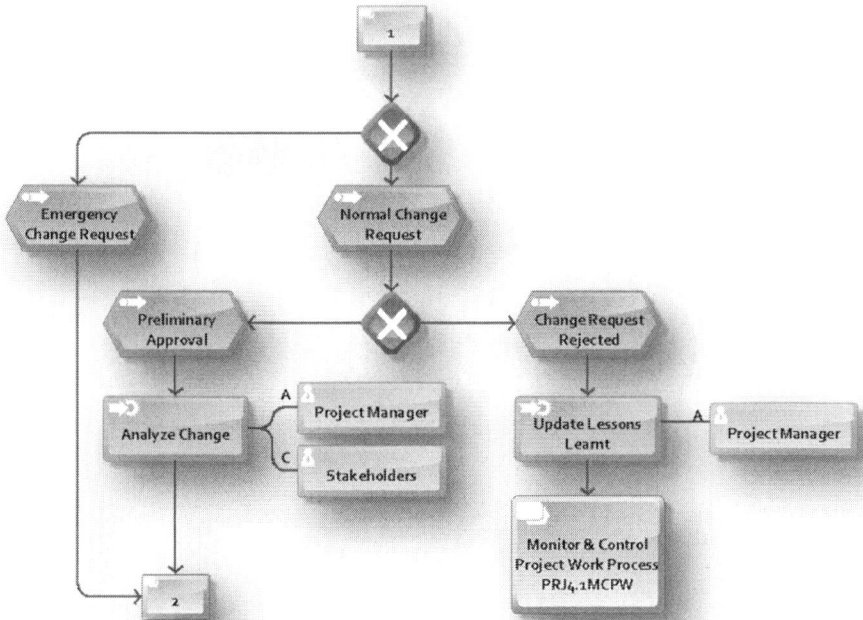

Perform Integrated Change Control Process (PRJ4.2PICC) Part 3

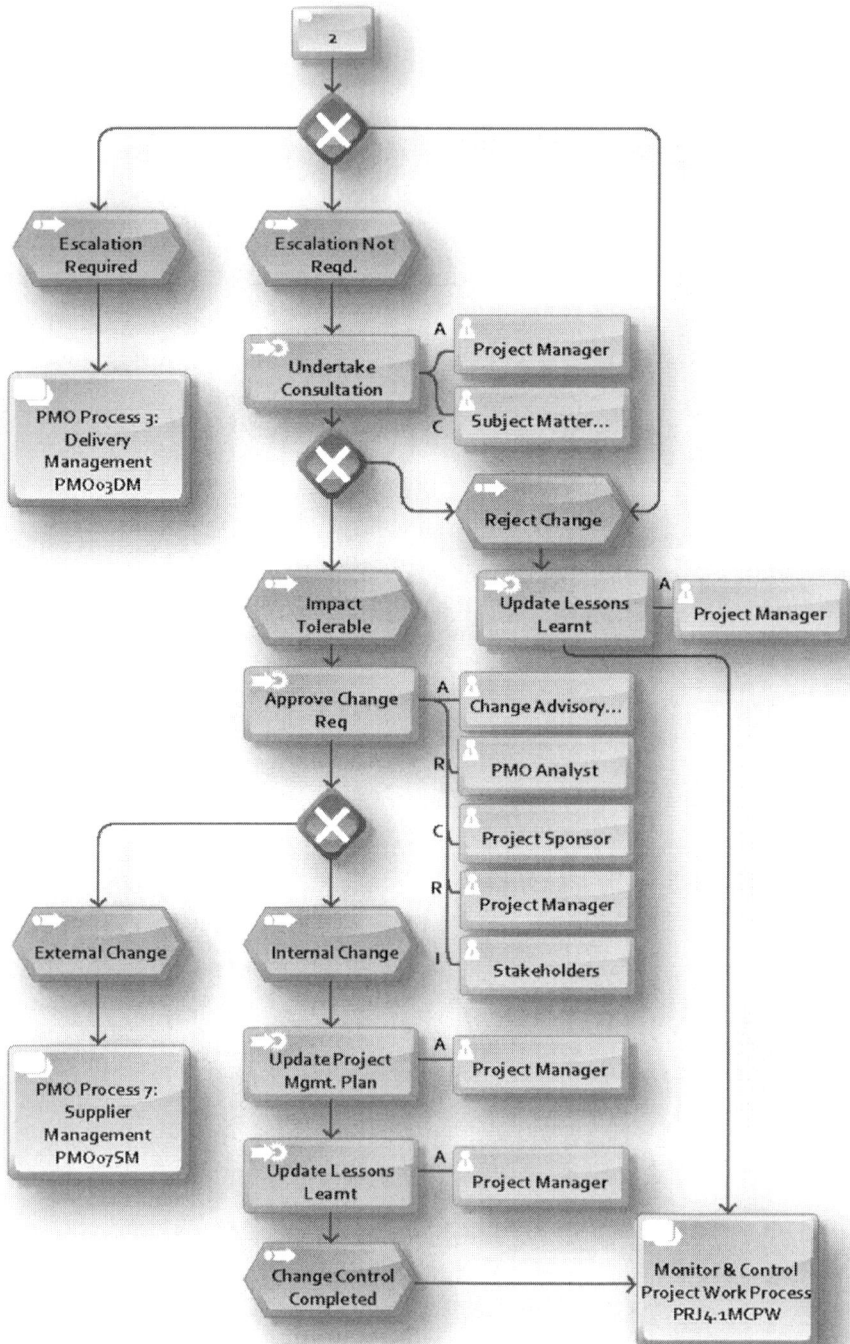

2

Escalation Required

Escalation Not Reqd.

Undertake Consultation
- A — Project Manager
- C — Subject Matter...

PMO Process 3: Delivery Management PMOo3DM

Reject Change

Impact Tolerable

Update Lessons Learnt
- A — Project Manager

Approve Change Req
- A — Change Advisory...
- R — PMO Analyst
- C — Project Sponsor
- R — Project Manager
- I — Stakeholders

External Change

Internal Change

PMO Process 7: Supplier Management PMOo7SM

Update Project Mgmt. Plan
- A — Project Manager

Update Lessons Learnt
- A — Project Manager

Change Control Completed

Monitor & Control Project Work Process PRJ4.1MCPW

Control Quality Process (PRJ4.7CQ)

The Control Quality (PRJ4.7CQ) process helps the project manager undertake quality measurements on the pre-final deliverables. The quality parameters are defined in the quality management plan created by the Plan Quality Management Process (PRJ2.6PQM) and implemented via Perform Quality Assurance Process (PRJ3.2PQA). The results of superior quality planning and the resulting quality processes should be evidenced via correspondingly good, quality control (QC) results.

The QC results are assessed to determine if any deviations are present, in the pre-final deliverables, from the defined baselines and accepted tolerances. If no changes are present, the final QC measurements are signed-off and the project manager, ideally , moves to Validate Scope Process (PRJ4.3VS) to procure final sign-offs. If a deviation from quality baselines is determined, then actions for correction are identified. Minor corrections, if any, are made directly. However, major corrections to the final deliverable are made though the Perform Integrated Change Control Process (PRJ4.2PICC). The Perform Quality Assurance Process (PRJ3.2PQA) is triggered to ensure that quality deficiencies do not occur henceforth.

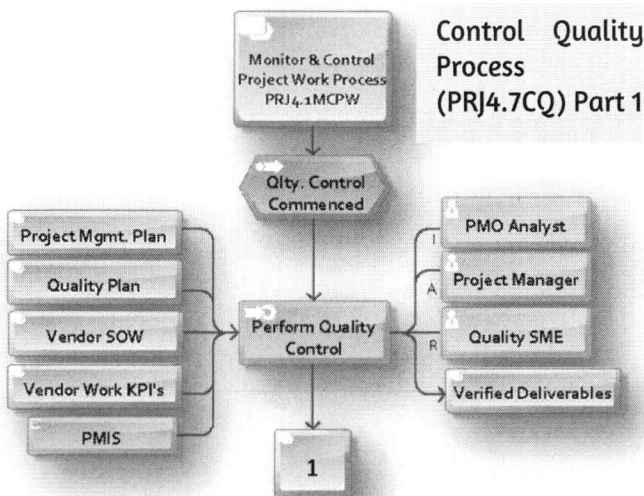

Control Quality Process (PRJ4.7CQ) Part 2

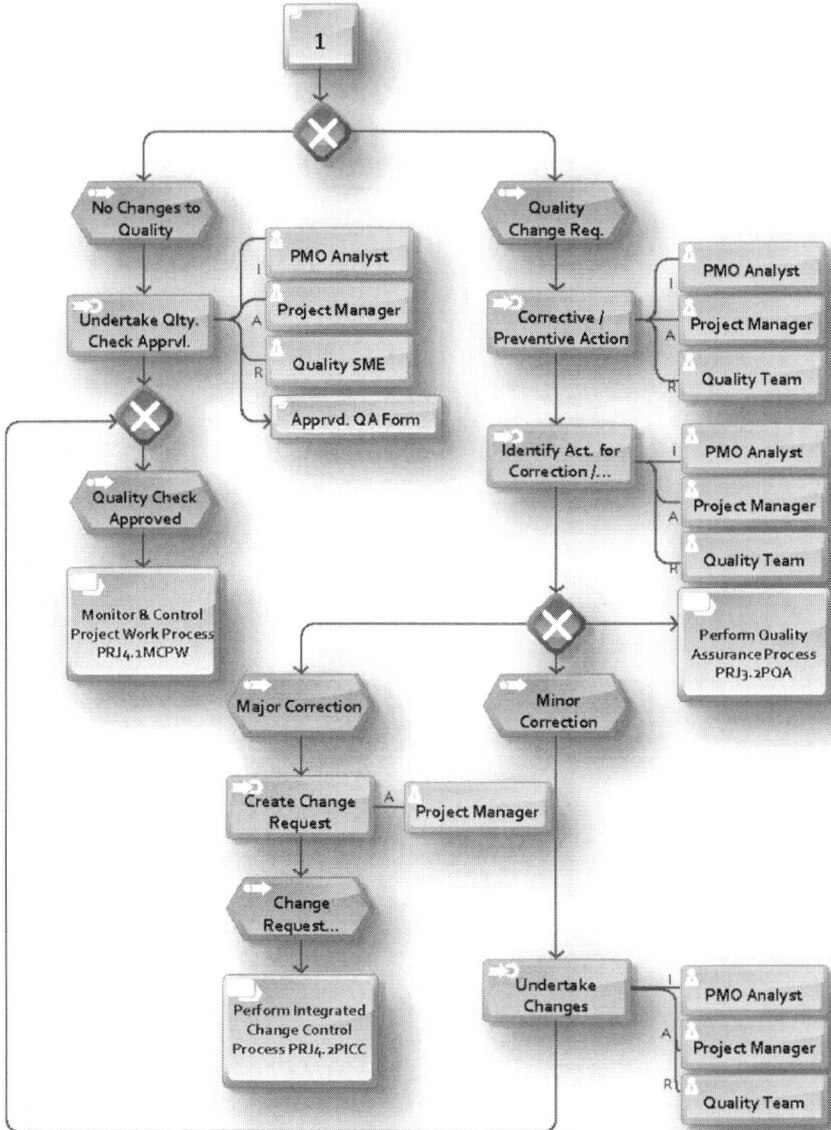

Validate Scope Process (PRJ4.3VS)

The validate scope process (PRJ4.3VS) is where the rubber meets the road. Weeks of project execution culminate in the PRJ4.3VS process, where the deliverables are approved and final sign-off is obtained.

This process enables the approval of QC-verified deliverables. If the final deliverable does not satisfy the requirements of the sponsor / stakeholders, minor changes are made and resubmitted for final sign-off. If all processes were followed thus far, there should ideally be no major changes being requested in the completed deliverables. If the project has other deliverables to execute before obtaining final-signoff, the project moves back into Direct & Manage Project Work Process (PRJ3.1DMPW) to complete the remaining work. Conversely, if this is the last piece of work, then post sign-off, the project moves briefly into Direct & Manage Project Work Process (PRJ3.1DMPW), only for the purposes of linking to the final Close Procurements & Project Process (PRJ5.1CP)

Validate Scope Process (PRJ4.3VS) Part 1

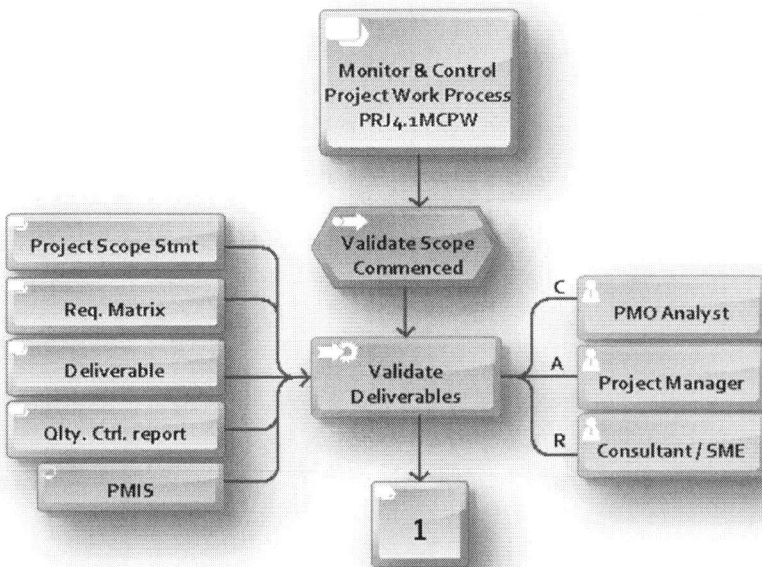

Validate Scope Process (PRJ4.3VS) Part 2

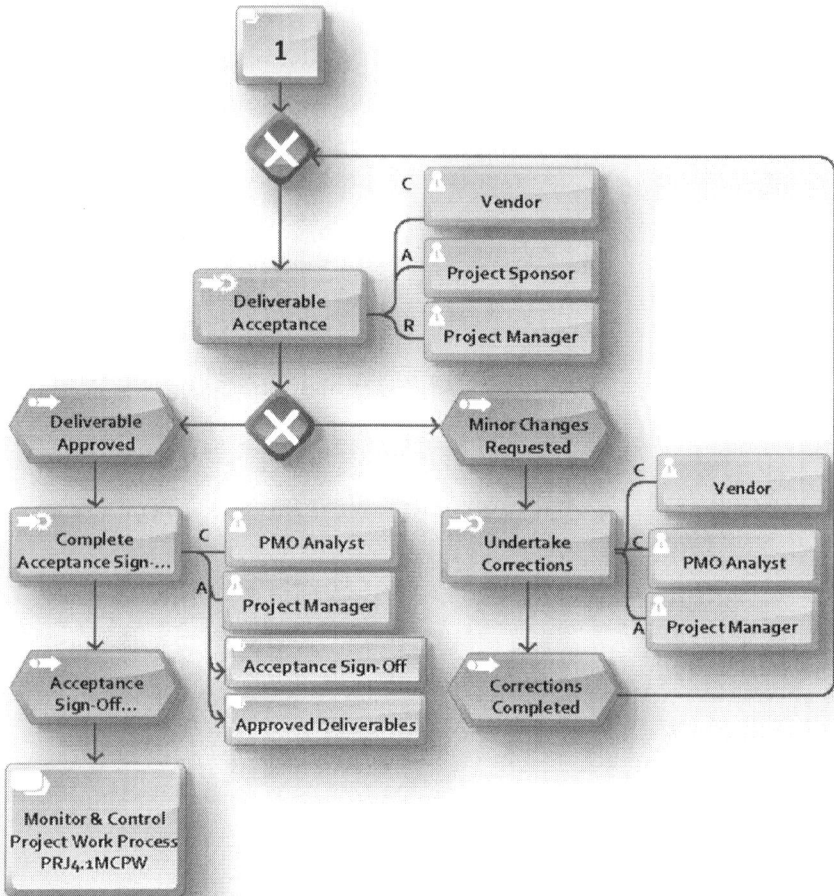

Control Scope Process (PRJ4.4CS)

The Control Scope Process (PRJ4.4CS) is invoked whenever any change to scope is requested or when the project manager decides to reconcile work being done on the ground with the planned scope. Whenever the project manager undertakes scope reconciliation, and a change in scope is detected, corrective action is taken, to bring the creeping scope back on track.

Alternatively, a change in scope could be requested, in which case, the requested change is considered for inclusion and project documents are re-baselined. If the scope change, is significantly large, the project manager collates the changes required and raises a change request through the Perform Integrated Change Control Process (PRJ4.2PICC). Smaller changes, however, are implemented immediately.

Control Scope Process (PRJ4.4CS) Part 1

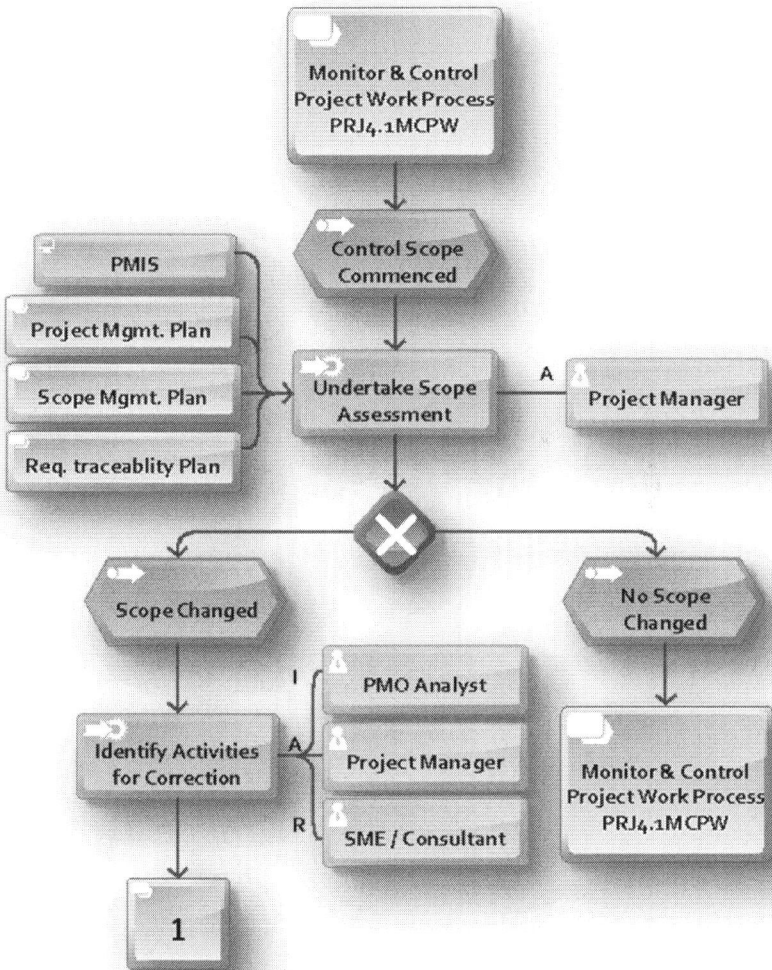

Control Scope Process (PRJ4.4CS) Part 2

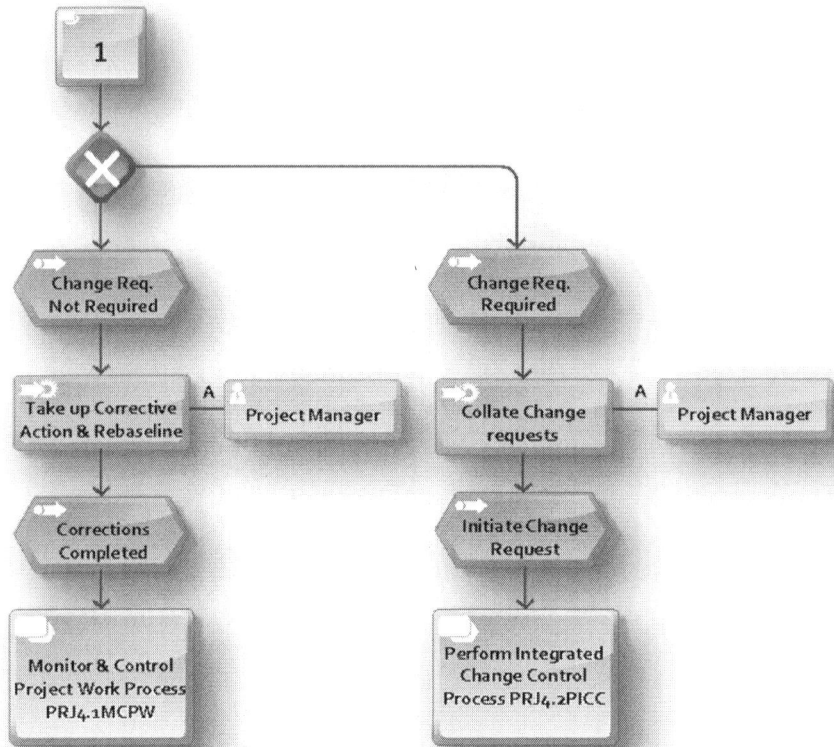

Control Schedule Process (PRJ4.5CS)

The Control Schedule Process (PRJ4.5CS) ensures that the project progresses as per the baselined schedule. Periodically, or randomly, as the situation may warrant, the project manager undertakes a review of the schedule to monitor progress against baselines. Whenever the project manager undertakes schedule reconciliation, and a change in schedule is required, due to slippage of activities, corrective action is undertaken to return the schedule to reflect reality. If the schedule change, is significantly large, that a change request is required, the project manager collates the changes required and raises a change request for approval through the Perform Integrated Change Control Process (PRJ4.2PICC). If the changes required are of minimal impact, they are implemented and the schedule is brought back on track and re-baselined. The frequency of checks is suited to meet the needs of the project. A guide-line would be to reconcile a strategic project on a daily basis and to reconcile a small project, once every two to three days.

Control Schedule Process (PRJ4.5CS) Part 1

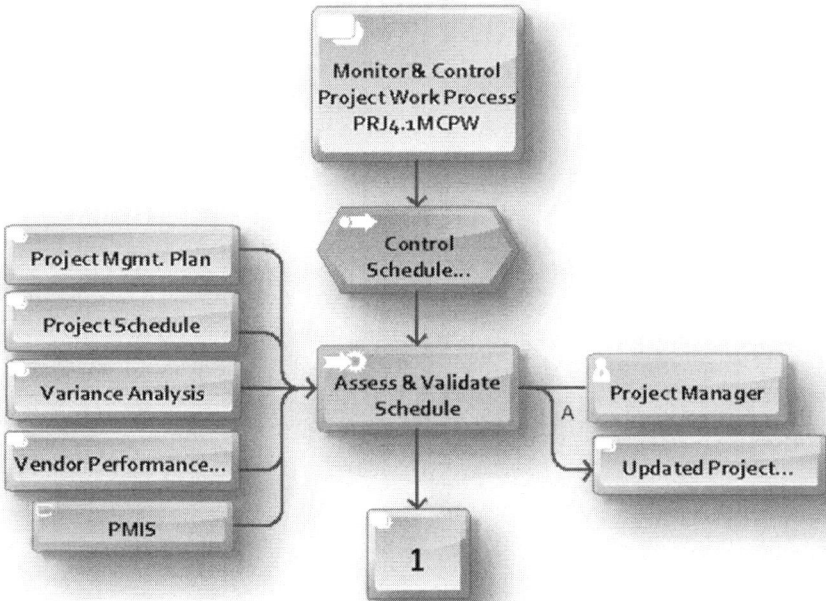

Control Schedule Process (PRJ4.5CS) Part 2

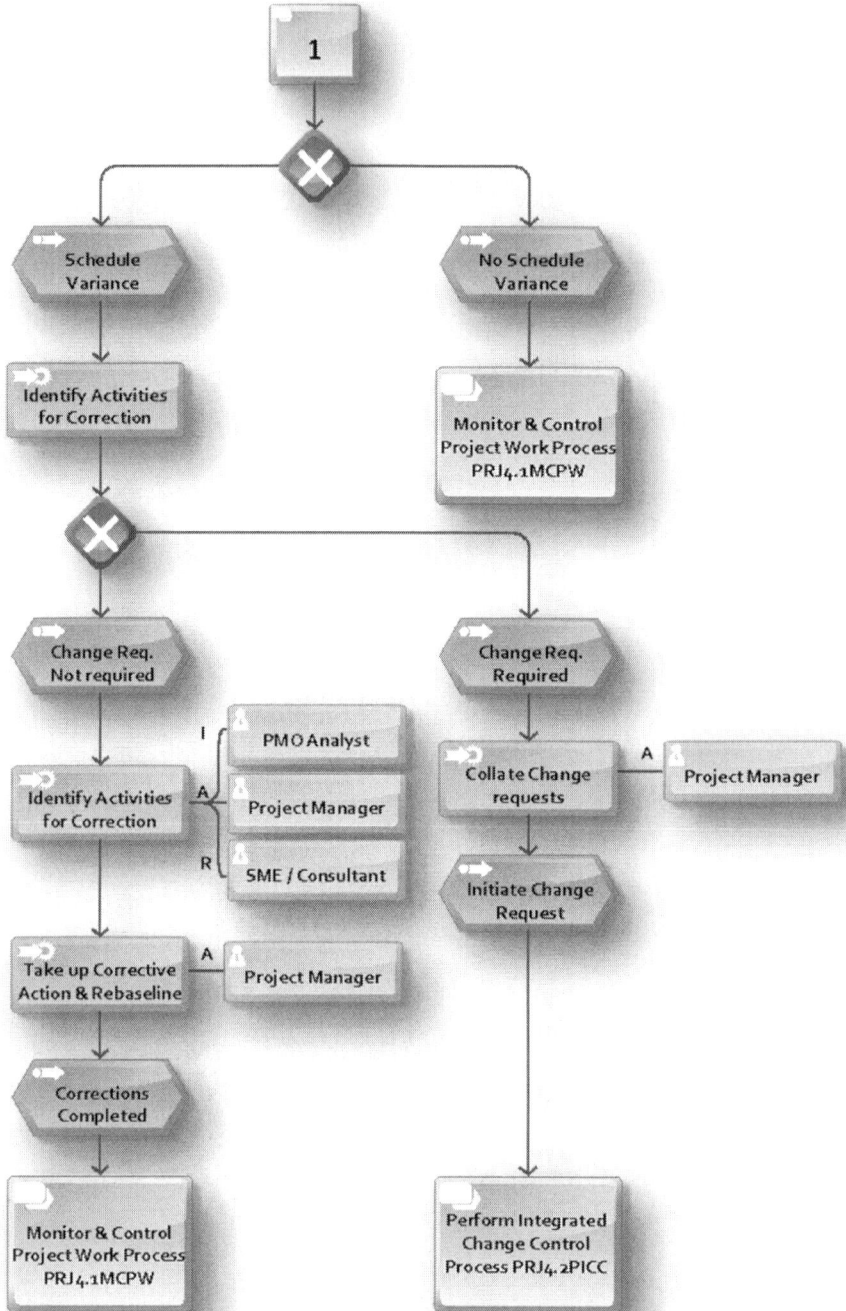

Control Costs Process (PRJ4.5CC)

The Control Costs Process (PRJ4.4CC) is invoked whenever the project manager decides to reconcile costs against approved budgets. Whenever the project manager undertakes cost reconciliation, and a change in budget is anticipated, corrective action is undertaken to bring costs back on track. Techniques such as Earned Value Management (EVM) are used to anticipate cost variations. If the budget change is significantly large that a change request is required, the project manager collates the changes required and raises a change request for approval through the Perform Integrated Change Control Process (PRJ4.2PICC), which upon approval is added to the project funding and project documents are re-baselined. If the changes are minimal, additional finding is provided immediately for requests that are within allowable limits.

Control Costs Process (PRJ4.5CC) Part 1

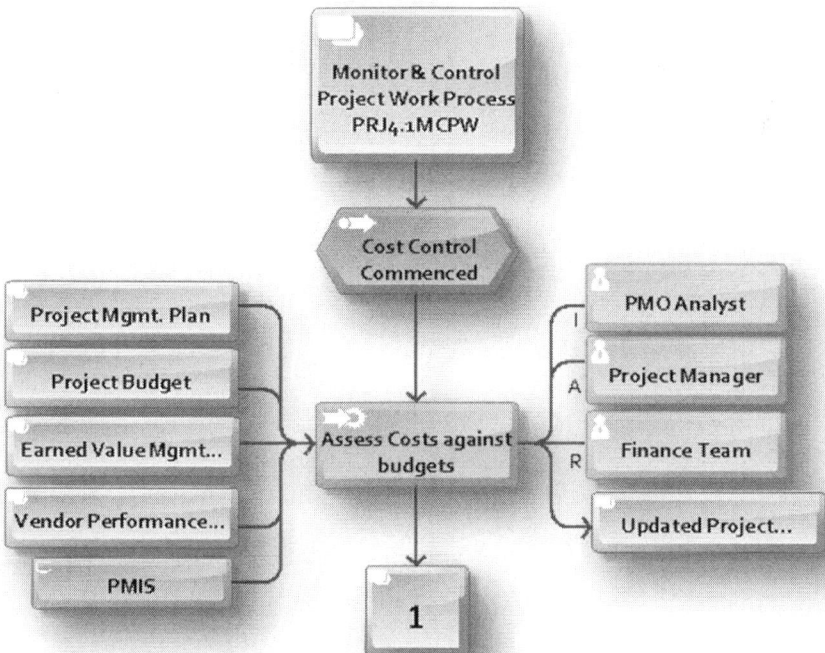

Control Costs Process (PRJ4.5CC) Part 2

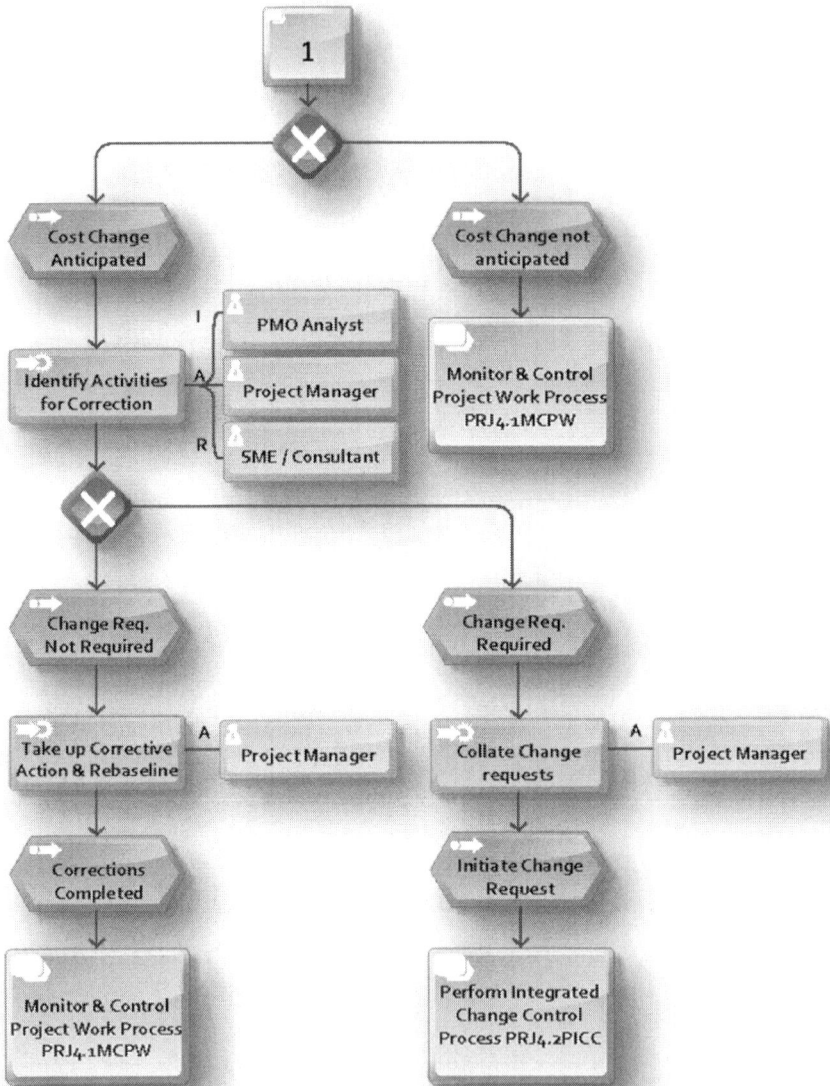

Control Risks Process (PRJ4.8CR)

The Control Risks Process (PRJ4.8CR) helps the project manager monitor and track identified risks, through formal planned risk meetings. During these meetings, the risk register and the current watch list of low-ranking risks are reviewed, to check if any of them have changed in severity. If an increase is noted, a re-planning of the mitigation strategy takes place in conjunction with the assigned risk owner.

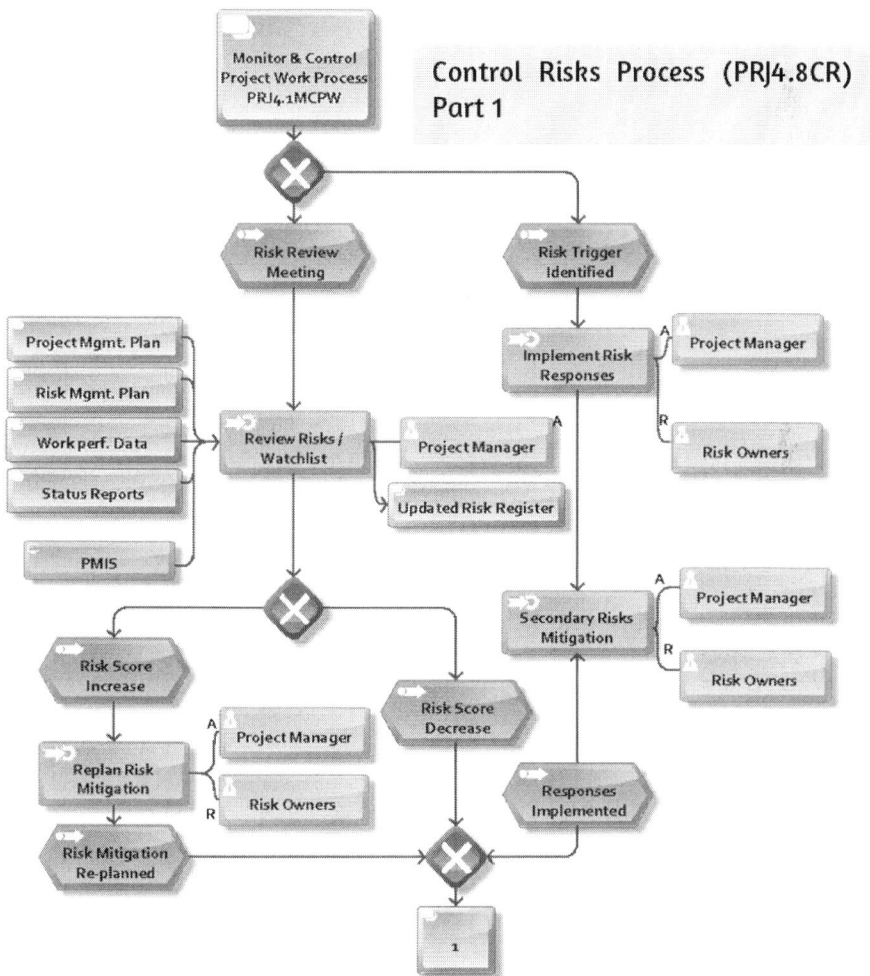

If an identified risk trigger occurs, then the planned mitigation for the risk is immediately implemented, again in conjunction with the assigned risk owner, who is assumed to have the most information about the various parameters of this specific risk. During implementation of the primary mitigation plan, any secondary risks that were identified are also mitigated.

The risk register is updated with the new responses and updated scores. A post-implementation review of the risk responses are done to determine the effectiveness of the responses. The findings are documented on the PMIS and the project manager returns to monitoring and controlling the project.

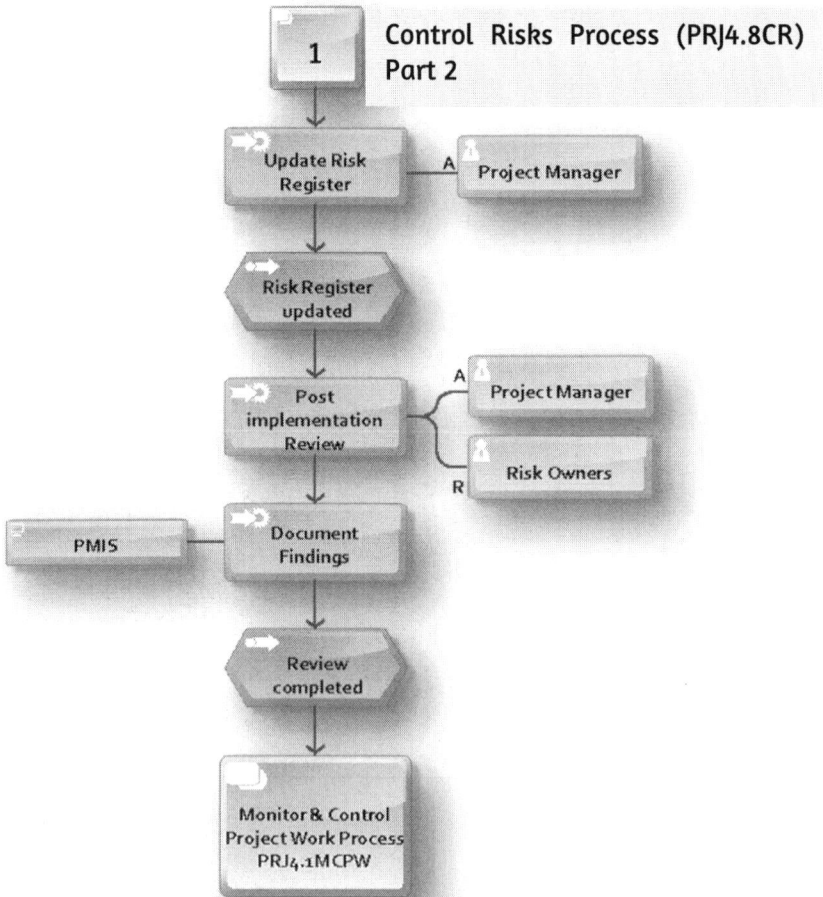

Control Risks Process (PRJ4.8CR) Part 2

Control Procurements Process (PRJ4.9CP)

The Control Procurements Process (PRJ4.9CP) ensures that outsourced work is delivered according to the requirements set forth in the contract and as agreed by the organization and the performing vendor. Each time this process is invoked, an audit of the vendor takes place including records administration, safety and interim quality of the deliverables. The methodology adopted by the vendor is also scrutinized to ensure that it is in-line with the organization's requirement (provided this is also a contractual obligation). Any deviation is given an opportunity to be fixed and perpetual deviations may warrant a contractual amendment or even revocation of the contract. This part of the process is handled by the PMO Process 7: Supplier Management [PMO07SM]. If the audit goes through smoothly and no deviations are identified, then lessons learned during the audit are documented and the project manager returns to monitoring and controlling the project.

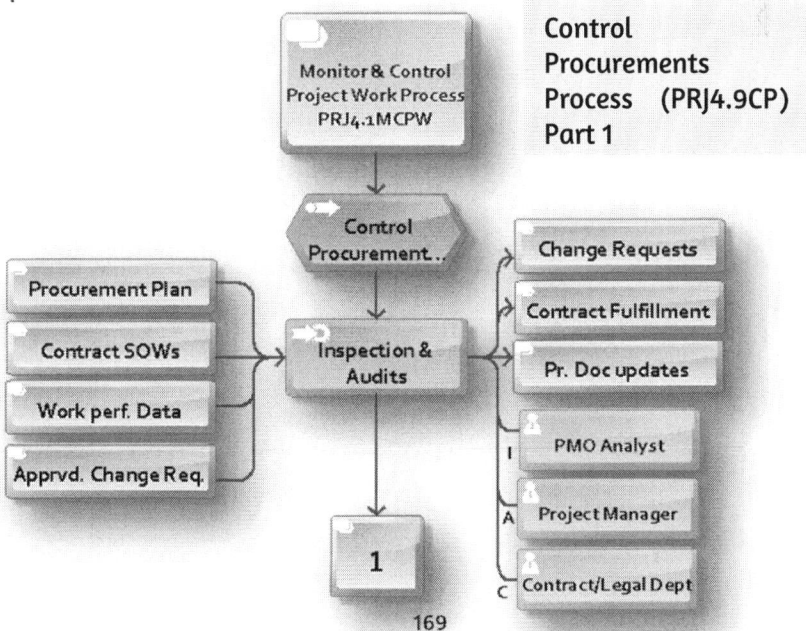

Control Procurements Process (PRJ4.9CP) Part 2

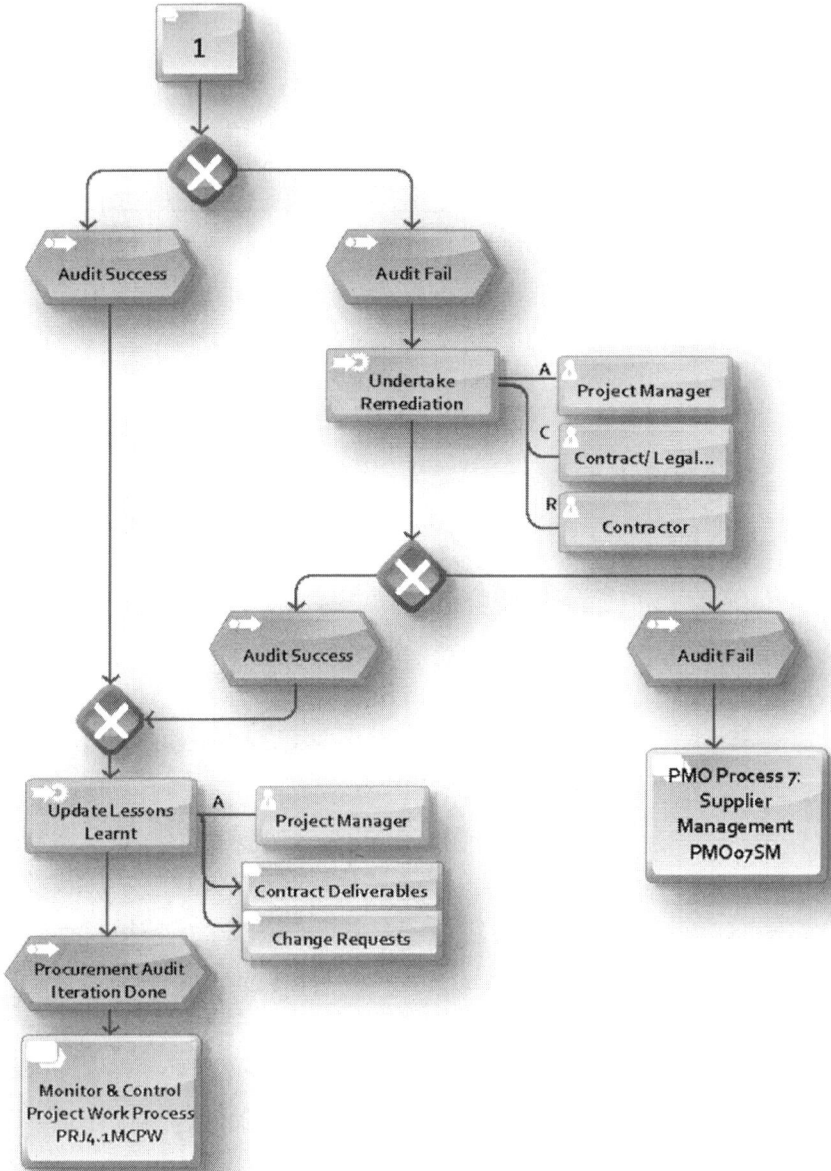

1

Audit Success

Audit Fail

Undertake Remediation

A Project Manager

C Contract/Legal...

R Contractor

Audit Success

Audit Fail

PMO Process 7: Supplier Management PMO07SM

Update Lessons Learnt

A Project Manager

Contract Deliverables

Change Requests

Procurement Audit Iteration Done

Monitor & Control Project Work Process PRJ4.1MCPW

Control Communications & Control Stakeholder Engagement Process (PRJ4.10CCS)

The Control Communications & Control Stakeholder Engagement Process (PRJ4.10CCS) helps the project manager measure the effectiveness and efficiency of the communications management process. This is done by periodically assessing stakeholder satisfaction, to ensure that the reports are meeting the needs of the stakeholders and the information provided is helping in the organizational decision making process. This is ensured by feeding the project-level reports into the PMO level reporting process PMO Process 6: Reporting [PMO06R] for inclusion into all high level

Control Communications & Control Stakeholder Engagement Process (PRJ4.10CCS) Part 1

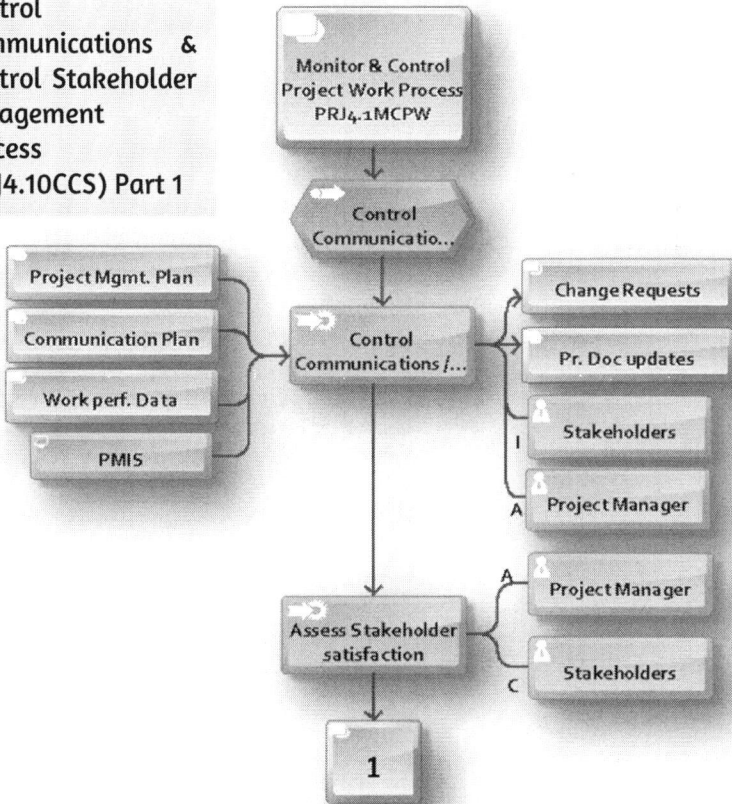

Monitor & Control Project Work Process PRJ4.1MCPW

Control Communicatio...

Project Mgmt. Plan

Communication Plan

Work perf. Data

PMIS

Control Communications /...

Change Requests

Pr. Doc updates

I Stakeholders

A Project Manager

A Project Manager

Assess Stakeholder satisfaction

C Stakeholders

1

reports that the PMO produces for strategic decision making.

If any of the stakeholders express dissatisfaction, attempts are made to fix the issue at the project level. If those attempts prove to be futile, the project manager escalates the issue through PMO Process 3: Delivery Management (PMO03DM) for top-level resolution as, dissatisfied stakeholders possess a great risk to project objectives, potentially derailing any work that the project has accomplished or planned.

Control Communications & Control Stakeholder Engagement Process (PRJ4.10CCS) Part 2

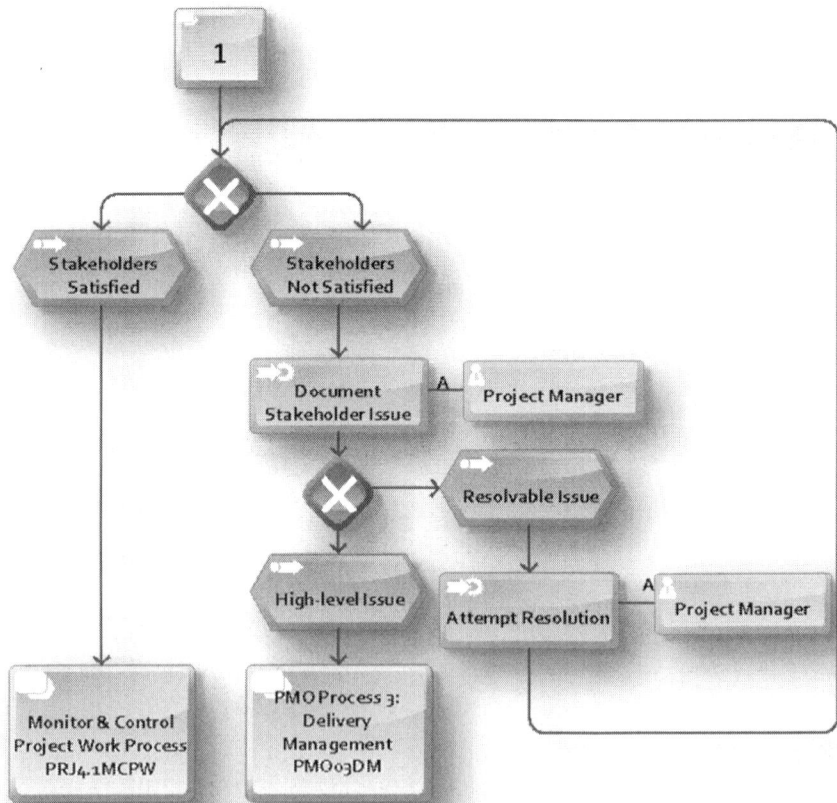

Closing Phase Processes

The closing phase processes of the Utopian PMO, help the project manager bring the project to a successful closure. The closing phase consists of a single all-encompassing process that at a high-level ensures that:

- Projects are closed in a consistent manner and all lessons learned are documented for enriching the OPAs.

- Resources (including the project manager) are released appropriately and contracts closed as per legal requirements.

- Handing over to PMO Process 8: Benefits Realization Management (PMO08BR) to await the materialization of intended project benefits.

Close Procurements & Project Process (PRJ5.1CP)

The Close Procurements & Project Process (PRJ5.1CP) contains the final steps to be performed before a project can be closed. Though the deliverables of the project are ready, several important activities are still required to be performed. The project can attain closure in several ways. The most common and the obviously preferred way is to have the project complete all its deliverables and successfully obtain sign-off. The other ways that a project can be closed, albeit abnormally, are when a material breach of the contract has taken place or when an enterprise-level project risk, jeopardizing the organization as an entity has been identified and no mitigation exists. In both these cases, senior management has made all attempts at various levels to avoid this situation (ref: PMO Process 3: Delivery management (PMO03DM).

Once the PRJ5.1CP process is triggered through any one of the aforementioned events, a final check is made with the sponsor and/ or customer to confirm closure. The PMO analyst then undertakes a phase gate test to ascertain if the project has followed the methodology in its entirety and if all recommended deliverables have in fact been produced and approved. On the successful passage of a phase gate test, the project manager releases the project resources. Internal resources are released to other projects and outsourced resources are terminated or moved internally.

The project manager then updates lessons learned by the project in this particular phase including what they (the project team) did right and, would like to repeat what they did wrong. An end of phase report is collectively made by the project manager and the PMO analyst and is

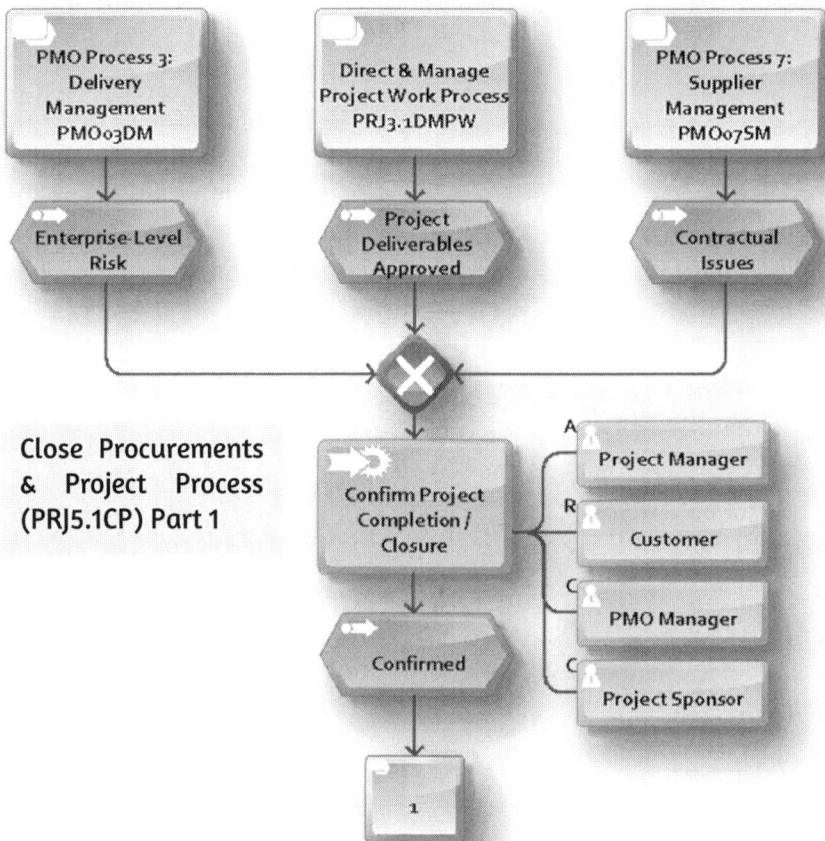

submitted to the PMO to archive as a part of the historical information database also known as the organizational process assets.

The completion of the lessons learned document effectively concludes the project and the project manager may now begin work on the closure activities for the contracts. This is accomplished by PMO Process 7: Supplier Management (PMO07SM), where the project manager is inter-

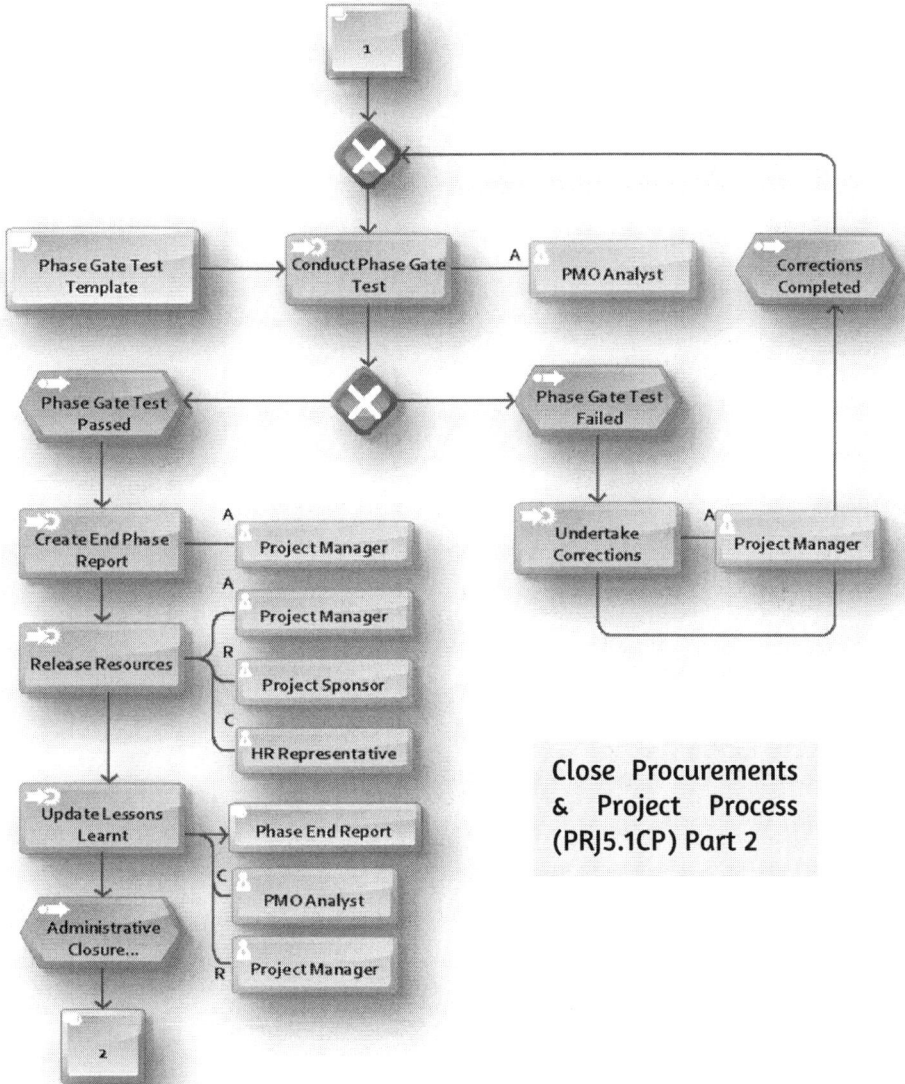

Close Procurements & Project Process (PRJ5.1CP) Part 2

viewed by the PMO manager on the procurement experience. Any subjective opinion (on the procurement) is also documented. The project manager is then released from the project and joins the pool of available project managers in the Utopian PMO's repository, with the experiences from the successful delivery of another project.

In case the project is part of a larger program, this process links to Program Closure Process (PGM3.1PC) and also to PMO Process 8: Benefits Realization Management [PMO08BR] to await intended project benefits to materialize.

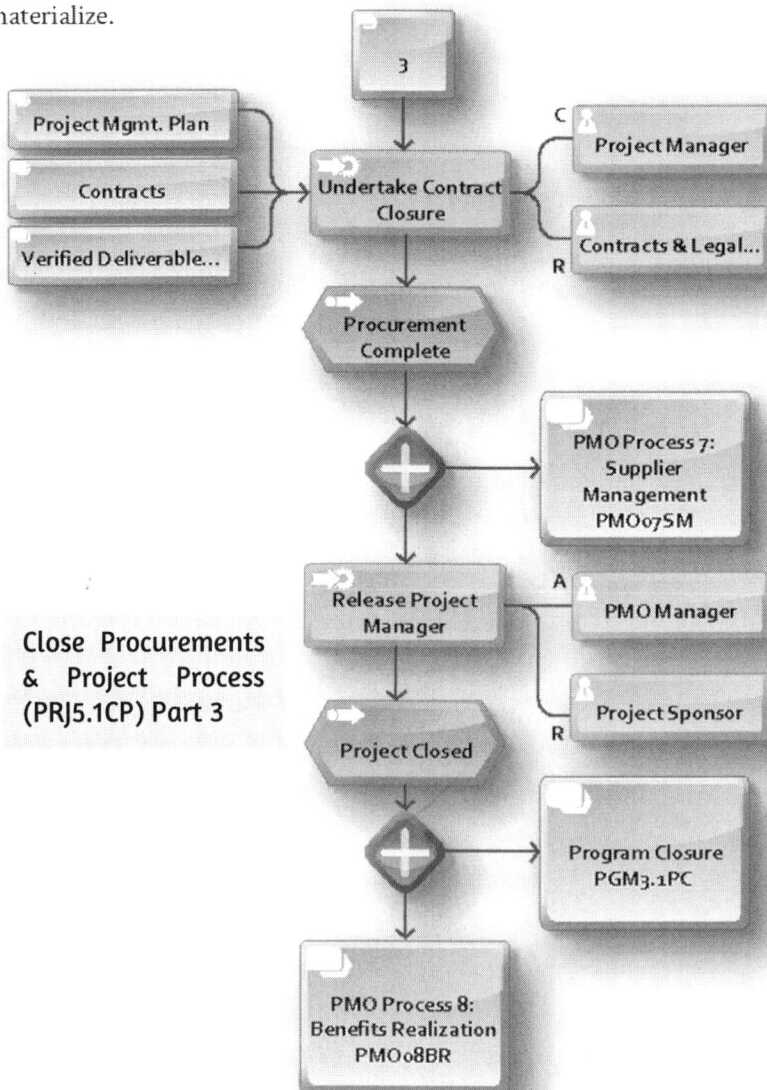

Close Procurements & Project Process (PRJ5.1CP) Part 3

The Develop Phase, Part 3

Program Management Processes for the Utopian PMO

This section provides a framework for program management, comprising of 3 processes encompassing the program management lifecycle. Features of the processes include:

- A framework for program management, interweaving the following into a cohesive whole:
    - Strategy
    - Business case
    - Project management
    - Benefits management
  providing for the most effective and efficient realization of an organization's strategy.

- Active involvement of the PMO at all key interfaces that feed-back into the PMO operational processes.

- Checks and controls built into the process to ensure maximum compliance to the processes.

Initiation Phase Processes

The Utopian PMO's program initiation process provides the necessary bridge between the PMO's Governance and Strategic Alignment Process (GSA) and organizational strategy. Any and all work executed by the Utopian PMO is in alignment with the organization's overall strategy. Once the GSA process confirms and checks for this essential alignment, a decision is made to decide if the proposed initiative is best delivered as a project or as a program. If it is determined that the initiative is best run as a program, then Program Start-up Process (PGM1.1PSU) is triggered.

Program Start-up Processes (PGM1.1PSU)

Once an approved and, strategically validated business case is received, the first course of action for the head of the PMO, the PMO manager, is to assign a PMO Analyst to the program. Unlike a project-level PMO analyst, who may be assigned to one or more projects, a PMO analyst for a program is usually dedicated to one single program. Acting on behalf of the PMO, the PMO analyst, mentors and monitors the program, keeping the delivery in strict alignment with the accepted practices of the PMO.

Once a PMO analyst is assigned, the PMO manager assigns a competent program manager whose skills suits the requirements outlined in the business case. Care should be taken to ensure that only competent program managers are selected. Program management requires a totally different skill set than what project management requires. Project managers with a few years of project management experience are usually automatically upgraded to a program manager without a specific validation of their program manager's skills. Any globally accepted program management credential (such as the PgMP®) can help provide the necessary validation of a person's program management skills and experience. The first remit of the newly assigned program manager is to create the program charter using the approved business case and program statement of work as inputs. The created program charter is taken through an approval process and upon final approval, is published on the Project Management Information System (PMIS).

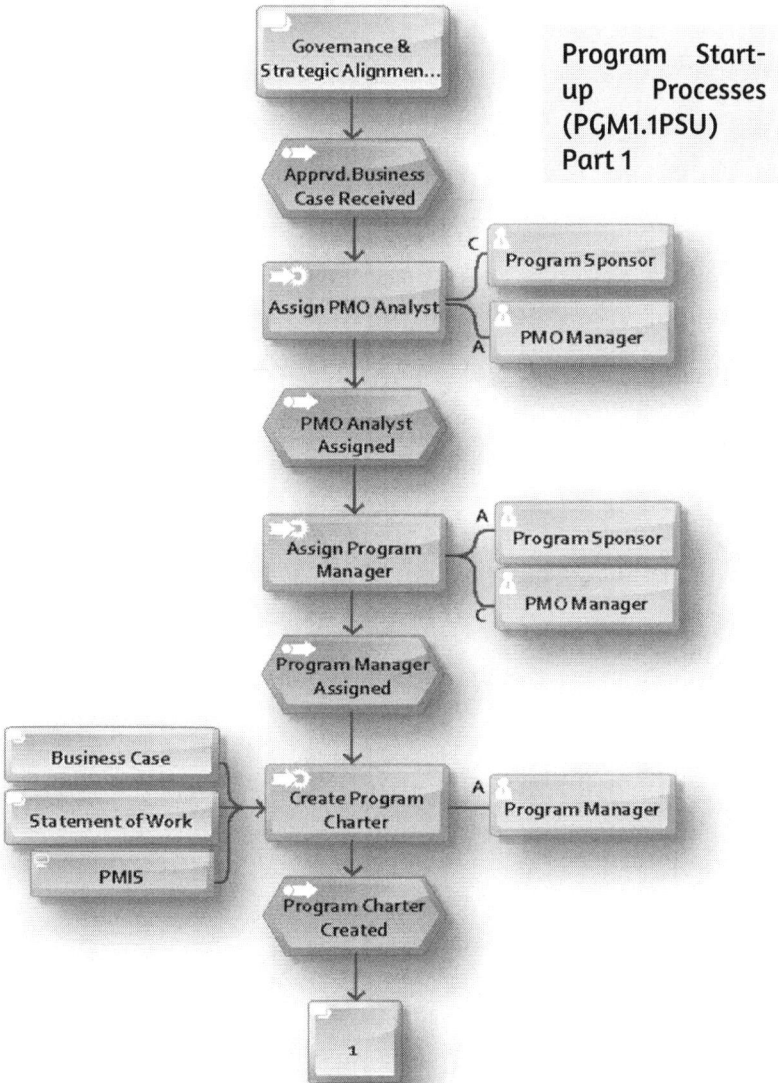

After successful approval of the program charter, the program manager produces the next critical program management deliverable, the stakeholder register. The stakeholder register identifies all positive and negative stakeholders associated with the program. The program manager collects information for the stakeholder register via a number of

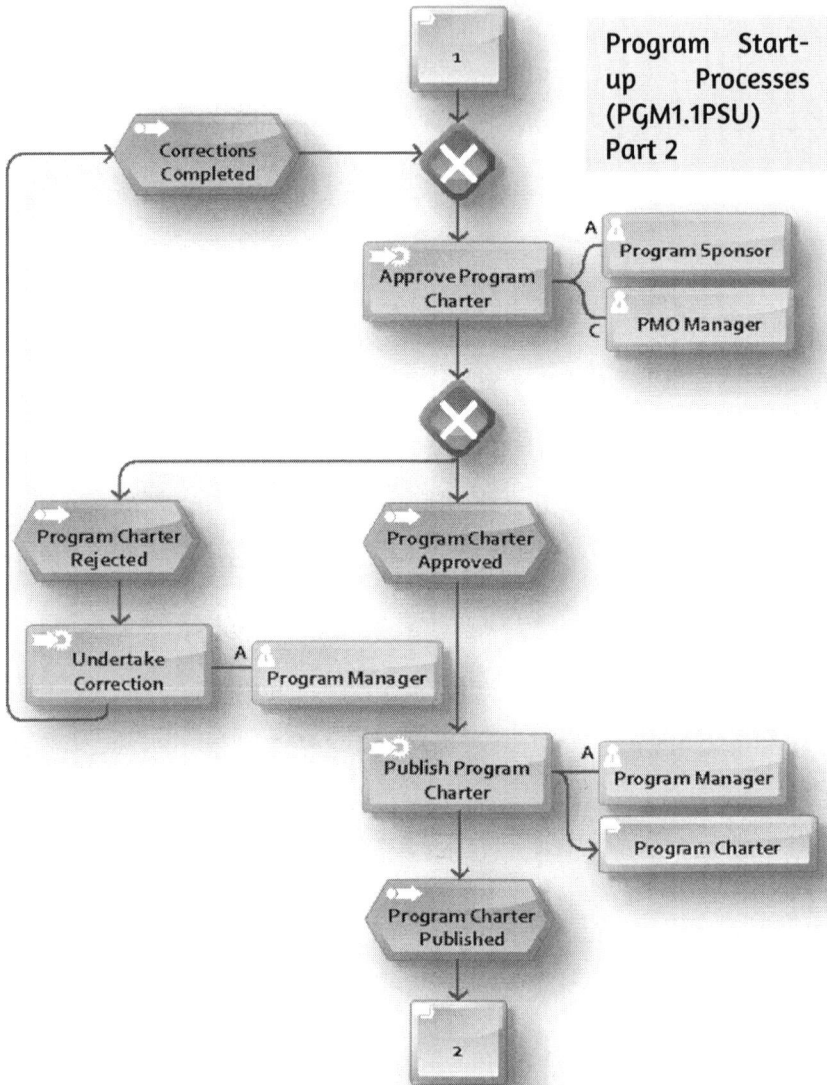

Program Start-up Processes (PGM1.1PSU) Part 2

information gathering techniques including but not limited to looking at historical information as well as by interviewing key contacts in the organization. The completion of the stakeholder register signals the end of the program initiation. The program manager notifies the PMO and the program then passes through a phase gate test.

The PMO analyst is primarily tasked with conducting the phase gate test. Any non-compliance detected is worked out with the program manager and an opportunity is provided to bring the program back on track. The program manager, then documents the lessons learned by the program in this particular phase including what they (the program team and the team-members of the program's constituent projects) did right and would like to repeat and what they did wrong. An end of phase report is collectively made by the program manager and the PMO analyst which is submitted to the PMO to archive as a part of the historical information database also known as the organizational process assets. The program, then moves to the next phase of the lifecycle viz. planning.

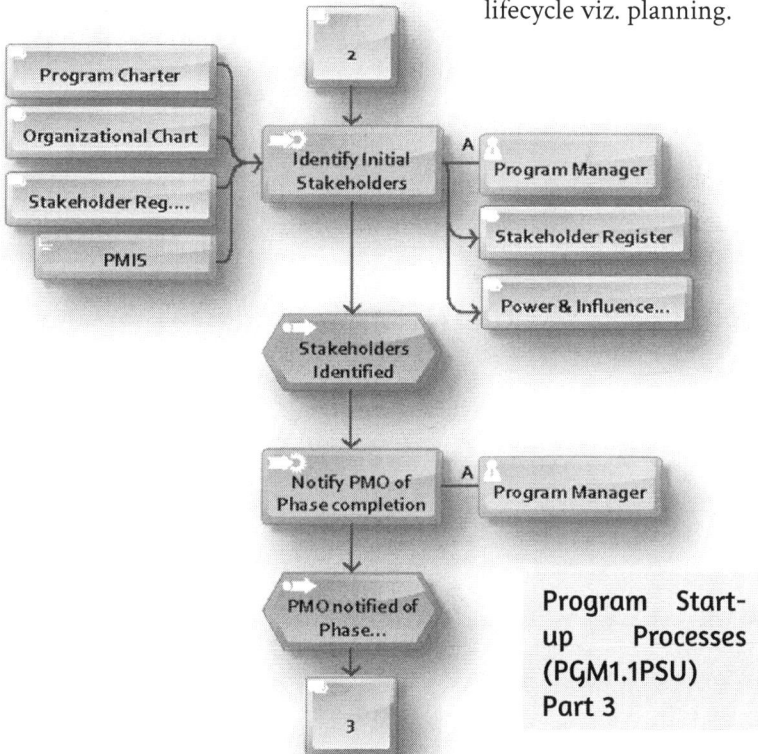

Program Start-up Processes (PGM1.1PSU) Part 3

Program Start-up Processes (PGM1.1PSU) Part 4

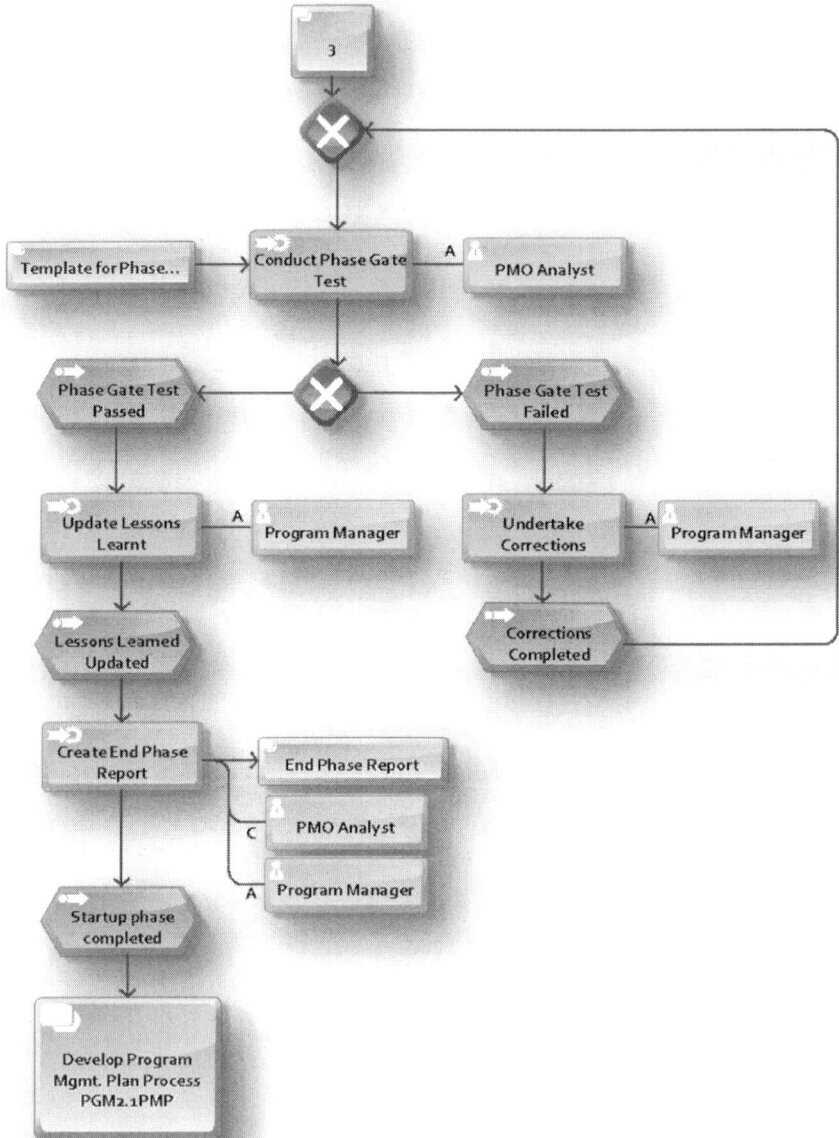

Planning Phase Processes

The Utopian PMO's program planning processes, help create the planning backbone for the program, the program management plan. The sum total effort of the planning process is directed towards developing a clear, articulate and efficient planning tool, that will help a program manager deliver a program that falls within its scope, time and cost boundaries. The program planning process also helps determine the sub-components of the program, spawning the program's constituent projects.

Developing the Program Management Plan Process (PGM2.1PMP)

The successful completion of a phase gate test concludes the program start-up process (PGM1.1PSU) and Developing the Program Management Plan (PGM2.1PMP) is triggered

The PGM2.1PMP process, holds the responsibility of program planning within its remit. The PGM2.1PMP process moves from activity to activity till all the sub-plans that make up the program management plan are created. The first step towards creating the program management plan is creating a stakeholder management plan. This activity is specific to defining a plan to manage the identified stakeholders and ascertaining whether a qualitative or quantitative measurement model is to be used. A recommended technique for effective stakeholder management is to score each stakeholder based on their power and influence on the program and then multiplying to get each stakeholder's score that helps the program manager determine the approach to take whilst managing their expectations.

The completed stakeholder management plan is given a walkthrough with the program sponsor who makes inputs and changes as required. The updated and approved stakeholder management plan is published on the PMIS for purposes of information recording, dissemination and collaboration.

Once the stakeholder management plan is finalized, work begins on the next part of the program management plan, i.e. collecting the requirements and solidifying everything into a base lined scope, which then forms the precursor to all the other planning activities in the program. The program manager then begins work on collecting the actual requirements that is expected of the program. The stakeholder register created during the previous activity helps provide guidance on whom and how to approach for the program requirements.

The requirements are consolidated, conflicting items nullified, and the next output of this process, the scope management plan is created. This plan elucidates a methodology to manage scope on the program. In the next steps, the final, agreed work, the program is expected to accomplish is put together in the form of the scope statement. The program is expected to deliver the scope detailed in this document, nothing more and certainly nothing less. The detailed scope document is put through a rigorous validation and approval process and the program scope is baselined.

The creation of the scope statement with the agreement of all stakeholders puts the program manager in a much better position to truly understand the program and the expected outputs. The program manager is now able to make concrete plans with the assurance of having a baselined scope in hand.

The development of a critical planning tool, the WBS (Work Breakdown Structure) begins. The WBS is a hierarchical decomposition of the program scope broken down into smaller elements. At the lowest level, the elements of a WBS are called work packages. The act of breaking down the program scope into work packages is called decomposition. The level to which to decompose a program's scope depends on the complexity and specific needs of a program. Too less and it doesn't aid in planning and conversely too much decomposition can make the management of the WBS very difficult. However, used correctly, the WBS is immensely invaluable.

Once the scope is broken down meaningfully into work packages, the activities required to accomplish each work package can be defined. The list of activities can now be ordered in the sequence in which they can potentially be executed. Activities, in an ideal world , would be executed in linear fashion but in the real world various constraints actually define the order of execution. An estimation of the effort required is carried out for each identified activity through any known qualitative and/or quantitative methods. Resources are assigned to activities with the involvement of the organization's HR representatives to ensure that shared resources are not over allocated. Once activities are listed, ordered and allocated resources, the expected durations can be assessed, again using any known qualitative and/or quantitative methods.

At this stage the program manager essentially has an ordered list of activities, with estimated durations and resources, preferably on a program scheduling tool, to help manage and monitor progress against recorded tasks. The program schedule is baselined and published on the PMIS.

The next activity of the PGM2.1PMP process, is to create a list of projects that are required to be spawned to deliver the program scope. Each project is delineated with a clear statement of work (SOW) and cross dependencies between the proposed projects are identified. These SOWs are used during the project initiation processes (PRJ1.1PSU), to help formulate a project's initial documents.

The financial case section, of the business case for the program contains a preliminary budget estimate for the program and by approving the business case for an initiative, an organization implies that it understands the costs involved in executing the initiative.

However the program has undergone further elaboration and the creation of a complete schedule with resource and time estimates puts the program manager in a better position to review the initial estimates provided in the business case to check if they still possess merits. The program manager then begins to assess the cost associated with performing each activity detailed in the schedule. An estimation of the costs involved is again carried out through any known qualitative and/or quantitative methods. This estimate is then compared against the initial estimates provided in the business case. In an ideal scenario, the business case estimates and the activity level estimates must not have significant deviation from each other. The level of deviation acceptable is usually mandated by the organization. It is usually set to be about ± 15%. If the two estimates are within the prescribed tolerances, then the new budget for the program is revised, the sponsor provides the necessary approvals, the program manager updates the lessons learned and the process moves to the next activity of the planning lifecycle

However, if the variation between the two estimates are outside allowable limits then the PMO Process #3 Delivery Management [PMO03DM] is triggered which then undertakes the necessary activities to provide organizational visibility to bring this conundrum to a conclusion.

The completion of the cost estimation activities triggers the next activity in the planning lifecycle, i.e. the quality planning activity . This activity creates a detailed plan to manage the activities pertaining to quality assurance and quality control on the program. The specifics of the plan include the acceptable level of quality, which is typically defined by the customer, and describes how the program will ensure this level of quality in its deliverables and work processes. Quality management activities ensure that the program deliverables meet stated or prescribed requirements and that work processes are performed efficiently and as documented. The plan also ensures that both preventive and corrective action is taken to ensure quality is consistent. Also included in this plan are methodologies, responsibilities, budgets, metrics and other quality tools including checklists. The program manager uses the parameters stated in the requirements documentation to determine final quality requirements for the product. A plan that facilitates meeting the defined quality criteria is then created. The program manager may also avail the expertise of a quality management SME in matters that require a detailed quality analysis. The completed quality management plan is published on the PMIS.

After establishing the quality management protocols on the program, the program manager's next course of action is to establish a solid base for management of the human resources assigned to the program. Key program roles and responsibilities are defined and documented in the plan including the creation of a RACI matrix for all identified program tasks. To effectively manage resources working on the program, organizational charts and reporting hierarchies are created and documented in the HR management plan. It would also serve in the best interests of the program manager to study and understand various organizational behavior and motivational theories to help define an approach to managing resources. The management of resources is a subjective topic and must be tailored to meet the unique requirements of each program. Also, any limitations arising out of the physical location of the program (and its constituent project's) team members are analyzed for any potential conflicts. For e.g.: virtually located, key-resources. Care must be taken to avoid considering limiting planning to only the human resource component and all other resources such as materials and equipment must also be taken into account. A hierarchical decomposition of resources by type can be used and such a diagram is known as a Resource Breakdown Structure (RBS). An elaborate rewards and recognition system is also developed as a part of this plan, to influence and promote team performance. The completed HR management plan which considers all potential HR management aspects, is published on the PMIS.

One of the key responsibilities of a program manager, is to maintain effective communications with the team and with all stakeholders. To do this, an effective communications management plan is pertinent. An effective communications management plan must document, in detail, how the program manager intends to communicate with the identified stakeholders of the program. This involves identifying the information needs for each of the stakeholders, their reason for wanting this information, and the preferred medium of communication. Also important, is the requirement to document the information needs of the program and the program manager. This includes the various pieces of information that the program needs from the stakeholders to make timely decisions. The completed communications management plan which considers all potential communication management aspects such as the ones discussed above, is published on the PMIS.

The next activity pertains to risk management and covers the entire gamut of risk management activities on a program, from the identification of risks to qualitative and quantitative assessments and culminating in developing mitigation plans for the identified risks. The first step is the creation of a risk management plan detailing the methodology, roles, categories of risk, definitions and most importantly the risk tolerances of the organization. A start-up company, will have significantly higher risk appetite than an older traditionally-run company. The risk management plan will also include a high-level initial assessment of risks on the program. Since this plan provides the entire framework for managing risk on the program, impetus exists for creating an all-encompassing risk management plan. The next step is the identification of risks. Several techniques exist to undertake a detailed identification of risks including not limited to simple methods such as interviewing and brainstorming to more in depth ones such as the Delphi technique. Care is taken to ensure that the identification of opportunities is not missed. A detailed risk / opportunity register is produced with a list of risks / opportunities and includes various categories under which to categorize the identified risks. The risk / opportunity register is then published on the PMIS for purposes of information dissemination and storage.

The next step of the process assesses each identified risk based on pre-established rating scales. The rating scales are established based on the risk appetite of the organization ascertained in the risk management planning phase. If the program itself is deemed too risky to continue, then PMO Process 3: Delivery Management PMO03DM is triggered for appropriate escalation and the top management is tasked with deciding its fate. Each risk or opportunity is segregated and treated according to commonly accepted strategies for dealing with risks and opportunities. Risks are avoided, transferred or mitigated while opportunities are shared, enhanced or exploited. A passive strategy for both risks and opportunities is to simply accept the risk, a decision that requires no process to accomplish. The identified treatment is formulated into a mitigation plan and is either implemented straight away or stored for implementation when a risk or it's triggers materialize. The individual projects that are closest to the risk event are issued mitigation plans and become part of the project's risk management plans. These instructions are updated on the PMIS and linked to the project's risk management activities via the Plan Risk Management Process (PRJ2.9PRM). This concludes one iteration of risk management planning on the project and further iterations are performed as required to mitigate all identified risks on the program to an acceptable level.

The final sub-plan of the program management plan is the procurement management plan. The procurement management plan is only created if any of the program deliverables are outsourced. The program manager need not be concerned with this part of the process if all of the program work is accomplished internally.

The procurement management plan concerns itself with creating a statement of work for each of the items planned to be procured, the types of contracts, the criteria for evaluating potential vendors and other procurement related documents. The completed procurement management plan which considers all potential procurement management aspects such as the ones discussed above, is published on the PMIS.

Once the final sub-plan, i.e. the procurement management plan is finalized, the completed program management plan is taken through a review and approval process with the program sponsor playing a key role. The PMO analyst facilitates the process and the approved program management plan is published on the PMIS for organizational review. The publishing of the program management plan signals the end of the planning phase and the program manager notifies the PMO of the completion of the phase. The PMO analyst then undertakes a phase gate test to ascertain if the program has followed the methodology in its entirety and if all recommended deliverables have in fact been produced and approved. On the successful passage of a phase gate test, the program manager updates the lessons learned by the program in this particular phase including what they (the program team) did right and would like to repeat and what they did wrong. An end of phase report is collectively made by the program manager and the PMO analyst and is submitted to the PMO to archive as a part of the historical information database also known as the organizational process assets.

The completion of the planning phase triggers the constituent projects, the execution of which, in totality, will deliver the scope of the program. For each project to be spawned by the program, the Project Start Up (PRJ1.1PSU) process is triggered with the project statement of work (SOW) and inter-project dependencies provided as initial documents.

Developing the Program Mgmt. Plan Process (PGM2.1PMP) Part 1

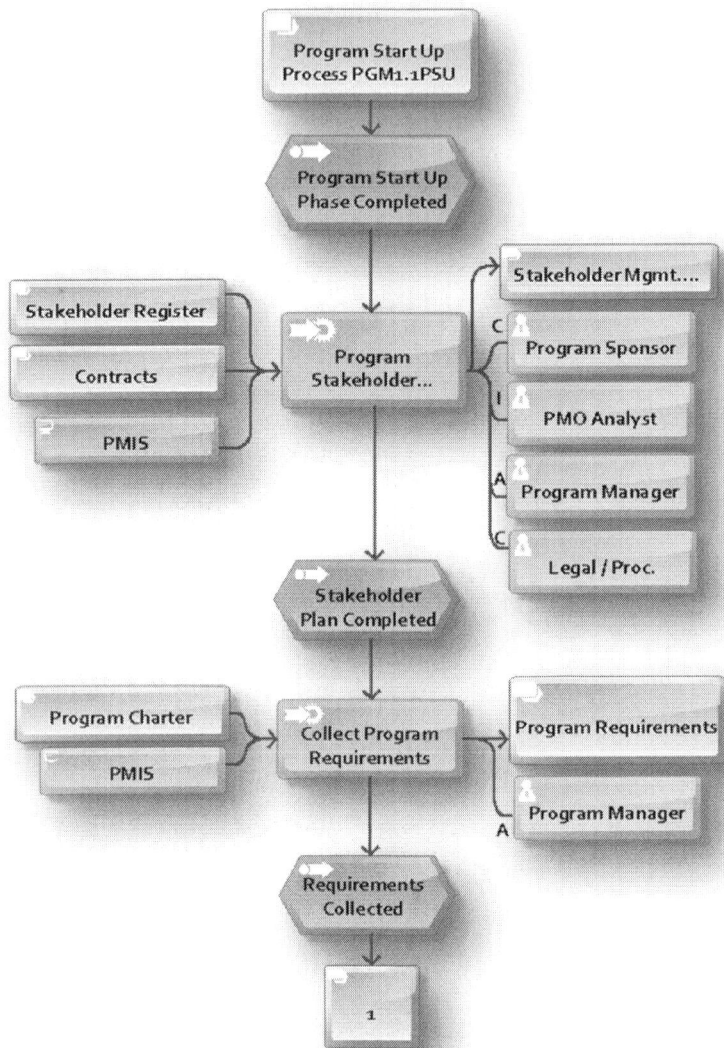

Program Start Up
Process PGM1.1PSU

Program Start Up
Phase Completed

Stakeholder Register

Contracts

PMIS

Program
Stakeholder...

Stakeholder Mgmt....

Program Sponsor

PMO Analyst

Program Manager

Legal / Proc.

Stakeholder
Plan Completed

Program Charter

PMIS

Collect Program
Requirements

Program Requirements

Program Manager

Requirements
Collected

1

Developing the Program Mgmt. Plan Process (PGM2.1PMP) Part 2

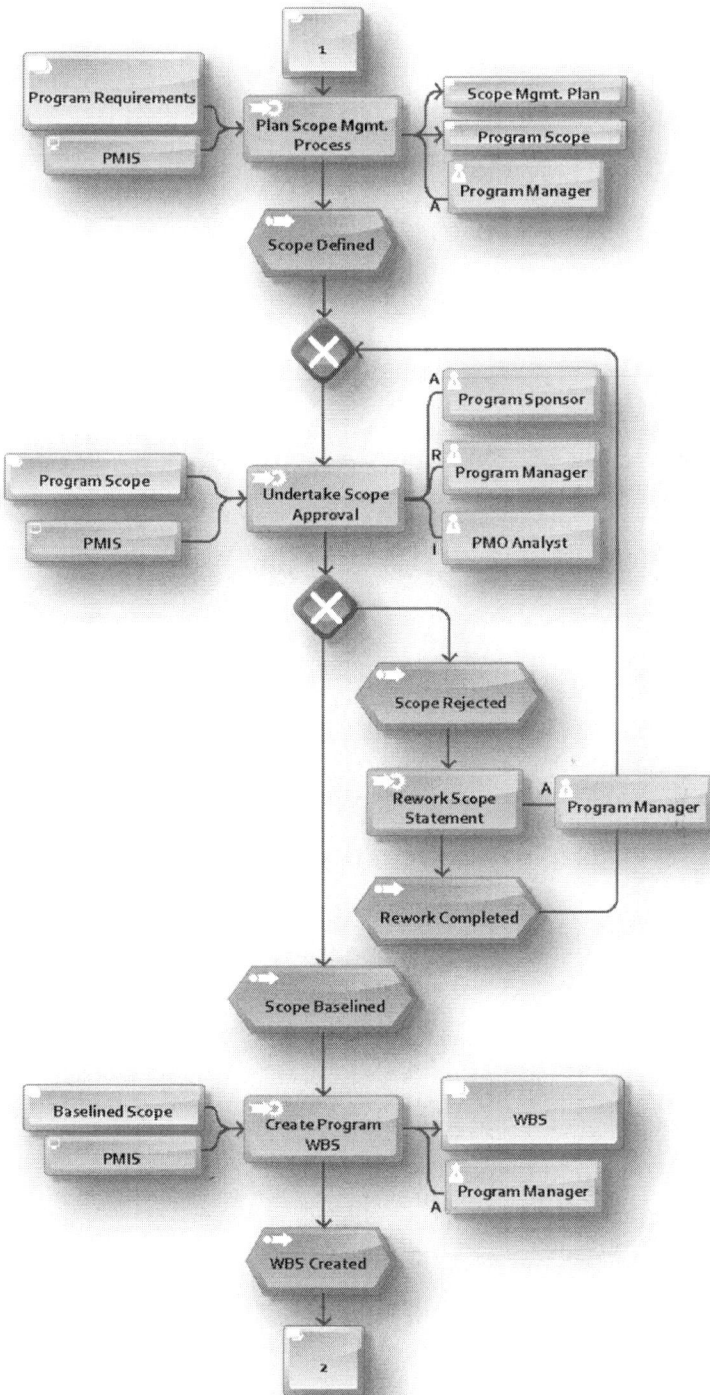

Developing the Program Mgmt. Plan Process (PGM2.1PMP) Part 3

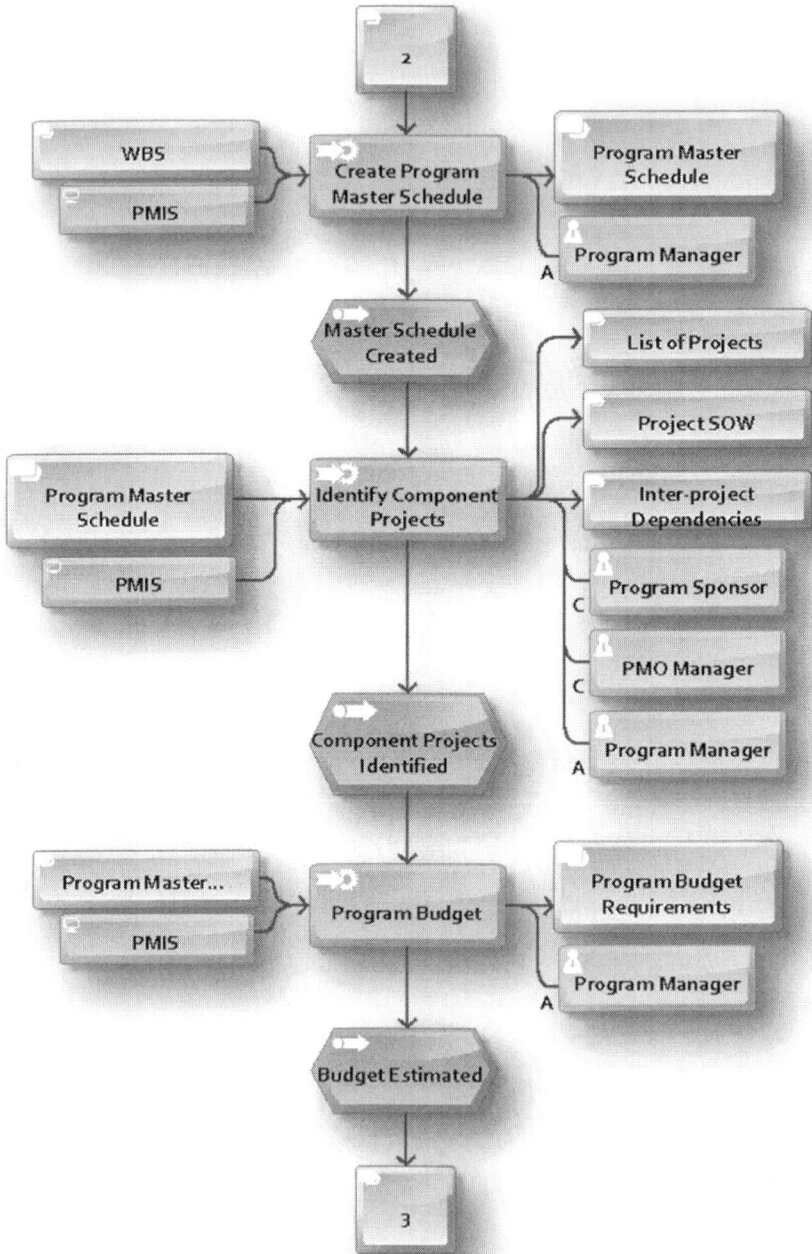

```
                              [2]

   WBS                   Create Program          Program Master
                         Master Schedule            Schedule
   PMIS
                                                  Program Manager
                                              A

                         Master Schedule         List of Projects
                            Created
                                                   Project SOW

   Program Master        Identify Component       Inter-project
     Schedule               Projects              Dependencies

        PMIS                                     Program Sponsor
                                              C
                                                   PMO Manager
                                              C
                         Component Projects      Program Manager
                            Identified        A

   Program Master...                           Program Budget
                         Program Budget         Requirements
        PMIS
                                                Program Manager
                                              A

                         Budget Estimated

                              [3]
```

Developing the Program Mgmt. Plan Process (PGM2.1PMP) Part 4

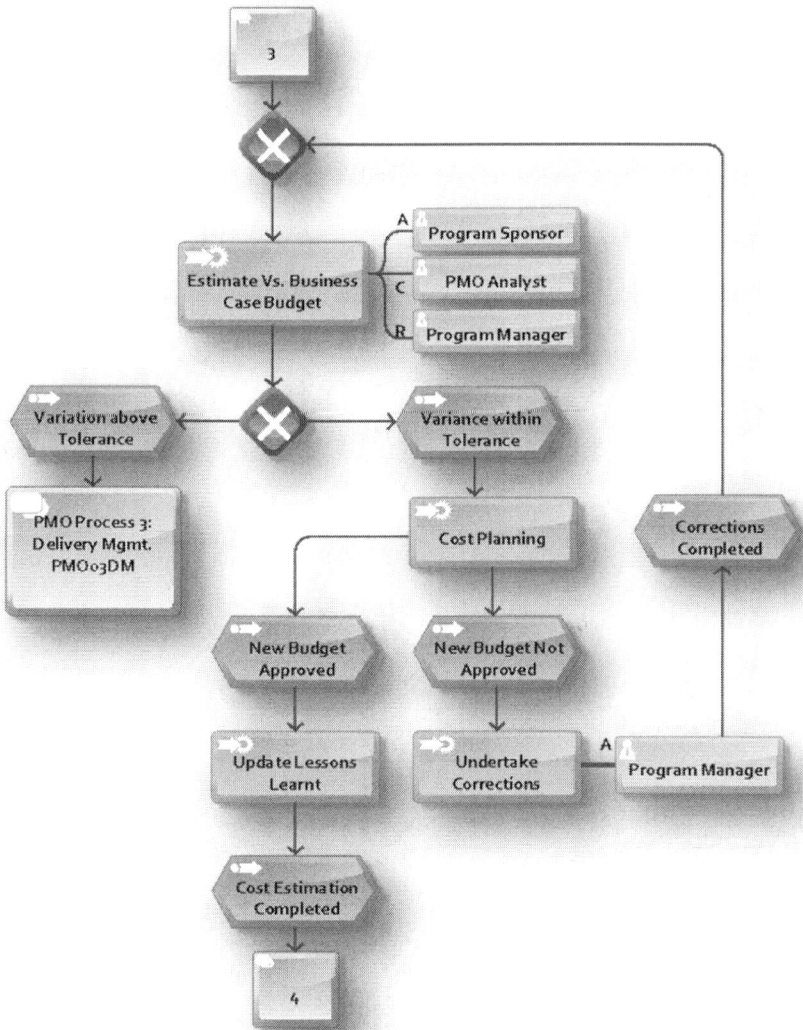

Developing the Program Mgmt. Plan Process (PGM2.1PMP) Part 5

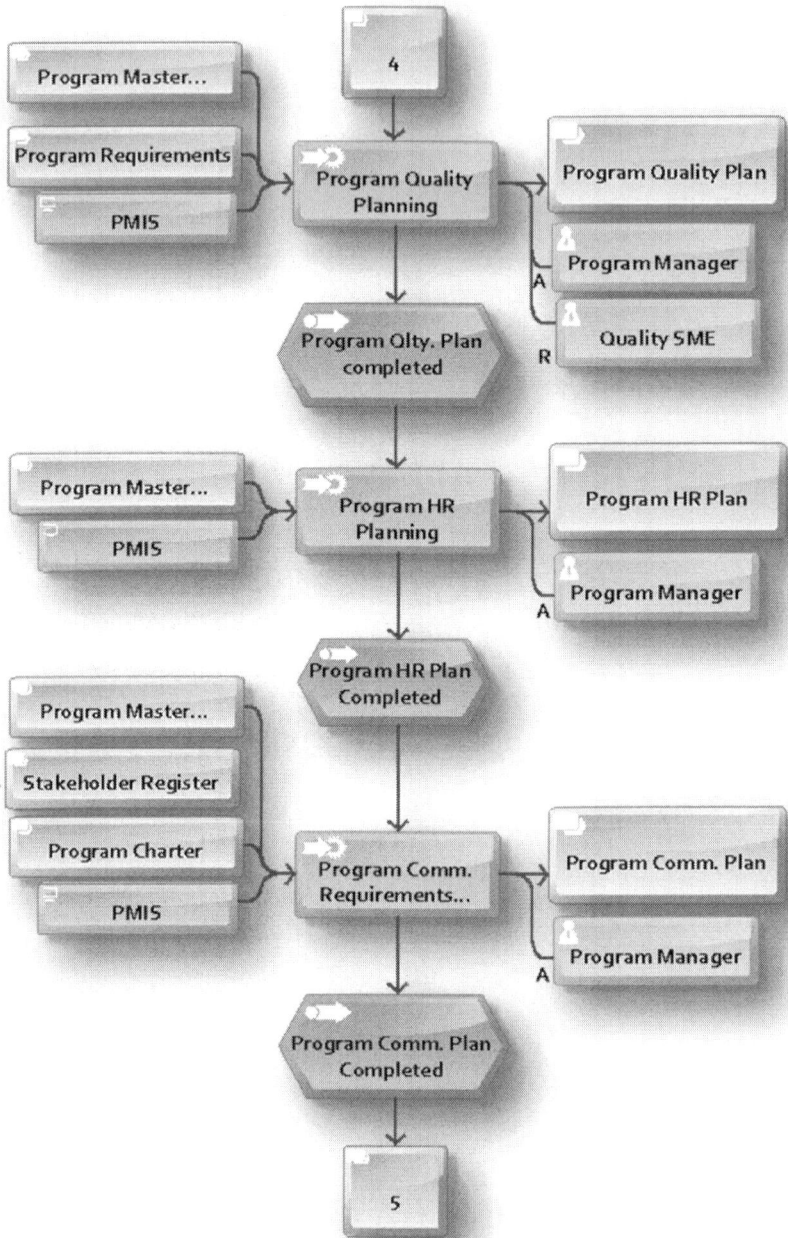

Program Master...

Program Requirements

PMIS

4

Program Quality Planning

Program Quality Plan

Program Manager

Quality SME

Program Qlty. Plan completed

A

R

Program Master...

PMIS

Program HR Planning

Program HR Plan

Program Manager

A

Program HR Plan Completed

Program Master...

Stakeholder Register

Program Charter

PMIS

Program Comm. Requirements...

Program Comm. Plan

Program Manager

A

Program Comm. Plan Completed

5

Developing the Program Mgmt. Plan Process (PGM2.1PMP) Part 6

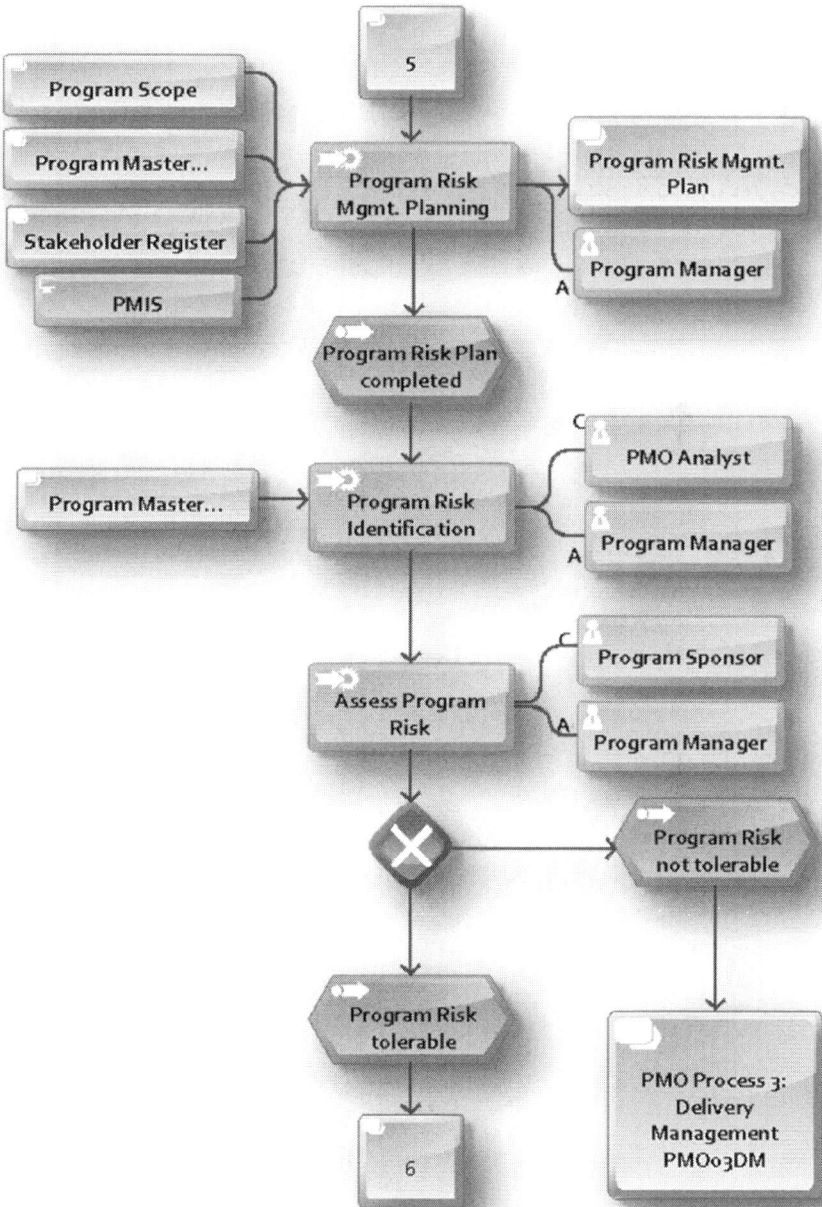

5

Program Scope

Program Master...

Stakeholder Register

PMIS

Program Risk Mgmt. Planning

Program Risk Mgmt. Plan

Program Manager

A

Program Risk Plan completed

Program Master...

Program Risk Identification

PMO Analyst

C

Program Manager

A

Assess Program Risk

Program Sponsor

C

Program Manager

A

Program Risk not tolerable

Program Risk tolerable

6

PMO Process 3: Delivery Management PMO03DM

Developing the Program Mgmt. Plan Process (PGM2.1PMP) Part 7

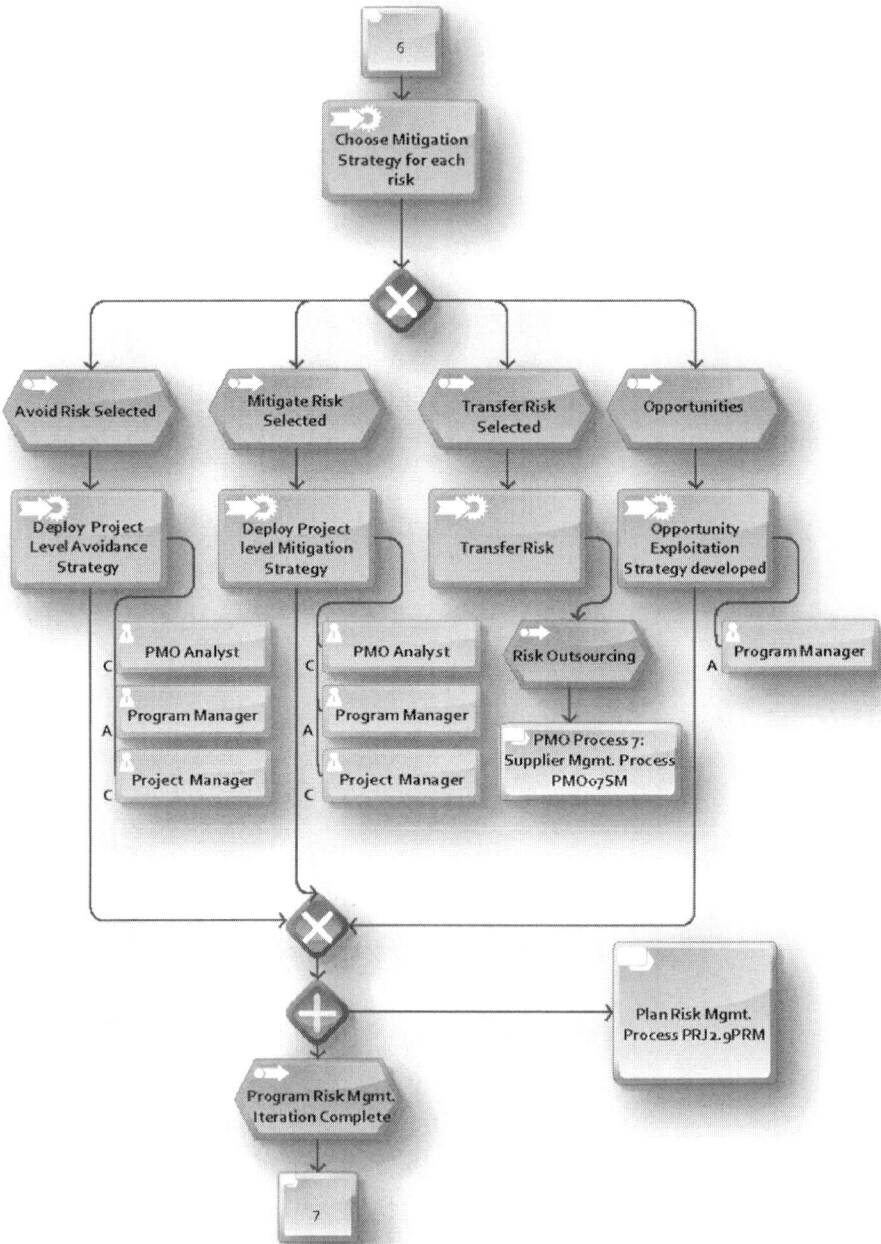

Developing the Program Mgmt. Plan Process (PGM2.1PMP) Part 8

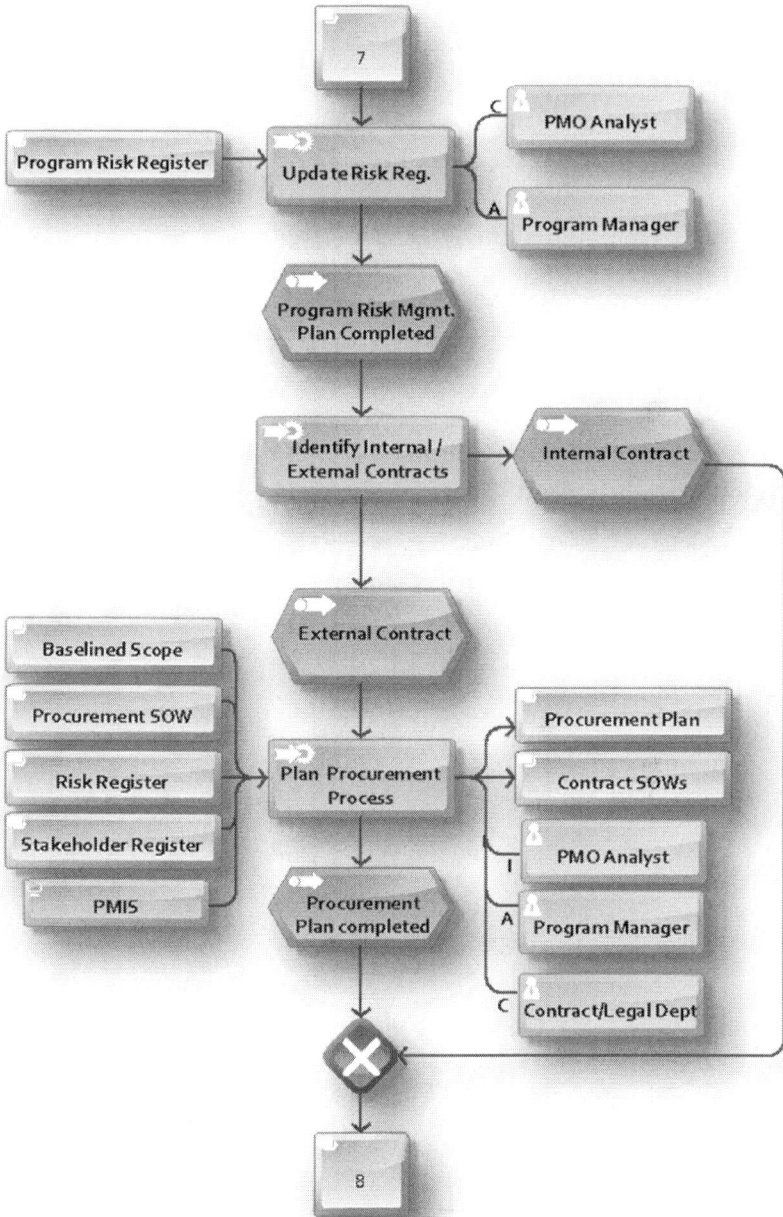

```
                            ┌─────┐
                            │  7  │
                            └─────┘
                               │
                               ▼                        ┌──────────────┐
┌──────────────────────┐  ┌──────────────┐         C   │  PMO Analyst │
│ Program Risk Register │─▶│ Update Risk Reg. │        └──────────────┘
└──────────────────────┘  └──────────────┘         A   ┌──────────────────┐
                               │                        │ Program Manager  │
                               ▼                        └──────────────────┘
                        ┌──────────────┐
                        │ Program Risk Mgmt. │
                        │  Plan Completed    │
                        └──────────────┘
                               │
                               ▼
                        ┌──────────────────┐       ┌──────────────────┐
                        │ Identify Internal /  │──▶│ Internal Contract │
                        │ External Contracts   │    └──────────────────┘
                        └──────────────────┘
                               │
                               ▼
                        ┌──────────────────┐
                        │ External Contract │
                        └──────────────────┘
┌──────────────────┐           │
│ Baselined Scope  │           ▼                    ┌──────────────────┐
└──────────────────┘    ┌──────────────────┐       │ Procurement Plan │
┌──────────────────┐    │ Plan Procurement │──┐    └──────────────────┘
│ Procurement SOW  │───▶│     Process      │  ├──▶┌──────────────────┐
└──────────────────┘    └──────────────────┘  │   │  Contract SOWs   │
┌──────────────────┐           │               │   └──────────────────┘
│  Risk Register   │           ▼            I  │   ┌──────────────────┐
└──────────────────┘    ┌──────────────────┐  │   │   PMO Analyst    │
┌──────────────────────┐│ Procurement      │  │   └──────────────────┘
│ Stakeholder Register ││ Plan completed   │ A│   ┌──────────────────┐
└──────────────────────┘└──────────────────┘  │   │ Program Manager  │
┌──────────────────┐           │               │   └──────────────────┘
│      PMIS        │           │            C  │   ┌──────────────────┐
└──────────────────┘           ▼               │   │ Contract/Legal Dept │
                            ┌──✕──┐             │   └──────────────────┘
                            └─────┘
                               │
                               ▼
                            ┌─────┐
                            │  8  │
                            └─────┘
```

Developing the Program Mgmt. Plan Process (PGM2.1PMP) Part 9

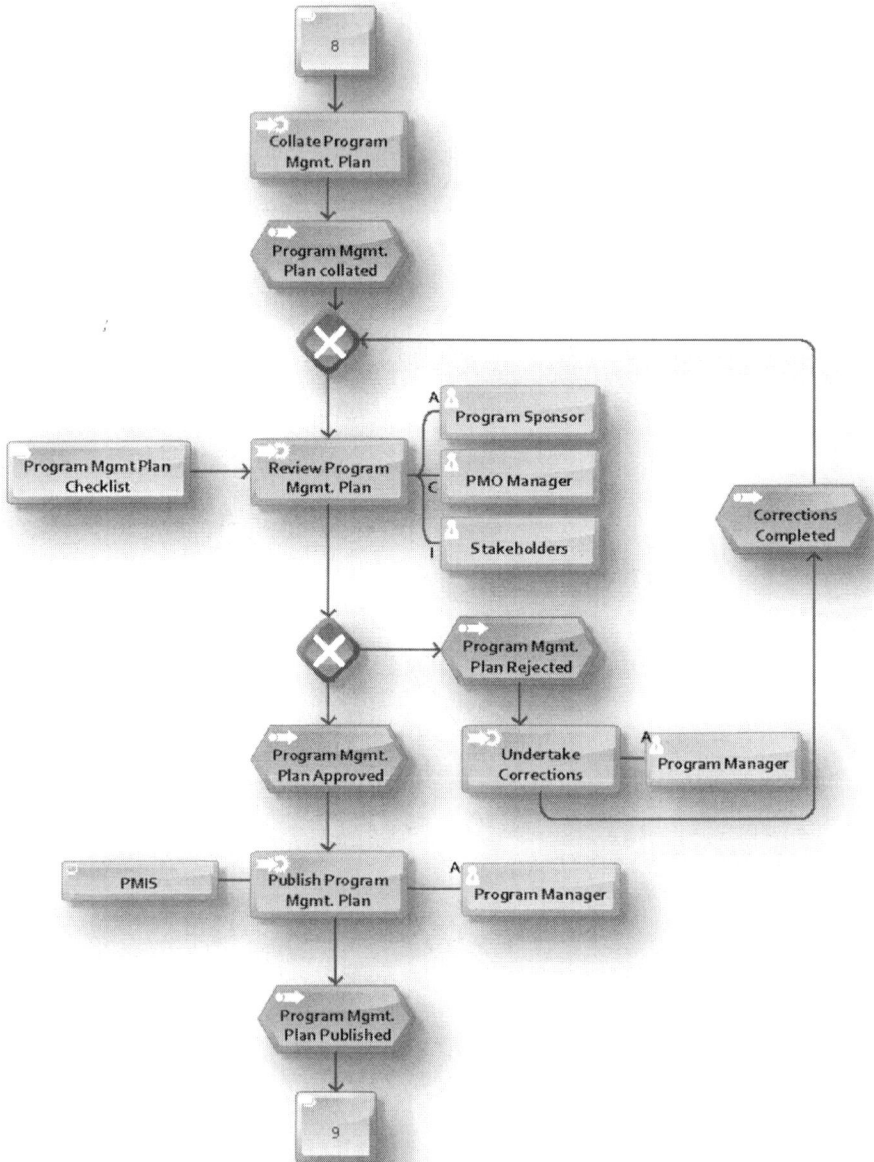

Developing the Program Mgmt. Plan Process (PGM2.1PMP) Part 10

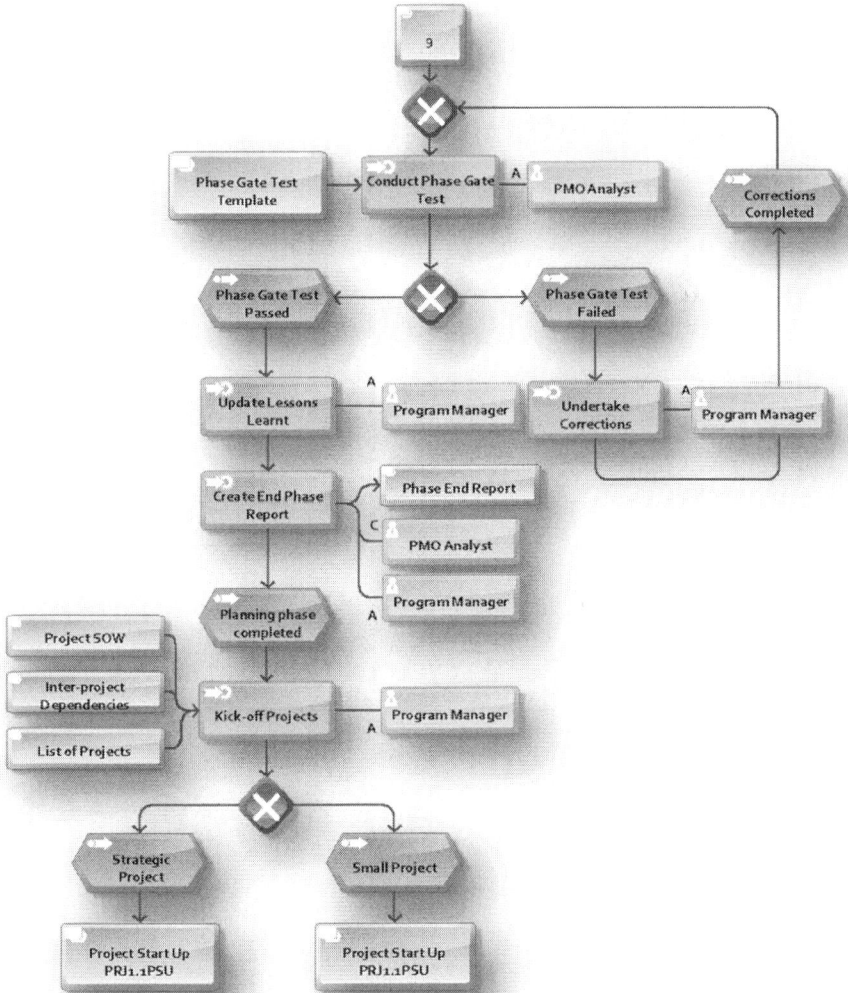

9	

Phase Gate Test Template → Conduct Phase Gate Test — A — PMO Analyst

Corrections Completed

Phase Gate Test Passed ← ✕ → Phase Gate Test Failed

Update Lessons Learnt — A — Program Manager

Undertake Corrections — A — Program Manager

Create End Phase Report

Phase End Report
C — PMO Analyst
A — Program Manager

Planning phase completed — A

Project SOW
Inter-project Dependencies
List of Projects

Kick-off Projects — A — Program Manager

Strategic Project

Small Project

Project Start Up PRJ1.1PSU

Project Start Up PRJ1.1PSU

Closing Phase Processes

The program closing phase of the Utopian PMO helps the program manager bring the program to a successful closure. The closing phase consists of a single all-encompassing process that at a high-level ensures that:

- Programs are closed in a consistent manner and all lessons learned are documented for enriching the OPAs.

- Resources (including the program manager) are released appropriately and contracts closed as per legal requirements.

- Handing over to PMO Process 8: Benefits Realization Management (PMO08BR) to await intended program benefits to materialize.

Close Procurements & Program Process (PGM3.1CP)

The Close Procurements & Program Process (PGMJ3.1CP) contains the final steps to be performed before a program can be closed. Though the deliverables of the program are ready, several very important activities are still required to be performed. The program can attain closure in several ways. The most common and obviously preferred way is to have the constituent projects in a program complete all its deliverables and successfully obtain sign-off. The other ways that a program can be closed, albeit abnormally, are when a material breach of the contract has taken place or an enterprise-level program risk, jeopardizing the organization as an entity has been identified and no mitigation exists. In both these cases, senior management has made all attempts at various levels to avoid this situation (ref: PMO Process 3: Delivery management (PMO03DM).

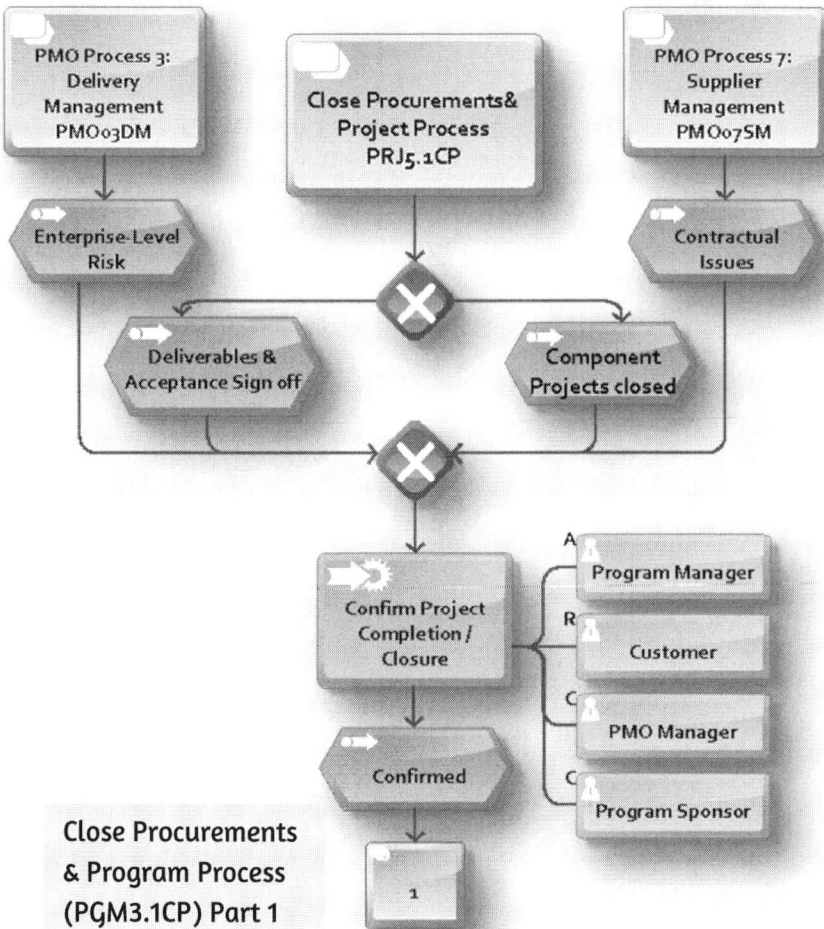

PMO Process 3:
Delivery
Management
PMOo3DM

Close Procurements&
Project Process
PRJ5.1CP

PMO Process 7:
Supplier
Management
PMOo7SM

Enterprise-Level
Risk

Contractual
Issues

Deliverables &
Acceptance Sign off

Component
Projects closed

Confirm Project
Completion /
Closure

A Program Manager

R Customer

C PMO Manager

C Program Sponsor

Confirmed

1

**Close Procurements
& Program Process
(PGM3.1CP) Part 1**

Once the PGM3.1CP process is triggered through any one of the aforementioned events, a final check is made with the sponsor and/ or customer to confirm closure. This process also includes the closure activities for open program contracts. This is accomplished by PMO Process 7: Supplier Management (PMO07SM), where the program manager is interviewed by the PMO manager on the procurement experiences and any personal views (on the procurement) are documented. The PMO analyst then undertakes a phase gate test to ascertain if the program has followed the methodology in its entirety and if all recommended deliverables have in fact been produced and approved. On the successful passage of a phase gate test, the program manager releases the program resources. Internal resources are released to other programs and outsourced resources are terminated or moved internally. The program manager then updates the lessons learned by the program in this particular phase including what they (the program team) did right and would like to repeat and what they did wrong. An end of phase report is collectively made by the program manager and the PMO analyst and is submitted to the PMO to archive as a part of the historical information database also known as the organizational process assets. The program manager is then released from the program and joins the pool of available program managers in the Utopian PMO's repository with the experiences from the successful delivery of another program.

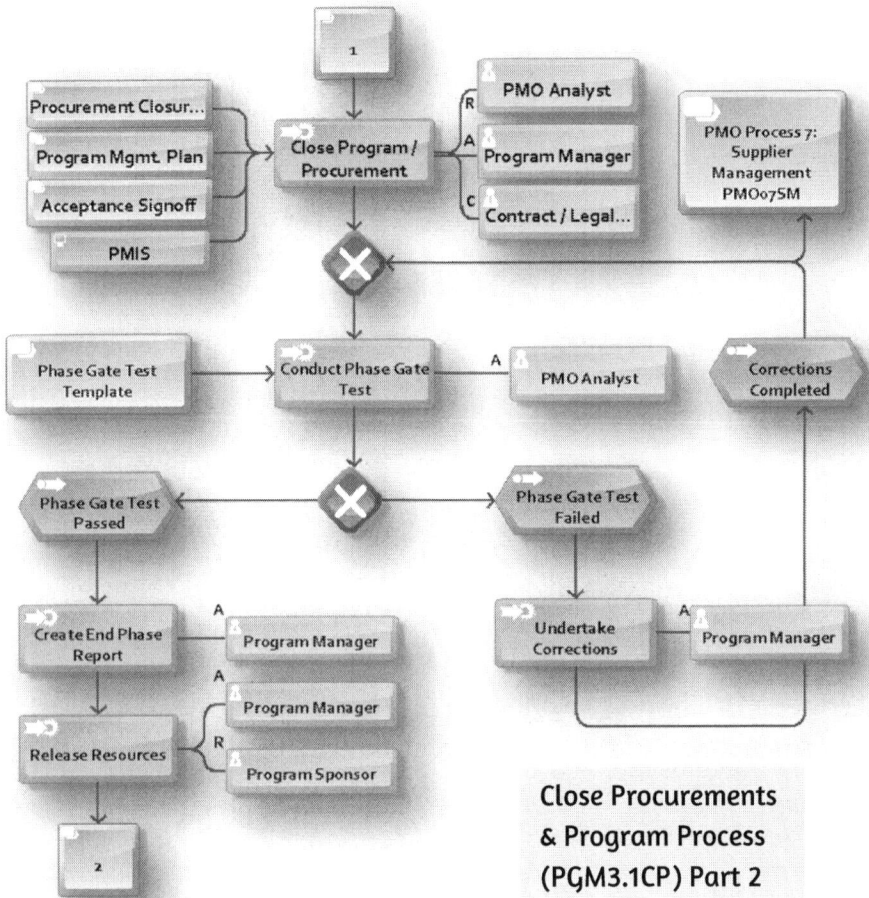

Close Procurements & Program Process (PGM3.1CP) Part 2

The process then links to PMO Process 8: Benefits Realization Management (PMO08BR) to await intended program benefits to materialize for subsequent measurement and documentation. The attainment of intended (and unintended) benefits stand as a program's ultimate success and all of the Utopian PMO's program management and project management process drive home this critical aspect.

Close Procurements & Program Process (PGM3.1CP) Part 3

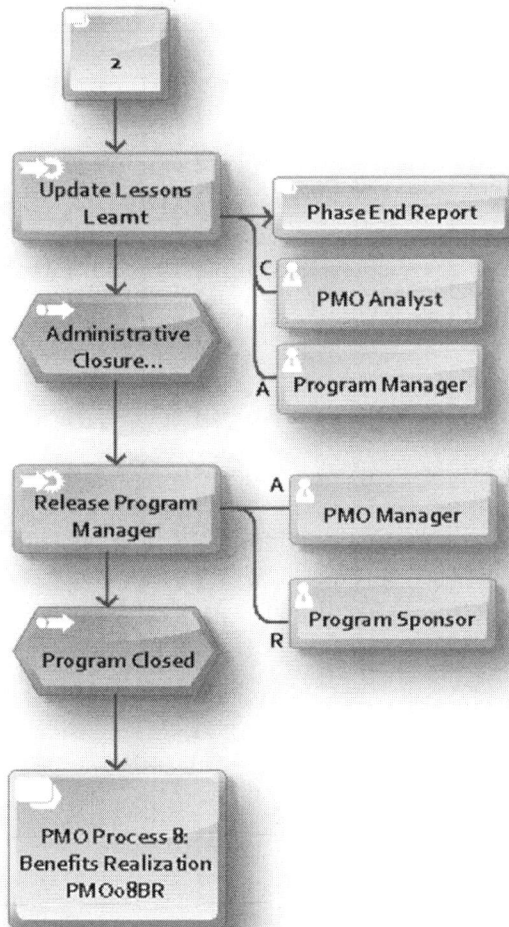

Chapter 7
The Deploy Phase

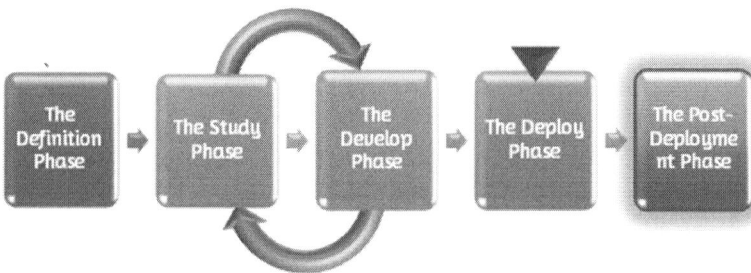

Change Management considerations

T he Utopian PMO, when implemented correctly, is a colossal transformation, which the organization must be comfortable with. The ability of the BPR team to manage and adapt the organization to be receptive to this change is an important part of the PMO reengineering effort.

The primary hurdles of the BPR team when executing a change so large and drastic is the persistent attitudes of the existing staff refusing to adapt to the proposed changes. If the BPR project has been adequately advertised and the organization is expecting change, a part of this resistance may be alleviated. However, staffs who are working at the lower levels of the organizational structure may perceive the BPR effort to be bureaucratic and may not realize the strategic motives behind this. The BPR team also needs to understand the multi-faceted nature of change. Changing over to refined or improved processes alone will not bring about the desired change. If process practitioners are not briefed about the need for change and adequately trained in their new roles, the general tendency is to slowly drift back into the tried, tested and inefficient "previous state".

The deploy phase can be treated as a project within the larger PMO reengineering initiative. This ensures that the objectives of change management in ensuring organizational-wide acceptance of the new PMO processes are attained. The Deploy phase can be broadly divided onto the following sub-phases (4 Ds), in order to be able to meaningfully manage and deploy the change.

- Delineate
- Define
- Disburse
- Defend

Following the 4Ds process to implement a change, ensures that a powerful, clear, shared vision for change is implemented and percolated throughout the organization.

Most of the resistance to a BPR implementation, stems from the fear of layoffs, as most BPR projects usually project savings from down-sizing an organization, as a quick-win for the BPR project in lieu of the actual far-reaching strategic advantages that a real BPR effort brings. In fact, a properly executed BPR exercise will "right-size" the organization and result in added roles, as staff responsibilities become more organized and defined, more often than not, requiring additional people to do work.

Delineate

The driver for change, as envisioned by the senior management must first be defined in the form of a story that is able to portray the end stage of the change in layman terms. The delineate stage comprises of laying out the activities required to define this end state in a manner that is both articulate and fits the needs of the organization undergoing the change. This stage also defines the organizational resources that are committed to helping the BPR team with the change management activities. The committed organizational resources, nominated as "Change Agents", push for transformation within each of their departments. The PMO manager , is nominated the "change champion" and leads the "change agents" in their endeavor. The change champion also works closely with the BPR team in creating material for the awareness campaign that fits the style and thinking of the organization. The change manager helps secure time from the leadership to participate in creating campaign material and a road map for implementing this change. The road map is set-up with campaigns with increasing amounts of intensity. At the beginning of the BPR program, campaigns may be limited to posters and other passive marketing material, advertising the progress on the BPR program and a countdown announcing the arrival of a reformed PMO. Intriguing questions could potentially be posted at strategic place in the organization most frequented by staff, such as at communal areas.

Examples questions could be:

"Are you delivering value through your projects?"

"Is your project resource-hungry?"

These questions could arouse the curiosity of the staff who then follow the campaigns more intensely hoping to satisfy their inquisitiveness. As the BPR program progresses, the change management activities can be ramped up to include targeted workshops, Q&A sessions and talks.

The BPR team could also use the expertise of a professional visual design company to create high-impact marketing materials. Irrespective of the approach taken, a crystallized set of benefits must be articulated periodically to the organization to keep the momentum and anticipation going.

Instances where extensive involvements of the change champion or change agents are required, are noted, planned and their agreement obtained in advance. The key to effectively garnering change agent support lies in identifying those stakeholders who are most affected by the existing state of affairs and those who would benefit the most by the new operating model. The support and effort from change agents must be enthusiastic, and not something done due to organizational mandates. The energy demonstrated by the change agents must be contagious and must be able to permeate the thick walls of persistence that usually resist change.

The distribution of the change agents must be suited to meet the needs of the organization. For a centralized PMO, that services a network of organizations, the change agents must be represented in each of the branches and a decentralized approach to change management must be taken.

The change plan must factor into account, key stakeholders who are or never were proponents of the BPR program. These stakeholders are usually ones who perform legacy processes and have usually spent a significant amount of time in the organization. A tailored approach to communicating with each opposing stakeholder must be defined and executed. The BPR team could assist each of the change agents in demonstrating quantifiable facts and figures to win the support of these stakeholders. At the same time, the BPR team must understand that winning the support of all the stakeholders in an organization is never the intent of change management, but rather the approach should be to win the support of a significant portion of the stakeholders in an organization. There will always exist some migration between the supporting and non-supporting camps after the new processes take effect.

The "defend" phase must be able to ensure that this migration is positive. The belief that the proposed change is beneficial, is usually at its peak when the actual change management activities are in progress and the recommendation is that the BPR team takes full advantage of this state, to ensure quick and lasting transformation.

The BPR team also incorporates lessons learnt from previous implementation exercises in the same organization, especially from those, who have experienced prior organization-wide transformations. The resistance to change is lesser, for those organizations who have experienced prior beneficial transformations. Conversely, the BPR team will face heightened resistance to change especially in those organizations which have had one or more failed transformation efforts in their history. The author has had the experience of successfully reengineering a PMO, which had 2 prior reengineering attempts that failed. In situations such as these, the BPR team might find themselves having to use extensive and often creative measures to convince the organization that curative change is beneficial.

The delineate phase also ensures that change management activities inculcate the values of the "to-be" culture into the organization. The Utopian PMO extolls a culture of reporting, learning and documentation. Change agents and the change champion must promulgate these values through workshops and other planned activities. Practicing project managers and other related roles must be allocated time to attend and learn from these highly beneficial workshops.

The first batch of workshops is limited to a hand-picked team of practitioners who will be using these processes as a part of their daily work. Members of this pilot team include project managers, program managers and PMO analysts. The selection of members for this team is made under the recommendation of the PMO manager. Any feedback on the processes obtained at this stage is passed on to the BPR team, who after extensive rationalization may amend the reengineered processes and modify supporting documentation. The new processes, if aligned to those suggested in the previous section of the book, are automatically aligned to leading practice for project management, the PMBoK®. Hence any suggestions *may* only be superficial and not integral to the core working of the process. The BPR team must also ensure that the suggestions made are not an attempt to circumvent the controls built into each of the processes.

During these workshops, process owners are identified and each process owner is assigned one or more processes from the framework to own and manage. Going forward, the process owner is made responsible for understanding the processes under their remit, both in theory and practice. They are also trained to be able to provide subject matter expertise on the process and be able to provide training on the process themselves whilst constantly watching out for improvements to the process. Among the new PMO roles defined, is a PMO Maturity Assessor role. The process owners report on the performance of the processes by measuring process-related metrics, which are aggregated by the PMO maturity assessor to come up with a maturity level for the PMO. This is discussed further in the next section.

Once the BPR team is satisfied, by observing the performance of the pilot team, that the reengineered processes have no reasonable hope of failing in operation and they are fairly impermeable, the final set of processes are frozen and the workshops continue for the rest of the organization

The workshops could be planned in such a way that they are repetitive, enabling staff to attend these programs based on their availability and work load. A time-table for the workshops published ahead of time helps encourage participation. Also, the nature of these workshops must be participant-led as opposed to a traditional instructor-led approach. Role playing and discussing real-life scenarios are recommended methods ensuring the new model is properly understood. Simulation of mock projects with a step-by-step run through of the remodeled processes can simplify understanding and enhance acceptance. If a new PMIS system is a part of the BPR project, training on the new system is provided along with process training and the extensive use of the PMIS in each of the new processes is highlighted.

The workshops must concurrently run at different levels, allowing participants to choose a workshop based on their knowledge levels and current roles. The objective of these workshops must be to close any gaps in knowledge between the current methodology and the "to-be" methodology and in the process bring all resources in the organization to the same level of understanding.

The workshops are designed such that any person attending these trainings can choose a path that enables them to learn progressively more and more about a topic until they possess knowledge on these processes, at a level that is sufficient to help them perform their job better and easier.

To Sum up:

- Change management is a critical activity in the BPR program, requiring a defined approach for successfully migrating the organization from the present model to the reengineered model. The first phase of change management for a BPR exercise focuses primarily on process workshops.

- A specific time-period is set for conducting the workshops depending on the volume of training and the BPR team's assessment of the organization's current state. A detailed time-table containing the proposed workshop details is published in advance.

- Concurrent workshops for developing expertise in the different areas of project management are organized (Viz. Risk, Scope, Cost, etc.).

- Each area in project management has two levels of workshops, the basic and the advanced levels, allowing attendees to choose the workshop(s) that would benefit them the most profoundly.

The delineate phase can be considered a success if:

- This phase, through its myriad activities, changes legacy beliefs/traditions and sets expectations for the upcoming change.

- It produces a unique customized change management approach that transforms existing skills to those required to operate and run the Utopian PMO.

- The BPR team successfully paves way for the expected behavior of the organization, one that is stepped in learning, documentation and controls.

- The leadership of the organization is receptive to change and they unanimously champion the Utopian PMO, extolling the benefits and virtues at available opportunities.

- Coaching and mentoring is adopted internally, process owners are available beyond the workshop duration to help with any process related queries.

- Change agents, at their respective locations, are available to answer any queries on the new PMO and help the organization quell the last bits of change resistance.

- The existing PMO gives up its individualistic nature and is fully apprised of the cohesive, team-dynamic, operating model that is to be implemented shortly.

- Any final environmental constraints that are a deterrent to the deployment of a Utopian PMO are ironed out.

Throughout this phase, the BPR team, the change champion and the change agents meet periodically to change the approach and strategy as well as share insights into departments and stakeholders needing a further push. A definite date for the cut-over to the new operating model is planned based on the findings established in this phase and other prerequisites essential for the cut-over, are planned in detail. The process owners, change agents, led by the change champion form a peer-driven internal change team, who carry on the momentum till the cut-over is complete and beyond.

Define

This sub-phase, defines that the various prerequisites for deploying the Utopian PMO and ensures that they are in place before cutting over to the new operating model. The framework of the Utopian PMO, as defined in the first chapter, rests not only on efficient processes but also on having the requisite human capital, which include the requisite number of staff with the accompanying skills required to perform their roles. The Utopian PMO also possesses opportunities for staff to create their own career path based on their growth and learning. This sub-phase also defines key skills required to establish a Utopian PMO with an environment that is conducive for improving employee engagement, retention, business processes and higher ROIs by staffing the Utopian PMO with leadership:

- That supports and encourages "self-learning" through on-demand learning portals.

- That supports experimentation, embraces change and openness to new ideas.

- That provides time for documentation and reflection of thoughts.

- That shows an appreciation for differences in opinion.

Also defined as a part of this sub-phase, is the new Utopian PMOs operating model which defines a clear scope and generic metrics for measurement which can be adapted to suit the needs of any kind of organization that wishes to deploy a Utopian PMO.

PMO Staffing –The PMO Manager

The leadership position for the Utopian PMO is the PMO manager, a powerhouse, who wields high strategic and executive power. This position, reporting to the CEO, must be filled by a person whose leadership skills reign supreme. A Utopian PMO, led by a resource with poor leadership skills will stall and catastrophically derail all the reengineering efforts put in by the organization. It would be inadvisable to move an existing staff member to fill this position purely based on their availability in the organization, unless the candidate expresses demonstrable leadership and diplomacy. The ideal candidate must focus on talent management, resource management, benefits realization tracking, strategic alignment and risk management, all the core virtues of a Utopian PMO. It is especially important that the Utopian PMO manager possesses significant risk management experience and the ability to solve problems at the core by devising lasting solutions. Most importantly, the PMO manager must have the ability, confidence and charisma to influence people and get the organization to comply with the PMO's mandated processes and also win the trust of the organization while nullifying misconceptions.

Key Functions:

- Establish the PMO organization structure, hiring and managing staffing requirements in line with strategic objectives.

- Oversee the delegation of work to Project Managers, Program Managers, and PMO Analysts.

- Set annual performance targets for individuals, the team, conducts performance reviews of resources and improves the maturity of the PMO.

- Provide ongoing motivation, coaching, guidance, feedback and mentoring support to the team.

- Manage the workload of program managers, project managers and PMO analysts in the PMO and help remove obstacles to their success.

- Manage third party vendor agreements.

- Coordinate and conduct post-implementation reviews of projects / programs.

Pre-requisites:

- 10-20 years of progressive project / program / portfolio management experience.

- Post-graduate degree or equivalent.

- Ph.D. in project management strongly preferred.

- One or more of the following: PMP® / PgMP® / PfMP/ PMI-RMP® / PMI-SP® / CUEX Certified.

The PMO Analyst

The team of PMO analysts forms the delivery arms of the PMO. They are represented in each and every project / program that the organization undertakes and provides coaching and mentoring services to the PMO while helping projects finish on time by supporting the project team in the development of plans, execution of the project and monitoring activities. However, a PMO Analyst's primary responsibilities are to track & monitor progress, co-ordinate delivery dates, maintain financial controls and project management information systems. The PMO analyst also aids in conducting organizational studies and recommends process improvement suggestions. Besides providing project related support, a PMO analyst also helps the PMO in delivering key functions, such as the ability to provide ad-hoc reports. [Ref: PMO Process #6: Reporting PMO06R] and conduct phase gate tests.

Key functions:

- Provide accurate advice to the project teams , to enable them set the overall strategy and delivery.

- Deliver strategy and policies set by the PMO and implement decisions taken by the PMO quickly; and within a clear performance framework.

- Handle PMO governance requests and ad-hoc report requests.

- Take personal responsibility for the delivery of timely and appropriate governance & risk decisions.

- Manage performance effectively, attending all appropriate governance meetings and providing regular performance reports to the PMO.

- Provide timely, accurate and clear advice based on evidence and accurate data.

- Ensure that the PMO Manager is kept informed about risks and operational issues which might affect the strategy of the organization.

- Manage all PMO audits, ensuring completion of agreed actions within due dates to facilitate successful closure.

- Manage a log of project deliverables including actually documenting the deliverables on the PMIS.

- Identify, produce and publicize improvements to the PMO processes and frameworks.

Pre-requisites:

- 3-5 years of project support experience.

- Under-graduate degree or equivalent.

- One or more of the following: CAPM®/ PMP®/ PgMP® / PMI-RMP® / PMI-SP® / CUPA1/ CUPA2.

The Program Manager

One of the most important aspects to hiring a program manager lies in understanding that a program manager is not just an experienced project manager. Program management requires a different set of skills, that are more governance and less operational in nature than that of a project manager's. A program manager is assigned as soon as a program comes to life and is responsible for taking the program all the way to completion by overseeing day-to-day activities including the following key functions:

- Providing governance and leadership for the entire program and its constituent project by ensuring regular reviews and accountability in the management of (sub)projects, stakeholders and suppliers.

- Planning the program and identifying component projects.

- Aligning the component projects to the objectives of the program.

- Multi-tasking activities between the component projects while providing the necessary integration and prioritization between tasks.

- Using inter-personal skills to manage the resources on the program / constituent projects whilst ensuring that component projects are not deprived of their individuality.

Pre-requisites:

- 7-10 years of progressive program management experience.

- Post-graduate degree or equivalent.

- One or more of the following: PgMP®/ PMP® / CUPGM.

The Project Manager

The project manager in a Utopian PMO is the final link in the chain that delivers strategy for an organization. The strategic objectives processed through the various steps in a Utopian PMO, finally materialize as strategic outputs. The project manager helps maximize the achievement of strategic success by planning and managing a project's activities.

Key functions:

- Collect a comprehensive and detailed set of requirements from all identified stakeholders and translate those project deliverables.

- Accomplish human resource objectives by recruiting, selecting, orienting, training, assigning, scheduling, coaching, counseling, and disciplining employees; communicating job expectations;

planning, monitoring, appraising, and reviewing job contributions; planning and reviewing compensation actions; enforcing PMO policies and procedures.

- Achieve operational objectives by contributing information and project status reports to feed strategic plans and reviews; preparing, completing and implementing project management plans, identifying trends in quality and implementing change.

- Meet financial objectives of the project by forecasting requirements; preparing a budget; scheduling expenditures; analyzing variances; initiating corrective actions.

Pre-requisites:

- 10-15 years of progressive project management experience

- Post-graduate degree or equivalent

- One or more of the following: PMP® / PgMP® / PfMP®/ PMI-RMP® / PMI-SP® / CUPM1/ CUPM2

The PMO Maturity Analyst

The PMO maturity analyst is a role unique to the Utopian PMO, who is responsible to ensure that the Utopian PMO is constantly on the path of improvement. Since the function of this role is seldom full-time, it is suggested that a senior PMO analyst be assigned the responsibilities of this role in addition to the regular duties of a PMO analyst. The Utopian PMO's maturity model is fully explained in the following chapter and the different progressive levels that the Utopian PMO could potentially mature into are defined. To quickly summarize, the first phase of the maturity model drives a PMO to take the onus to develop its capability to what has defined as one having a highly desirable or near perfect qualities, a Utopian PMO. Once a

PMO reaches the zenith in this aspect, the maturity improvement model pushes for continued delivery excellence by assessing the number of years in existence and the number of projects delivered whilst in Utopian operating mode.

Operating continually at the Utopian levels for extended periods, whilst delivering strategic projects adds further points to the PMO's maturity, increasing its position in the classification levels. This model is primarily self-sustinent in the fact that it does not require external information to help in its maturity assessment.

To successfully execute maturity assessments, the PMO maturity analyst plays a key role by performing the following functions:

- Assess and define current maturity levels of the PMO.

- Define a roadmap to reach the penultimate and subsequently the ultimate levels of PMO maturity.

- Measure, assess and improve on the 9 strategic Utopian PMO areas of operation, based on the scoring levels defined in the following chapters.

- Work with the PMO process owners on improving the processes as well the alignment with other processes in the project and program management framework

Pre-requisites:

- 5-7 years of PMO analyst experience

- Post-graduate degree or equivalent

- One or more of the following: PMP® / PgMP® / PfMP®/ PMI-RMP® / PMI-SP®/ CUMA/CUPA2

PMO Delivery - Skills Assessment Framework

The program manager and the project manager are two delivery roles described above that the Utopian PMO relies on, for achieving delivery success. Each delivery resource possesses delivery skills at various levels of proficiency, the measurement of which is based on the parameters defined by the Successful Delivery Skills (SDS)® framework defined by the UK Cabinet Office. Each skill can have one of the following proficiency levels:

Level 0 – Not Tested

Level 1 – Awareness: Describes someone who is dependent on others for direction, is learning the skill and when facing something new or unusual has to refer to procedures, manuals, other team members etc., for guidance. The assesse may only ever need awareness of particular skills, or may be gaining experience in the skill. It is important to note that attending training does not automatically mean that the assesse's proficiency level will increase. Once the assesse has received training, reinforcement of the learning is done by using the skills. As people learn at different rates, there is no set time limit for the assesse's level to increase.

Level 2 Practitioner: Describes someone who can cope with standard problems/common situations, is competent at day-to-day application of the skill, and is able to present concepts, information and solutions. At this level the assesse can deal with most standard problems and will need to refer to an expert for non-standard issues and problems. The assesse will still be using a variety of development activities to increase their experience and proficiency level e.g. reading manuals, white papers etc. and on the job training. The assesse will still need go on training courses and these will probably be at an advanced level. The assesse will probably stay at this level for some time.

Level 3 – Expert: Describes someone who can cope with unusual/non-standard problems and issues, is aware of alternative options and approaches to situations, can guide or advise others in this skill and is able to look ahead and anticipate. Training alone will not take the assesse to an expert level. It is experience in the job, as well as using the skill and other development activities that will develop the assesse's proficiency level. Not only is the assesse capable but confident in applying the skill in ordinary and unusual situations. Others will seek the assesse out for advice and may involve them in coaching/mentoring activities.

Level 4 – Innovator: Describes someone who is seen as setting an example to others, is a recognized expert and visionary in the field, provides broad guidance to others in the application of their skills to related areas, is a 'thought leader' in their field (shows advanced thinking, develops innovative approaches) and stretches others' thinking and challenges them to excel.

Program Manager's Skill Assessment Framework

The program mangers skills can be broadly broken down into the following key areas:

- Program management techniques/methodologies
- Program definition
- Program governance
- Managing the change process

For each key area, the skills and the proficiency level required are:

Program management techniques/methodologies – Required Level 4

The program manager is responsible, on behalf of the program sponsor, for successful delivery of the new capability. The role requires the effective coordination of the projects and their interdependencies, and any risks and other issues that may arise. As the program is implemented, changes to policy, strategy, or infrastructure may have an impact right across the constituent project portfolio, or across programs. The program manager is responsible for the overall integrity and coherence of the program, and develops and maintains the program environment to support each individual projects within it - typically through the PMO

Program definition – Required Level 4

Defining a program is a crucial process. It is where the detailed definition for the program is done and it provides the basis for deciding whether to proceed with the program or not. The initial justification and case for the program has to be developed into a more rigorous view of its outcomes and how the organization needs to change to deliver them.

The program brief is used as the starting point for refining the program's objectives and targets into the program definition, which defines what the program is going to do, how it going to do it, who is involved and the business case for the program. The governance framework is developed, which defines the strategies for quality, stakeholders, issues, risks, resources and planning and control. Plans are developed providing information on the resources, dependencies and timescales for delivery and realization of benefits.

Program governance - Required Level 4

Governance is concerned with accountability and responsibilities; it describes how the organization is directed and controlled. In particular, governance is concerned with policies - the frameworks and boundaries established for making decisions within the program by the PMO, and the context and constraints within which decisions are taken. The program manager's arrangements for governance will form an integral part of the wider arrangements for the organization, management and policies of the organization as a whole; i.e. governance will need to be consistent with the wider governance issues in the organization.

Managing changes - Required Level 4

The skill requirements of a program manager with regards to change management are two- fold. One is to prevent unnecessary changes to the objectives of the program and second is the change management requirements of the deliverables of the program. Both concepts of change management are only unified only by the term but both have differing objectives. The first type of change management requires the efficient use of the PMOs governance and change control processes to manage and control change. The second kind of change refers to the program manager's ability to perform adequate change management activities in the organization to create an acceptance of the program's deliverables within the organization.

Project Manager's Skill Assessment Framework

Skill Set	Level	Specific Skill Requirements
Business case management	Level 3	- general principles and processes for developing a business case - idea generation techniques - analysis and evaluation techniques
Requirements management	Level 4	- clarify requirements and prepare an outline strategy for agreement with stakeholders - verify that specified activities/resources will deliver agreed requirements - validate requirements against delivery

224

of project outputs

- ensure that any assumptions on which estimates are based are clearly stated and communicated

Planning and control	Level 4	- verify that sufficient information on the project exists to prepare an appropriate work/product breakdown structure

- derive the activities required to achieve project outputs, to the level of accuracy and detail needed for scheduling and resourcing

- produce a work breakdown structure which meets the specified requirements for the project

- verify that schedules are formatted to facilitate shared understanding and implementation

- identify critical and sub-critical paths and include adequate contingency to reflect risks

- monitor progress against the schedule, manage exceptions and re-schedule as appropriate.

PMO regulatory requirements	Level 5	- Understand the Utopian PMO's regulatory requirements for each process
		- Comply with and produce the requisite project management deliverables
		- Participate in voluntary and involuntary project health checks
		- Create timely and accurate reports to feed into organizational reports
		- Provide feedback on suppliers upon completion of contracts
Risk management	Level 5	- identify all perceived and relevant areas of risk and their implications for the project
		- identify roles and responsibilities for risk management
		- access sources of information and advice
		- analyze, evaluate and prioritize risks and potential consequences. Develop and recommend response options for reducing risk to a level of acceptability
		- influence monitor and control the risk environment

Quality management	Level 4	- verify whether quality assurance procedures are appropriate and sufficient to meet requirements
		- ensure that commitment to quality assurance procedures is obtained from those responsible for applying them
		- ensure data is gathered and recorded in accordance with agreed quality assurance procedures
		- initiate effective remedial action to correct the causes of non-conformance and limit their effect
		- produce and maintain records in line with requirements needed for quality audits.
Procurement management	Level 3	- identify elements of the project to be procured through contractual agreements and confirm these with interested parties
		- identify and evaluate key objectives and criteria for the procurement strategy and communicate with stakeholders
		- verify that the specifications or work/product breakdown structure for

the project are suitable to allow outsourcing to proceed

- prepare tender lists for elements of the project to be contracted out, that are sufficient to attract competitive bids from contractors capable of meeting specified project objectives

- conduct research to determine the means/options for procuring resources

- evaluate identified options against constraints and criteria and select the preferred options for further analysis

Creating and leading a project team	Level 5	- create the appropriate organizational structure for a project

- ensure delegation of work is consistent with achieving the project objectives, in keeping with the policies and values of the organization

- clearly define responsibilities and limits of authority of the team

- where team resources are insufficient, reach agreement with relevant people on the prioritization of work or re-allocation of resources

- provide clear feedback that is based on

objective assessment of their performance against agreed objectives, ensuring feedback acknowledges achievements

- give feedback that provides team members with constructive suggestions and encouragement for improving future performance against work and development objectives

- present feedback in a way that retains respect for the individual and the need for confidentiality, giving the team opportunities to respond and contribute to how they could improve performance in the future

Acting as a change agent	Level 4	- create and maintain project issue logs and requests for change
		- understand human aspects and factors influencing change
		- Lead project change management along with the PMO Analyst
Performance management	Level 4	- evaluate performance management processes against project objectives

Project closure and handover	Level 4	- define, record and agree the state of the project at handover with the relevant stakeholders
		- verify that the project's objectives have been achieved to the agreed schedule, costs, and quality criteria
		- ensure that all deliverables are handed over according to agreed procedures
		- resolve any hand-over problems in a way which maintains an effective working relationship with the sponsor

PMO Career Path for a PMO Analyst

PMO Analyst to PMO Maturity Analyst

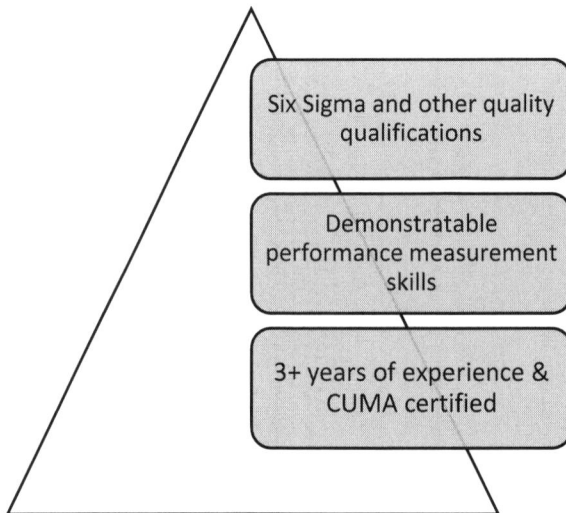

Six Sigma and other quality qualifications

Demonstratable performance measurement skills

3+ years of experience & CUMA certified

PMO Analyst to project manager

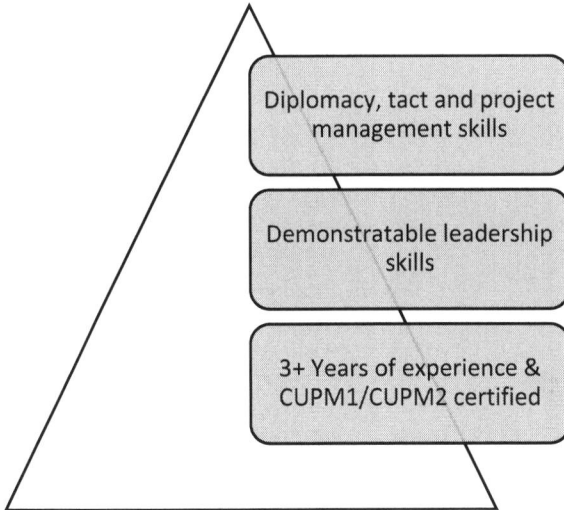

Diplomacy, tact and project management skills

Demonstratable leadership skills

3+ Years of experience & CUPM1/CUPM2 certified

PMO Career Path for a PMO Maturity Analyst

PMO Maturity Analyst to project manager

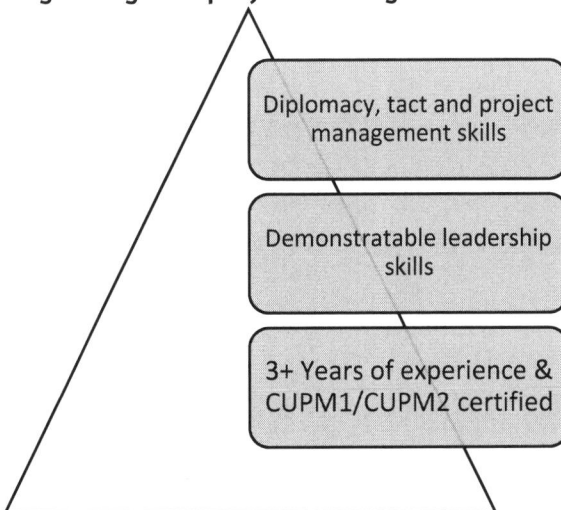

Diplomacy, tact and project management skills

Demonstratable leadership skills

3+ Years of experience & CUPM1/CUPM2 certified

PMO Career Path for a Project Manager

Project manager to program manager

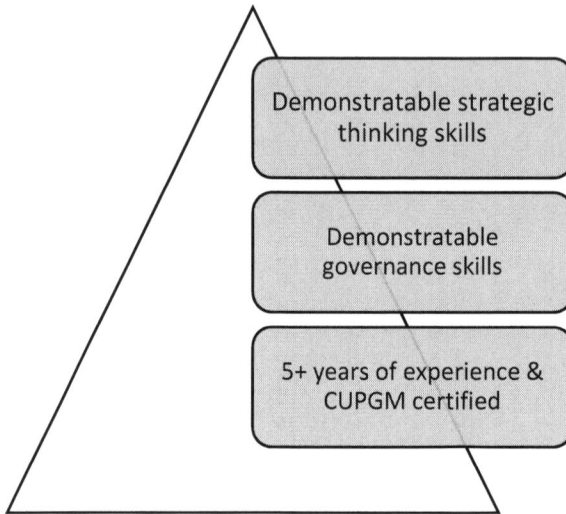

Demonstratable strategic thinking skills

Demonstratable governance skills

5+ years of experience & CUPGM certified

Project manager to PMO manager

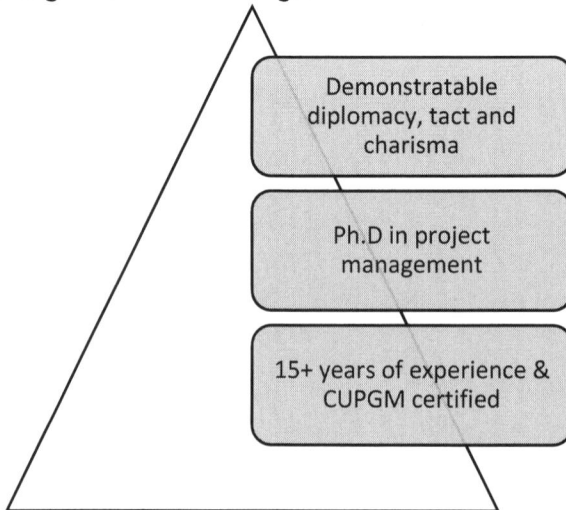

Demonstratable diplomacy, tact and charisma

Ph.D in project management

15+ years of experience & CUPGM certified

PMO Career Path for a Program Manager

Program manager to PMO manager

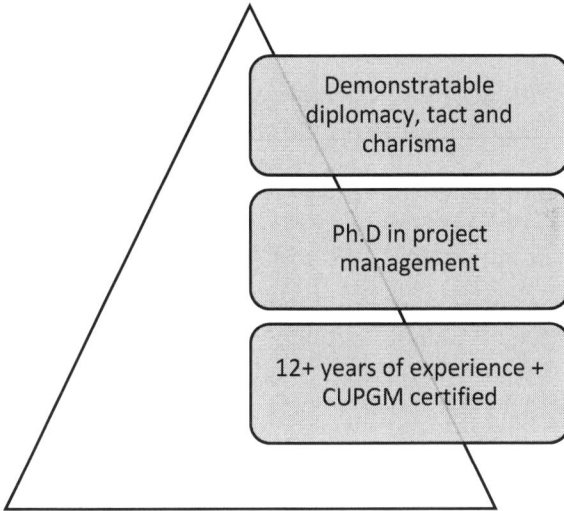

Utopian PMO Staffing Levels

PMO Manager: The Utopian PMO manager is a senior, strategic , C-level, position, reporting directly to the CEO and is staffed by *one* PMO manager who manages all responsibilities for that role. If the situation requires, a senior program manager can assist the PMO manager in shouldering some of the routine decision making responsibilities, during periods of elevated engagement levels. However, the ultimate accountability for the functioning, delivery and governance of the Utopian PMO rests with the singular PMO manager.

Program Manager: The Utopian PMO prides itself on providing superior program delivery support. A program, with its collection of interdependent projects, requires a focused effort on managing the program and its constituent projects whilst assigning priorities to conflicting requirements. To provide the extended dedication that is required to manage such an effort, a 1:1 ratio is recommended when assigning programs to program managers.

Project Manager: The Utopian PMO's superior delivery of projects relies on extensive controls and documentation requirements which in-turn calls for a project manager's complete involvement and support. To be able to deliver the requirements of the Utopian PMO's project delivery frameworks, the following ratios of projects to project managers is recommended based on the classification of the project.

Small Projects : The assumption is that the project management activities may take around 20% of the total project effort for a project classified as "small". If the 20% effort equates to the number of working hours per week (usually 35 hours/week) then this one project that becomes a full time job for the project manager. If 20% is more than 35-40 hours then the project manager's effort is supplemented by adding PMO analysts. If this 20% is less than 35 hours/week then the project manager will have time to take on more projects.

Strategic Projects: To be able to deliver strategic projects with the intensity and project excellence requirements of the Utopian PMO, a project to project manager ratio of 1:1 is recommended

PMO Analyst: The Utopian PMO relies extensively on the PMO analyst role to be able to perform key governance and planning activities on a project / program. This role dedicates time extensively to a project and is responsible for supporting the project manager in the project's day-to-day management. To be able to facilitate this level of support and dedication, the following ratios of projects to PMO analysts is recommended based on the classification of the project.

Programs: The assumption is that the program governance and documentation activities may take around 50% of a PMO analyst's effort for a process intensive framework such the Utopian PMO. The higher assignment percentage for programs is due to the additional governance support that a program inherently requires. Thus, the ratio of programs that can be assigned to a PMO analyst is recommended to be approximately 2:1

Small Projects: The assumption is that the project governance and documentation activities may take around 30% of a PMO analyst's effort for a process intensive framework such the Utopian PMO's. Thus, the ratio of small projects that can be assigned to a PMO analyst is recommended to be approximately 3:1

Strategic Projects: To be able to deliver strategic projects with the intensity and project excellence requirements of this kind of a PMO, a PMO analyst expends approximately 50% of the available effort. Thus, the ratio of strategic projects that can be assigned to a PMO analyst is recommended to be approximately 2:1

PMO Analysts / PMO Maturity Analysts with shared workload: PMO Analysts who have taken up some of the project manager's workload or have their time distributed between small, strategic projects and or PMO maturity assessment roles, the recommended workload distribution is as per the following model:

$$1 - \left[\left[2 - \eta_{eff} \right] \left[\frac{Pgm}{2} + \frac{P(sm)}{3} + \frac{P(st)}{2} + \frac{PM(st)}{3} + \frac{PM(sm)}{4} + P_{mat} \right] \right]$$

Where:
- η_{eff} is the **efficiency** of the resource [assessed qualitatively / quantitatively]
- $P(sm)$ is the **number of small projects** assigned to the PMO resource

- $P(st)$ is the **number of strategic projects** assigned to the PMO resource
- $PM(st)$ is the **number of strategic projects** to which the PMO analyst is supporting the project manager
- $PM(sm)$ is the **number of small projects** to which the PMO analyst is supporting the project manager
- P_{mat} =0.3 if the PMO analyst also has the responsibilities of a PMO Maturity analyst.

For example:

A PMO resource with a subjectively assessed efficiency of 80% (0.8) is assigned to one (1) strategic project and one (1) small project and no PMO maturity analyst responsibilities. The available capacity of this resource is calculated by substituting in the equation:

Available capacity:

$$1 - \left[[2 - 0.8] \left[\frac{0}{2} + \frac{1}{3} + \frac{1}{2} + \frac{0}{3} + \frac{0}{4} + 0 \right] \right] = 0$$

From the analysis, it can be inferred that the PMO analyst **is fully allocated and is not available** for further allocation based on estimated capabilities and present assignments

Another example:

A PMO resource with a subjectively assessed efficiency of 90% (0.9) is assigned the responsibilities of a PMO maturity analyst only. The available capacity of this resource is calculated by substituting in the equation:

Available capacity:

$$1 - \left[[2 - 0.9] \left[\frac{0}{2} + \frac{0}{3} + \frac{0}{2} + \frac{0}{3} + \frac{0}{4} + 0.3 \right] \right] = 0.67$$

From the analysis, it can be inferred that the PMO analyst **has a further 67% availability** for allocation based on his estimated capabilities and present assignments. The remaining capacity can be allocated to any combination of small, strategic projects or programs.

Re-issuing the PMO Charter

Irrespective of how the PMO has operated thus far, establishing a Utopian PMO requires an organizational mandate for the PMO to exist. This mandate is set-forth in the form of a PMO charter. The PMO charter provides authority for the PMO to function efficiently in the organization and an authority to commit organizational resources to achieve its goals. The PMO Charter is the authorization mandate for the PMO to exist

A Utopian PMO with its wide-spectrum of powers, especially needs a well-defined PMO charter to function as per its design specifications. Such a charter must, at a minimum contain the following elements:

- An executive summary
- PMO business need
- Services provisioned by the PMO
- PMO mission
- PMO guiding principles
- PMO metrics
- PMO stakeholders
- PMO resourcing
- Glossary

Each of the elements in a PMO charter must contain the following in detail:

Executive Summary: Describes an overview of the purpose, objectives, staffing, leadership, and critical success factors of the PMO organization. The name and title of the executive sponsor, who designated the creation of the PMO is explicitly stated.

PMO Business Need: Describes the current organizational pain points and the areas where the current PMO is inadequate such as those described in the business case for a Utopian PMO. Reasons could include the current PMO not having:

- Defined processes
- Organizational presence
- Involvement in the organization's project management community
- KPIs defined for all of its processes
- Benefits measurement team in place
- Periodic reporting in place
- Supplier management function
- Business relationship function

Services: Describes the portfolio of services that the proposed PMO is expected to provide, including future dates for services that have a deferred implementation date. The services offered may be of two kinds: strategic and operational and both are shown separately.

Strategic Services	Availability Date
Governance and Strategic Alignment	Immediate
Process Maturity Management	Immediate
Delivery Management	Immediate
Resource Management	Immediate
Quality Management , Compliance & Maturity	Immediate
Benefits Management	When available
Reporting	Immediate
Supplier Management	Immediate
Business Relationship Management	Immediate

Specific Operational Services	Availability Date
Project Delivery Management	Immediate
Program Delivery Management	Immediate
Risk Management	Immediate
Communications Management	Immediate
Training	Immediate
PMO Resource Management	Immediate

PMO Mission: Describes the high-level mission of the PMO of being a strategic engine, consuming organizational resources on one end and efficiently and effectively delivering strategic projects on the other with minimal operational losses.

PMO guiding principles: Describes the core values of the PMO. The Utopian PMO has the following as its values that guides everything that this PMO does:

- Deliver Success: Ensure that every delivery entrusted to the PMO is a strategic success.

- Support Excellence: Ensure that every activity undertaken by the PMO, strives to achieve excellence and all necessary steps to achieve this is taken.

- Train Accomplishment: Ensure that all strengths and ambitions of this PMO are percolated to the organization through effective training programs.

PMO metrics: Describes the metrics and KPIs that the PMO uses to define success. For every strategic service that the PMO offers, KPIs are defined and measured. A detailed list of KPIs for each strategic service is given in the following chapter of this book.

PMO Stakeholders: Describes the key stakeholders of the PMO. For the Utopian PMO, the stakeholders are at a minimum divided into two groups:

Executive Stakeholders

- The CEO / Organizational Head - Sponsor
- PMO Manager, directly reporting to the CEO
- Program Managers
- Project Managers
- PMO Analysts
- PMO Maturity Analysts

Customer Stakeholders

- Executive Directors / VPs
- Division Managers
- Rest of the organization

PMO Resourcing: Describes the current PMO resources, staffing plans, resource acquisition plans, recruitment plans to staff the Utopian PMO with the required roles / number of resources.

Glossary: Contains a list of terms and acronyms used in the charter.

Deploy

The BPR team at this point has successfully achieved the following:

- Identified and defined the need for a Utopian PMO.
- Presented and defended an elaborate business case deliberating the organization's need for a Utopian PMO.
- Studied the current operating model.
- Created exceptional process aligned to leading practices.
- Executed change management and marketing campaigns.
- And finally created a new charter extolling the upcoming PMO's virtues and benefits to the organization.

At this stage, if everything has proceeded correctly, the organization is at a stage, where it is highly receptive to having a strategic Utopian PMO implemented and operated. During the deploy phase of the BPR program, the final checks are made before the Utopian PMO is finally deployed into operation. The final check before deployment consists of a checklist-type assessment to determine if the pre-requisites to facilitate a successful cut-over to the new PMO are in place.

PMO Readiness Assessment

The readiness check for the PMO consists of ensuring the following domains of the organization are ready for this change.

- Technology

- Processes

- People

- Policies

- Strategy

Technology Readiness:

- The readiness check for technology consists of ensuring that any PMIS system upgrades that are planned as a part of the reengineering process are complete.

- Checks for IT system readiness may include system testing, stress testing, pilot testing or parallel testing. Once the new PMIS system is tested, the data stored on the "legacy" system is migrated to the new system.

- A detailed check of the migrated data is carried out to ensure errors whilst migrating have not crept in.

- Appropriate project workspaces have been created for the projects to start documenting extensively based on the new model.

- Appropriate user access rights to workspaces and reports have been provided based on the information security principles of "least privilege" and "need-to-know".

- Process workflow, escalation and flow of reports are aligned to meet the new flows specified by the reengineered processes.

Process Readiness:

- Specified templates, guideline documents and standard operating procedures are defined for each of the processes and empty slots for storing them on the PMIS are made for each project workspace.

- Any specific criteria used to make decisions on any of the processes (E.g.: Criteria to segregate small and strategic projects – PMO01GSA process) is defined explicitly.

- The interfaces between processes are checked for break-free latching and smooth hand-over.

- A pilot run of the processes are done with a few hand-picked projects of varying complexities.

- Feed-back received during the pilot run of the processes is incorporated and changes incorporated.

People Readiness:

- A skill inventory is carried out of the existing PMO staff to assess their suitability for the role requirements of the reengineered processes. Testing and assessment of the framework can be carried out internally, or if the organization's PMO fully aligns to the framework prescribed in this book, by using the testing and assessment services available at **www.theutopianpmo.com** that tests real-world application of the Utopian PMO's process frameworks and provides for different levels of certification for each of the PMOs roles.

- Roles missing resources are filled via acquisition, re-assignment of roles or assigning shared responsibilities.

- Surplus resources beyond the current and near future requirements of the re-engineered PMO are re-organized to other functional areas (if possible) or released.

- PMO staff are appraised of their new roles and responsibilities, HR contracts, remunerations amended and other legal requirements (if any) are satisfied

- The organization's information technology team is on standby to take the legacy systems off-line and is trained to support the new PMIS systems

Policy Readiness:

- The Utopian PMO charter is signed-off authorizing the PMO and explicitly depicting the PMO Manager role as a directly reporting to the CEO / organizational head. The charter is then archived along with other organizational documentation.

- Present projects, programs and initiatives underway are issued change requests to accommodate time and effort required to migrate to the new delivery model. These new change requests, will form the first of those changes to be processed by the Perform Integrated Change Control Process PRJ4.2PICC.

- Vendors and customers are apprised of the imminent changes and initiative-specific actions are undertaken to smoothen the transition and to keep them abreast of the progress.

Strategy Readiness:

- Projects and initiatives which have no business cases are noted and an assessment team is formed to study and understand if a strategic dependency exists for those initiatives to continue. If no compelling case can be proven, they are scrapped. Those that have a strategic purpose have new business cases documented.

- The organization's mission, vision and values are updated to incorporate references to the presence of a strategic engine in the organization.

- The strategic direction is modified to accommodate projects and market spaces which were hitherto out-of-limits for the organization due to the lack of a Utopian PMO.

Cut-over

The final step in the deploy phase is the cut-over to the new PMO operating processes. Once the readiness assessment has been completed and the items specified have been found to exist, a cut-over to the new, reformed way of working is undertaken. There exist two strategies for cut-over, the big bang approach and the phased approach.

Big-bang: In this scenario, all initiatives are required to use the new delivery model as of a particular date. The PMO assesses if any projects in the portfolio can be managed as a program and business cases are created accordingly. Program managers are assigned. Project managers and PMO analysts are assigned projects or take-over existing projects. All existing initiatives are given a specific time period to come into compliance. On a pre-defined date, the Utopian PMO is born into the organization.

Phased Approach: In this scenario, selections of initiatives are required to use the new delivery model as of a particular date. Any initiatives requiring pre-emptive work such as business cases are deferred for migration to the new operating model when ready. However, in this approach too, a final date is mandated by which all initiatives have to have migrated to the new model. Chaos is greatly reduced in this method , however the chance to relapse into the old ways of working, at least temporarily, is also higher in this approach. One or more cut-over dates are specified, if a high number of initiatives are underway in the organization, to allow each of them time to migrate in batches. In this approach, newly hired PMO staffs are given the time and opportunity to get themselves inculcated into the organization, instead of facing chaos on the first few days of work as the case would be in a big-bang migration approach.

The right approach to cut-over depends on the organization and its present environment. The BPR team is encouraged to use the method that is seen as a best fit from their observations of working in the organization thus far. Along with the BPR team's recommendation to the approach is the all-important need to have the approach vetted by the management of the organization being reengineered.

Defend

Any reengineering effort, however well executed, always faces the risk of failing, due to the organization relapsing to the old ways of working. A few reasons why this happens and how they can be avoided are listed below:

Senior management commitment wanes after go-live: Very often a BPR initiative is the brain-child of a newly appointed executive leader. To quickly secure acceptance in an organization, a BPR initiative is proposed, which is quickly forgotten after implementation, as other organizational priorities take over. The organization faces chaos and resistance as soon as the new operating model is unveiled and in the absence of executive management's support, the old methodology quickly takes over and the new methodology is relegated to a bunch of process maps. Often, the BPR team is blamed for a poor attempt at reengineering the organization. Therefore, the constant and undivided attention of the BPR initiative sponsor is mandatory to keep the organization focused on change.

Stakeholders seeking improvements immediately after go-live: As is often the case in any reengineering effort, the productivity is often low in the first few days (or weeks) after deployment of the new model. Only after the processes have been sufficiently incorporated into daily operations and its benefits realized by its practitioners, do the actual benefits materialize. Hence, anyone seeking immediate returns post-BPR, is quickly disappointed and promptly traverses to the camp of non-supporters. Any stakeholders looking for post-BPR improvements must only begin to do so after a minimum period of 90-180 days have elapsed. Employee retention, employee satisfaction and customer satisfaction metrics are often the first to show a rise.

The intensity of change management reduces after go-live: Change management is a continuous exercise and failure to continue activities such as campaigns and workshops quickly bring the intensity down. To counter this from happening, any quick wins that have materialized are broadcast through posters and other appropriate marketing materials. The PMO manager, through carefully coordinated approaches makes the PMO's presence felt and extolls its virtues at appropriate events. Also, onus is on the BPR team to create a culture of learning and curiosity as opposed to creating temporary change. Change agents must continue to play their role to keep the cogs of change in an organization moving, long after the BPR team has left.

Chapter 8
The Post-Deployment Phase

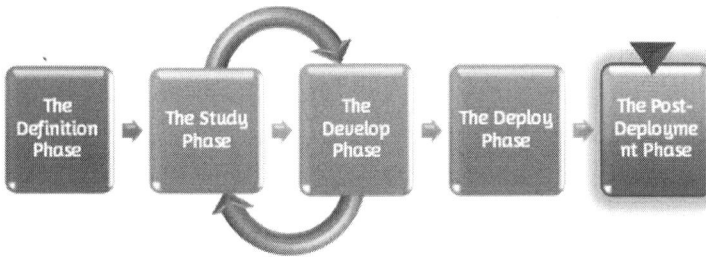

PMO Operational Metrics

After the successful deployment of the Utopian PMO, the post-implementation team runs the PMO in a directive approach, actively managing the projects along with the project managers and the PMO staff. This form of support is the safest and provides a conducive environment for the organization to adopt the newly engineered processes, under the watchful eye of the reengineering team. The post-deployment phase is usually limited to a period of not more than 180-days to enable just enough time for the processes to permeate into the natural flow of work but not long enough that the reengineering team becomes a part of the work-flow, that their subsequent disengagement actually disrupts future process flows.

In forward thinking and organizations highly receptive to change, the post-deployment phase is much lesser or may not exist at all, with the training provided in the deployment phase sufficient to enable the organization to cut-over to the new processes.

During the operational phase of the PMO, a constant monitoring of the PMO operational and delivery processes take place. This section attempts to define an objective system for measurement to ensure that the performance of the process themselves are always are always improving. Each strategic function of the Utopian PMO has KPIs defined, the measurement of which can help the organization determine how the PMO is functioning. For each KPI score, a desired objective is also stated and that provides the direction of progress. The scores obtained from these KPIs drive the overall maturity scores of the Utopian PMO.

KPIs for PMO Processes

PMO Processes	KPIs	Objective
Governance and Strategic Alignment PMO01GSA	Number of projects with no business cases	Zero
	Number of projects that are not aligned to strategy	Zero
	Number of projects which were found to be in violation of regulations	Zero
	Number of projects for which no feasibility studies were undertaken	Zero
	Number of projects that were later found to have conflicts of interest	Zero
	Number of projects that were later identified as program-type initiatives	Zero
	Number of projects that were improperly classified	Zero

Process Maturity Framework PMO02PM	Number of new processes incorporated without supporting framework elements	Zero
	Number of new processes for which familiarization was not conducted	Zero
	Number of new processes for which interfaces were only found during operation	Zero
	Number of processes for which improvements were found	High
Delivery Management Process PMO03DM	Number of instances where excessive performance slippage was not escalated	Zero
	Number of enterprise risks that were failed to be documented	Zero
	Number of strategic projects that followed the incorrect methodology	Zero
Resource Management PMO04RM	Number of performance improvement plans created for each PMO resource	High
	Number of PMO resources with insufficient performance	Zero
Quality Compliance Management PMO05QC	Number of KPIs found to be outside defined tolerances	Zero
	Number of non-compliant KPIs for which, an RCA fixed the problem	All
Reporting PMO06R	Number of initiatives that are not represented on the enterprise status report	Zero
	Number of Ad-hoc report requests serviced	All

Supplier Management Process PMO07SM	Number of vendors whose performance was found to be unacceptable	Zero
	Number of project managers with outsourced scope who were interviewed for establishing supplier performance	All
	Number of material contractual breaches that were not reviewed by the PMO	Zero
Benefits Realization Process PMO08BRM	Number of initiatives, for which the benefits established in the business case was recorded	All
	Number of benefits identified that materialized before the established date	High
	Number of new projects that were spawned due to initiatives not having conveyed intended benefits	All

KPIs for Key PMO Functions

PMO Functions	KPIs	Objective
Project Delivery	Number of projects that were delivered without changes to the original scope, cost and time estimates	All
	Number of projects that successfully pass the Utopian PMO's phase gate tests with minimal changes	All
	Number of failing projects that were brought back on track	All

	Number of project managers voluntarily subjecting their projects to checks	>75% of strategic projects
Program Delivery	Number of programs that were delivered without changes to the original scope, cost and time estimates	All
	Number of programs that successfully pass the Utopian PMO's phase gate tests with minimal changes	All
	Number of failing programs that were brought back on track	All
	Number of program managers voluntarily subjecting their programs to checks	All
Change Management	Number of change requests that bypassed the Perform Integrated Change Control Process PRJ4.2PICC	Zero
	Number of changes that abused the emergency change process by bypassing key steps	Zero
Risk Management	Number of risks that materialized which were not identified	Zero
	Number of risks whose impact and probability was greater than what was assessed	Zero
	Number of risks that were not properly documented in the risk register	Zero
	Number of risks for which the post-implementation review determined that the mitigation plans were insufficient	Zero

	Number of risks/opportunities that were failed to be identified during initial risk assessment	Zero
	Number of high score risks that were not analyzed quantitatively	Zero
	Number of risks that were passively accepted	Close to Zero
Communications Management	Number of reports that changed due to inconsistent information	Zero
	Number of days delay between report updation & change in status	< 24 hours
Training	Number of processes for which training workshops were not conducted	Zero
	Number of new PMO employees for whom Utopian PMO process and delivery framework induction was not conducted	Zero
	Number of employees who have remained in the same level in the UPMO assessment for more than a year	Zero
Resource Management	PMO resources attrition rate	Low
	PMO resources promoted during this appraisal cycle	At least 33%
	Number of times the same PMO resource was flagged for unsatisfactory performance	Zero
	Number of rewards and recognitions awarded during this appraisal cycle	At least 33%
	Number of resources whose project assignments were done based on skill set	All

Maturity Improvement

This book does not attempt to delve into the nuances of PMO benchmarking *against other non-Utopian PMO entities,* except suggesting that no tangible value can be drawn from this effort, especially if the sponsoring organization is aiming to achieve Utopian status insofar as its PMO operations are concerned.

Non-Utopian PMOs operating at efficiencies below the ones recommended in this book may benefit from inter-organizational benchmarking by comparing against peers to see how far ahead or behind they are from other organizations but the scores are in no way indicative of the direction in which the PMO is headed. PMOs by their very nature are complicated organizational entities with an existence almost organic in nature, that an apple to apple comparison can seldom be drawn between two apparently-similar PMO entities. In any case, most PMO maturity models only measure the maturity of project management processes in an organization, a unilateral measurement system hardly indicative of maturity.

A more accurate self-sustinent maturity model that takes into account more than one measurement factor is proposed:

PMO Maturity =
$\sum$ *Scores at the PMO assessment verticals* + $\sum$ *PMO* delivery
expertise

This approach considers the capabilities of the PMO and also awards a score for experience in running a PMO at an established threshold. As described before, a 4 level non-linear scale, comprising of the numbers 1,4,7 and 10 is suggested to ease the scoring process whilst helping to remove subjective errors. The first phase of the maturity drives a PMO to take the onus to develop its capability to what has defined as one having a highly desirable or near perfect qualities, a Utopian PMO. Once a PMO has reached the zenith in this aspect, the maturity improvement model pushes for continued delivery excellence by assessing the number of years in existence and the number of projects delivered, whilst in Utopian operating mode.

Operating continually at the Utopian levels for a certain periods whilst delivering strategic projects adds further points to the PMO's maturity increasing its position in the classification levels. This model is primarily self-sustinent in the fact that it does not require external information to help in assessing its maturity.

Maturity Factor	Allowable Scores			
	1	**4**	**7**	**10**
	Orwellian	Juvenile	Metamorphosis	Utopian
Score at the assessment verticals	NA	Max. score on 6/10 verticals	Max. score on 8/10 verticals	Max. score on all verticals
Years at Utopian Maturity level	0	5	10	10+
Strategic Projects delivered at Utopian Maturity	0	25+	50+	100+

This maturity model emphasizes that, organizations fix their PMO capabilities in the first phase of their long-term maturity improvement initiative and then, gather points as their experience and expertise incrementally increases with each successive year of operation as more projects are successfully delivered. The maximum score that an organizational PMO can achieve in this maturity model is 30, which is obtained when a PMO has excelled in all the nine verticals, in consistently delivering strategy for the organization via the successful execution of 100s of projects for over a decade. Intermediate maturity levels help an organization monitor and track progress, as it makes its way to the final stages of maturity. As each of the assessment verticals intrinsically emphasize improvement, ongoing PMO operations at the maximum thresholds defined, can in itself bring the PMO closer to being the perfect strategic engine, a *Pièce de résistance* for a top-performing organization.

The following intermediate stages of maturity are suggested to track and monitor long-term progress

Score	Maturity Level	Entry Criteria
1	Orwellian	None
4	Juvenile	Max. score on 6/10 verticals
7	Metamorphosis	Max. score on 8/10 verticals
10	Utopian	Max. score on all assessment verticals
10-20	Red Giant	Max. score on all assessment verticals with less than 10 years of operation
20-30	Supernova	Max score on all assessment verticals with at least 5 years of operation and successful delivery of at least 50 strategic projects

UPMO Knowledge Assessment & Testing

The Utopian PMO framework is an all-encompassing solution for reengineering a PMO, based on a framework of processes for PMO operations , two frameworks for project delivery and a light yet robust framework, for the delivery of programs. However, where the Utopian PMO processes truly stand out, is in possessing the much needed integration between these multiple frameworks and the incorporation of built-in controls for each process.

However, the reengineering of a PMO to a Utopian PMO brings the need to have everyone working in the PMO and with the PMO to have a common understanding of the Utopian PMO framework, processes and controls. The various roles within the Utopian PMO especially, need to possess substantial knowledge of the framework in order to be able to execute their day to day responsibilities. A testing framework to assess the understanding and application of the framework needs to exist, to segregate and promote those with a superior understanding of the processes and the PMO environment.

The UPMO knowledge assessment framework and tests available on *www.theutopianpmo.com* is recommended to examine, assess and certify knowledge on the principles, framework and processes on which the Utopian PMO rests. The Utopian PMO (UPMO) assessment is demarcated into the following tracks with various levels of progression and fixed entry criteria for each level. Also indicated is the qualification title / certificate provided on the successful passage of the requisite examinations. The various assessment tracks help PMO employees with different job functions to get certified in their line of work. Since the assessment is tailored to test understanding of the subject matter from an operational point-of-view, the management of a reengineered organization can rest easy in the understanding that a certified employee has the know-how to perform real world application of the framework and is immediately able to demonstrate superior productivity and understanding of the work environment as a direct result of getting certified.

UPMO Testing and Assessment Tracks:

Track	Level	Entry Criteria	Testing Objectives	Test type
Analyst	Certified UPMO Level 1 Analyst (CULA1)	None	- Knowledge of the Utopian PMO framework basics - Corresponds to Bloom's taxonomy Level 1 cognitive domain	Online - 40 Questions – Multiple choice objective
Analyst	Certified UPMO Level 2 Analyst (CULA2)	CULA1 Certified and PMP® Certified	- Ability to explain in detail the Utopian process framework for PMO, project and program management -Calculate problems on risk scoring and PMO analyst work load estimation - Corresponds approximately to Bloom's taxonomy at Level 3	Online - 40 Questions – Multiple choice objective

Analyst	Certified UPMO Expert Analyst (CEA)	CULA2 and PMP® Certified	- Ability to apply the Utopian process framework for PMO, project and program management to real-life situations	Online – 5 Questions – Essay type answers for a given scenario. Each answer is graded at 1,4,7 or 10 with 10 being the maximum and 1 being the minimum. The answers are graded for situational aptness, and understanding of the framework.
			-Calculate problems on risk scoring, PMO analyst work load estimation and measurement of benefits	
			- Corresponds approximately to Bloom's taxonomy at Level 3	
PMO Maturity Analyst	Certified UPMO Maturity Assessor (CUMA)	CULA2 and PMP® Certified	- Ability to apply the Utopian maturity assessment to measure the current PMO maturity levels	Online – 5 Questions – Essay type answers for a given scenario. Each answer is graded at 1,4,7 or 10 with 10 being the maximum and 1 being the minimum.
			- Corresponds approximately to Bloom's taxonomy at Level 3	

Project Delivery	Certified UPMO Small projects Manager (CUPM1)	PMP® Certified	- Ability to explain application of the Utopian small project delivery framework (DF3) to real-life situations	Online – 5 Questions – Essay type answers for a given scenario. Each answer is graded at 1,4,7 or 10 with 10 being the maximum and 1 being the minimum. The answers are graded for situational aptness, and understanding of the framework.
			- Demonstrate working knowledge of the Utopian PMO and program delivery frameworks (DF1)	
			- Demonstrate working knowledge of stakeholder assessment, risk management, requirements collection, project plan development and vendor management	
			- Corresponds approximately to Bloom's taxonomy at Level 3	

Project Delivery	Certified UPMO Strategic projects Manager (CUPM2)	PMP® Certified	- Ability to explain application of the Utopian strategic project delivery framework (DF2) to real-life situations -Demonstrate working knowledge of stakeholder assessment, risk management, requirements collection, project plan development and vendor management as well as knowledge of the Utopian PMO and program delivery frameworks (DF1) - Corresponds approximately to Bloom's taxonomy at Level 3	Online – 5 Questions – Essay type answers for a given scenario. Each answer is graded at 1,4,7 or 10 with 10 being the maximum and 1 being the minimum. The answers are graded for situational aptness, and understanding of the framework.

Program Delivery	Certified UPMO Program Manager (CUPGM)	PMP® Certified or PgMP® Certified	- Ability to explain application of the Utopian strategic program delivery framework (DF1) to real-life situations	Online – 5 Questions – Essay type answers for a given scenario. Each answer is graded at 1,4,7 or 10 with 10 being the maximum and 1 being the minimum. The answers are graded for situational aptness, and understanding of the framework.
			-Demonstrate working knowledge of stakeholder assessment, risk management, requirements collection, program plan development , vendor management and management of priorities as well as knowledge of the Utopian PMO and project delivery frameworks (DF2 & DF3)	
			- Corresponds approximately to Bloom's taxonomy at Level 3	

| Expert | Certified UPMO Expert (CUEX) | Either PMP® / PgMP® Certified and either CULA2 or CUMA or CUPM1 or CUPM2 or CUPGM certified | - Conduct an appraisal of the Utopian framework from time to time and develop modifications and improvements as required to meet evolving business needs

- Able to identify shortfalls in any process within the Utopian PMO framework and be able to justify it with an appropriate business case for change | Online – one 1000 word essay describing the nature of the deficiency in the implemented framework, the resulting issues and proposed solution to fix the same |

Notional Charging

Organizational entities that often deliver work in the form of services are considered in lesser light than entities that produce tangible deliverables. A PMO delivers strategy in the form of good governance in the delivery of initiatives. Since project managers, program managers and other delivery staff are seen producing actual deliverables, the organization is often left wondering about the benefits of having a heavy-weight Utopian PMO in place, once a certain amount of time has elapsed and the delivery team is perceived to be working independently of the Utopian PMO; but, in reality the link between governance and delivery has become so seamless that it creates the illusion of making the PMO work seem invisible.

To constantly drive home the value that the Utopian PMO delivers to the organization, a notional charging system, set-up rightly, can go a long way in demonstrating value. Notional charging is a system of charging the users of the PMO for actual services rendered *but* the charging is purely notional and no actual transfer of funds take place. Some organizations have successfully implemented complex notional charging systems in the form of service credits that are assigned to each organizational entity in the beginning of the year. Through the year, each entity exchanges service credits for services rendered or consumed. For example: the PMO charges 1000 service credits for each small project delivered and the PMO successfully delivers a HR portal project for the HR department and in the process earns 1000 service credits. These 1000 service credits can be used to purchase HR services for the PMO resources. For example, an urgent salary certificate can be purchased from the HR department by paying (back) 50 service credits.

However, a much simpler system of providing a menu of potential PMO services with specified prices, can help the PMO establish delivered value, in tangible terms. This number, computed annually, can be used to establish the costs of delivering initiatives and any suggestions of cost savings due to outsourcing or downsizing can easily be juxtaposed against this value to establish a concrete case for retaining the existing PMO.

The number of service credits / cost for delivering each kind of initiative is established by using a system similar to the following. First, the costs to deliver program, strategic and small projects annually, is established through historical information, after the newly re-engineered PMO has operated for a year.

The total annual operating budget of a PMO is spread out among the initiatives delivered in that calendar year. One operational-cost unit is the amount taken to deliver one initiative. However, all initiatives in a PMO do not cost the same in terms of effort. The Utopian PMO delivers 3 distinct types of initiatives. Towards this, an assumption is made to the effect that it takes approximately 60% of a PMO's operating cost for delivering strategic projects, 25% of a PMO's operating cost for delivering programs and 15% of a PMO's operating cost for delivering small projects. The low operating cost for delivering a program is due to the fact that most of the PMO related effort for a program, is in fact, distributed among a program's constituent projects. This split of the operating costs between types of initiatives is arbitrary and can be adjusted to reflect what the organization observes from practice. This is known as OCD or operational cost distribution.

In this example,

A PMO's annual operating cost is $100,000

Total portfolio delivered this year:

Type	Strategic	Small	Initiatives
Stand-Alone	5	15	20
Program 1	2	2	4
Program 2	1	1	2
Total Units	8	18	26

26 Project Initiatives + 2 programs = 28 Initiatives

Effort duration:

The average duration of each type of initiative in a PMO is estimated. If an initiative spans across this calendar period, then the duration is taken for the number of months in the calendar period, i.e. 12

For example: 2 programs which span the entire year and is expected to be delivered in 2 years will have their cumulative durations for this calendar year as 24 (12 months for program A and 12 for program B).

Another example: 8 projects, 7 of which spanned the entire year (and may spill over to the next year) plus 1 that took 6 months (this calendar year) to deliver. The total duration is (12x7)+(1x6) = 90 months

Type	Cumulative Duration	Units	Average
Programs	24 months	2	12
Strategic Projects	90 months	8	11.25
Small Projects	50 months	18	2.7

Cost of delivering each type of initiative:

PMO Annual Budget x OCD

Where OCD being the operational cost distribution is:

- 0.25 for programs
- 0.6 for strategic projects
- 0.15 for small projects

PMO Annual Budget : $100,000 (previous year's)

Operating costs for delivering programs annually	100,000 x 0.25	$25,000
Operating costs for delivering strategic projects annually	100,000 x 0.6	$60,000
Operating costs for delivering small projects annually	100,000 x 0.15	$15,000

$$Monthly\ Operating\ cost = \frac{Annual\ operating\ costs\ for\ a\ type\ of\ initiative}{Number\ of\ units\ x\ Average\ Duration}$$

PMO operational costs for 1 month of program delivery	$25,000 / (2x12)	$1041
PMO operational costs for 1 month of strategic project delivery	$60,000/(8x11.25)	$667
PMO operational costs for 1 month of small project delivery	$15,000/(18x2.7)	$308

From the above, a menu of notional costs for running each type of initiative can be indicated, to allow the organization, especially senior management, to know the cost of delivery by the Utopian PMO vs. outsourcing the effort.

For example: A 20 month program can now be estimated to cost the organization 20*1041$ = 20,820$ approximately in PMO effort

This value can now be used in a variety of planning estimates, especially when budgeting for PMO operational cost. The operational budgets can easily be estimated based on the portfolio size being proposed for any given budgeting period.

Chapter 9
Closing Notes

This book efficaciously demonstrates a methodology for reengineering a PMO to a best-in-class, machine that delivers strategy with utmost efficiency, creating a PMO known as the Utopian PMO

To begin doing this, a series of assessment questions are presented to check if the organization meets the necessary criteria to support the reengineering effort for a Utopian PMO. Once this is established, a solid case for reengineering the PMO is defined and necessary approvals procured. Then, the current state of maturity of the existing PMO is baselined and a revamp of the processes aligned to leading practices is done. Eight extremely cohesive and effective processes for PMO operation are used to form a support for the new PMO. Three delivery frameworks for delivering programs, strategic projects and small projects are described and used to form the PMO's delivery core. The program delivery framework has 3 processes, the strategic project delivery framework has 29 processes and the small projects delivery framework has 16 processes. All processes feature preemptive PMO involvement and built-in controls to allow for minimal process failures. An elaborate, multi-faceted change methodology is proposed with a clear implementation plan that includes various cut-over strategies to choose from based on the most suitable approach to migrate to the new PMO.

Then, new roles for the Utopian PMO are defined and the PMO is staffed with resources with the requisite skills. Reporting structures and career progressions for each of the PMO roles are explicitly defined. A brand new PMO charter ratifying the requisite authority and governance is drafted and signed-off by the powers that be. A final readiness check is done before the Utopian PMO comes into existence. KPIs to measure the operational efficiency of the Utopian PMO's processes' are defined, measurements obtained and are used to drive the maturity scores of the PMO. A knowledge and skills testing framework is presented to ensure that resources are constantly learning and progressing within the PMO. A framework for a notional charging system is also suggested to ensure that the Utopian PMO quantitatively demonstrates its value, to the organization.

The Utopian PMO, relentlessly delivers value, by living and breathing within every initiative that has the privilege of passing through its hallowed processes.

⚜

www.theutopianpmo.com

Index

Bibliography

A Guide to the Project Management Body of Knowledge (PMBOK© Guide): PMBOK© Guide. Newtown Square, PA: Project Management Institute, 2008. Print.

Hammer, Michael, and James Champy. *Reengineering the Corporation: A Manifesto for Business Revolution.* New York, NY: HarperBusiness, 1993. Print.

Manganelli, Raymond L., and Mark M. Klein. *The Reengineering Handbook: A Step-by-step Guide to Business Transformation.* New York: AMACOM, 1994. Print.

Managing Change. Cambridge, MA: Harvard Business Review, n.d. Print.

Maslow, Abraham H. *Motivation and Personality.* New York: Harper & Row, 1970. Print.

Kendall, Gerald I., and Steven C. Rollins. *Advanced Project Portfolio Management and the PMO: Multiplying ROI at Warp Speed.* Conyers, GA: J. Ross, 2003. Print.

Taylor, Peter. Leading Successful PMOs: *How to Build the Best Project Management Office for Your Business.* Farnham, Surrey: Gower, 2011. Print.

Office of Government Commerce, UK, *Successful Delivery Skills framework.*

ABOUT THE AUTHOR

AJAY KUMAR IS A CONSULTANT, WHO DISCOVERED A PASSION FOR PROJECT MANAGEMENT EARLY IN HIS CAREER. AFTER HIS MASTER'S DEGREE IN ROBOTICS, AJAY SPECIALIZED IN STRATEGY AND BUSINESS TRANSFORMATION, AND HAD THE PRIVILEGE OF WORKING IN MULTI-MILLION DOLLAR, PUBLIC-SECTOR REENGINEERING PROJECTS IN THE MIDDLE EAST, ASIA & NORTH AMERICA WHERE HIS CONTRIBUTIONS WERE HIGHLY RECOGNIZED. HE NOW CONSULTS IN PROJECT MANAGEMENT FOR ONE OF THE LEADING TRAINING COMPANIES IN THE WORLD, BASED OUT OF NEW YORK CITY.

APART FROM HIS MASTER'S IN TECHNOLOGY, AJAY IS ALSO A PMI® CERTIFIED PROJECT MANAGEMENT PROFESSIONAL - PMP®, PROJECT RISK MANAGEMENT PROFESSIONAL - PMI-RMP®, ITIL® V2 SERVICE MANAGER / V3 EXPERT, CERTIFIED INFORMATION SYSTEMS AUDITOR - CISA®, CERTIFIED INFORMATION SYSTEMS MANAGER - CISM®, CERTIFIED INFORMATION SYSTEMS SECURITY PROFESSIONAL - CISSP®, AND COBIT® CERTIFIED.

WE CAN EASILY FORGIVE A CHILD WHO IS AFRAID OF THE DARK; THE REAL TRAGEDY OF LIFE IS WHEN MEN ARE AFRAID OF THE LIGHT.

PLATO

7261378R00166

Printed in Great Britain
by Amazon.co.uk, Ltd.,
Marston Gate.